raised roof

Castelations raised

W42 W41

W11 W10 W9 W8 W7

C

W2 W3 W4 W25 W26 W26A W22

LUGGALA

LUGGALA

THE STORY OF A GUINNESS HOUSE

ROBERT O'BYRNE

with photography by James Fennell

CICO BOOKS

LONDON NEW YORK

Published in 2018 by CICO Books
An imprint of Ryland Peters & Small Ltd
341 E 116th St, New York, NY 10029
20–21 Jockey's Fields, London WC1R 4BW

www.rylandpeters.com

10 9 8 7 6 5 4 3 2 1

First published in 2012 by CICO Books
as *Luggala Days*

A CIP catalog record for this book is available from the Library of Congress and the British Library.

ISBN: 978 1 78249 634 2

Managing Editor: Gillian Haslam
Designer: Louise Leffler
Special photography: James Fennell (see page 255 for further photography credits)

Printed in China

DEDICATION
For Kathy Gilfillan, without whom this book would not have been conceived
and
In memory of Garech Browne, custodian of Luggala for half a century.

Contents

Introduction

by The Hon. Garech Browne

Through my mother, and through her memories and those of her sisters Aileen and Maureen, I feel as though I have been at Luggala over two generations. My mother told me about her childhood: how she and her sisters used to make little caves in the banks of the Clohogue River and tell ghost stories after dark in a cave above Spooks Corner, perhaps so named because of the eerie sound produced by wind whistling around and through the split trunk of a Scots Pine.

My grandfather, The Honourable Ernest Guinness, had rented The Lodge at Luggala and Lough Bray Lodge from Viscount Powerscourt since 1912. He and his wife stayed in Lough Bray while their three daughters went to Luggala. My grandfather had created his own special short-barrelled shotgun for grouse. The biggest bag for one day at Luggala and Lough Bray was 223 grouse on 3rd October 1912. In 1916, the year of the Easter Rebellion in Dublin, the grouse total for the season was 939.

I was first brought to Luggala by my father when I was two weeks old and shown to Sam Hamilton, the gamekeeper from Glaslough, County Monaghan, whose son Noel was to become one of my great childhood friends. When I was a child we came during the summer. My father shot grouse and stalked with, amongst others, Erskine Childers, who was to become President of Ireland, the architect Michael Scott, the British representative in Ireland, John Maffey, and the Spanish and Italian Ambassadors. The British representative had by far the greatest security. This was during what we in Ireland called The Emergency but in the rest of Europe was known as the Second World War. My father believed in Irish neutrality. My mother stalked at Luggala. She rode side-saddle with the Galway Blazers and drove us from Luggala to Roundwood and back in the Governess cart; she seldom motored. Tara and I used to play beside a dam which we built across The Piper's Brook.

My parents divorced in 1950, at which time Luggala became my mother's chosen spot, having been given to her

OPPOSITE: The Hon. Garech Browne, Luggala's current owner, walking on the drive in August 1999. He is wearing a tweed greatcoat with mother of pearl buttons made for him by London tailers Lesley and Roberts using fabric he had bought from Millar's of Clifden, County Galway.

ABOVE: Garech Browne painted by his friend, Anglo-Belgian artist Anthony Palliser. Although based in Paris, Palliser is a regular visitor to Ireland where he has embarked on a much-admired series of portraits of the country's notable writers.

as a wedding present by her father when she married my father. People were drawn to Luggala by my mother's wit and beauty and by the atmosphere and beauty of the place. I learned a great deal from the people my mother brought to Luggala and formed many friendships, most of which endured. Just as the word 'people' begins with the letter 'p', so do many of the different sorts of people who came here, painters, poets, pipers, peers, playwrights, performers, philosophers, presidents, princes, princesses, priests not excluding parsons, and photographers.

Without giving a list of names, I remember those who most affected Tara and myself. My mother's lover, Robert Kee, who much enjoyed the fishing at Luggala, was learning about recent Irish history. This enabled him to write his many books on Ireland. He would talk to us about his discoveries. Then there was Derek Lindsay, author of a wonderful novel called *The Rack* under the pseudonym A. E. Ellis and a play on Alfred Dreyfus performed at the National Theatre in London. Known as Deacon because his appearance was somewhat churchlike, he taught Tara and I about classical music, especially opera. We were particularly fascinated by the rediscovery of composers such as Vivaldi, Geminiani, Corelli, Albinoni, Cimarosa – we often heard their music in Venice – and the early operas of Monteverdi. Daphne Marchioness of Bath and Ricki Huston, wife of film director John Huston, were constant visitors at that time and taught us a great deal about the world. Daphne's future husband, Xan Fielding, had fought in Crete with Paddy Leigh Fermor during the war and I always remember Paddy, in a moment of enthusiasm, waving his arms and knocking the actress Hermione Baddeley onto the floor. She said nothing and returned to her seat. He never noticed. The poet Iris Tree, one of my mother's oldest friends, would also appear, as did Claud Cockburn with his family.

Perhaps the person from whom I learned most was Lucian Freud. He first came to Luggala with his wife Kitty. He subsequently married my cousin Lady Caroline Hamilton-Temple-Blackwood. He was painting my portrait at Luggala when the house caught fire in 1956, so he gave the unfinished smoked version to Caroline and started again. Lucian subsequently introduced me to many interesting people, including Francis Bacon, and brought me around the Louvre. Lucian brought Brendan Behan, Anthony Cronin and Patrick Swift to Luggala. Brendan and his wife Beatrice spent every subsequent Christmas at Luggala.

Luggala became a home to musicians and poets. Séamus Ennis's death hands, made by Edward Delaney, sit in my drawing room. Leo Rowsome without whose skills there might be no pipers in Ireland today. Neillidh Mulligan and Ronan Browne became friends of John Hurt in this house. Paddy Moloney and all The Chieftains were frequent visitors, as were people like Tommy Potts, Mrs. Crotty, the concertina player and publican from Kilrush, and Éamon de Buitléar who in his other role as wildlife expert, once told me that almost all mammals to be found in Ireland could be found at Luggala. I must not leave out the singers Máire Áine Ní Dhonnachadha, Seán 'ac Dhonnacha and Seosamh Ó hÉanaí, Seán Garvey, Dolores Keane, Dolly MacMahon and her husband Ciarán Mac Mathúna. There were cooks ranging from Theodora Fitzgibbon to Kylie Kwong.

The landscape at Luggala contains one of the few remaining 18th-century landscape gardens and includes two native Irish oak woods, described by the Foresty Department as 'scrub oak' and therefore of no value. No trees have been planted here to interfere with the La Touche landscape, apart from some conifers by the 7th Lord Powerscourt. I have tried to recreate and reinstate some of the La Touche vision of Luggala. Although they had an extraordinary knowledge of botany, I felt at liberty to replace a few trees that had succumbed to age with interesting species. There are trees associated with people and places I love. Gloria MacGowran planted a sycamore in memory of Samuel Beckett, Gerald Hanley planted a crab apple, my mother planted a medlar, Marianne Faithfull a weeping wych elm, the Rolling Stones, with the exception of Keith Richards, planted ginkgos around Tara's grave, as did Seamus Heaney.

Some of the horse chestnuts represent Glenmaroon, where I was born. The London plane reminds me of my childhood at Castle MacGarrett and the Catalpa is the same as several planted by Lucian Freud at Coombe Priory where I spent many weekends while at school at Bryanston. I learned everything that I knew about plants and trees from Mr Alfred Williams, head gardener at Castle MacGarrett, who came with my mother to Luggala, and from the 19th-century Irish gardener William Robinson's book *The English Flower Garden*.

All four continents are represented at Luggala. Trees from Japan and Korea seem to flourish here. I am currently planting the great Irish plant hunter Augustine Henry's discoveries from China, Indian trees from the sub-continent, especially those from the Himalayas flourish. There have always been deodars at Luggala. Some eucalypts are happy as are North American and some Central American trees. As far as climate permits we have introduced trees I find remarkable. A metasequoia I planted years ago was only found to be extant in 1944. Others include the Japanese Sciadopitys, a *Zelkova Carpinifolia* from the Caucasus, the longest known living tree *Pinus Longaeva*, both Redwoods and the Wollemi discovered in 1994.

On the front of the house is a robust pink double dog rose. Possibly originating in the wild, it has been there since the La Touche time. Outside what was my mother's bedroom there is a Victorian rose which cannot be reproduced from cuttings. In the courtyard is planted a white double dog rose, which John Ducie rescued from a fallen-down Gate Lodge to the La Touche estate at Bellevue in 1992. Another rose planted here is known as Cooper's Burmese Musk. This was acquired by the Coopers of Markree Castle from Lady Wheeler-Cuffe and her husband Sir Otway, both from Kilkenny, who laid out the Royal Botanic Garden in Burma near Maymyo and Mandalay. She discovered the rose in north-eastern Burma in 1918. She was the first lady director and many of her botanical paintings are in the Botanic Gardens at Glasnevin.

Luggala is a place of primeval colours: the greys, greens and browns of the landscape, the darkness of the lake, the whiteness of the beach, the yellow of the primrose and the gorse, the contrast of the bluebells and the purple of the heather. And finally, to borrow from Frederick May's orchestral composition, sunlight and shadow.

The Hon. Garech Domnagh Browne (25th June 1939–10th March 2018)

OPPOSITE: Garech Browne photographed by Peter Knaup, standing at the top of the Luggala estate. Below him and stretching to the south is Lough Tay, which, with its dark waters and pale shoreline, is often said to bear a resemblance to a pint of Guinness.

The Guinness Family Tree

Arthur Guinness (founder of family brewery) 1725–1803

Sir Benjamin Lee Guinness 1798–1868 m. **Elizabeth Guinness** 1813–1865

Anne Lee Guinness
1839–1889

Arthur Edward Guinness
1st and Last Baron Ardilann of Ashford
1840–1915

Captain Benjamin Lee Guinness
1842–1900

Edward Cecil Guinness
1st Earl of Iveagh
1847–1927
m. **Adelaide Maria Guinness**
1844–1916

Rupert Edward Cecil Lee Guinness
2nd Earl of Iveagh
1874–1967

Hon. Arthur Ernest Guinness
1876–1949
m. **Marie Clothilde Russell**
1880–1953

Walter Edward Guinness
1st Baron Moyne
1880–1944

Aileen Sibell Mary Guinness
1904–1999

m. 1st 1927: **Flight Lieutenant Hon. Brinsley Plunket** (1903–1941), divorced 1940

Neelia Clothilde Plunket (1929–1992)
Doon Aileen Plunket (1931–)
Maria Lee Plunket (1933–1936)

m. 2nd 1956: **Valerian Stux-Rybar** (1919–1990), divorced 1965

Maureen Constance Guinness
1907–1998

m. 1st: **Basil Sheridan Hamilton-Temple-Blackwood**, 4th Marquess of Dufferin and Ava (1909–1945)

Lady Caroline Maureen Hamilton-Temple-Blackwood (1931–1996)
Lady Perdita Maureen Hamilton-Temple-Blackwood (1934–)
Sheridan Frederick Terence Hamilton-Temple-Blackwood, 5th Marquess of Dufferin and Ava (1938–1998)

m. 2nd 1948: **Major Harry Alexander Desmond Buchanan**, divorced 1954

m. 3rd 1955: **John Cyril Mande**

Oonagh Guinness
1910–1995

m. 1st 1929: **Hon. Philip Leyland Kindersley** (1907–1995), divorced 1935

Gay Kindersley (1930–2011)
Tessa Kindersley (1932–1946)

m. 2nd 1936: **Dominick Geoffrey Edward Browne, 4th Baron Oranmore and Browne** (1901–2002), divorced 1950

Hon. Garech Domnagh Browne (1939–)
m. 1981 **Princess Harshad Purna Devi, Jadeja of Morvi**
Unnamed baby (b. and d. 1943)
Hon. Tara Browne (1945–1966)
m. **Noreen Ann (Nicki) MacSherry**

Dorian Browne (1963–)
Julian Browne (1965–)

Miguel Ferreras (see pages 164–165)

The Owners of Luggala

1788–1828: Peter La Touche

1828–1830: Peter II La Touche

1830–1840s: Peter III La Touche

1840s–1857: David Charles La Touche

1857–1904: Mervyn Wingfield, 7th Viscount Powerscourt

1904–1937: Mervyn Wingfield, 8th Viscount Powerscourt

1937–1970: Lady Oranmore and Browne

1970–1977: The Hon. Garech Browne (since 1977, part custodian of Luggala)

CHAPTER ONE

Luggala: The Beginning

'To the west of the Djouce mountain is Luggelaw, a richly verdant vale, beautifully contrasting with the rugged severity and dreary barrenness of the other parts of this wild and romantic district. This delightful place is commonly visited from Roundwood, and has, under the auspices and by the taste of the La Touche family, been rendered one of the most interesting scenes in the county. The approach to it is over the southern shoulder of the Djouce mountain; and on passing the summit of a ridge which previously presented only bold undulations of dark heath-clad mountains, a sudden turn of the road presents a fine view of Lough Tay, overshadowed by the vast granite precipice of Carrigemann on the opposite side, rising in rugged cliffs perpendicularly to the height of 1000 feet. A little further, on the opposite side of the road, an opening discloses a fine view of an extensive glen in the mountain, the precipitous sides of which are richly planted to a certain height, above which they are thinly clad with heath.

At the head of the glen are some meadows of beautiful verdure, and a fine lawn shaded by overhanging woods, on which is a handsome lodge in the early English style, built by the late David La Touche, Esq., and now the residence of Robert D. La Touche, Esq. The lodge, which is open to visitors by permission of the family, is approached by a road through the wood, near the margin of the lake, a fine sheet of water comprising 72 Irish acres, and abounding with trout and char. On the side above the house a new hanging walk has been constructed among the plantations, commanding a view of the glen and lake below, and a splendid mountain vista across the lower extremity of Lough Dan, terminating in a prospect of the unrivalled mountain of Lugnaquilla.'

FROM SAMUEL LEWIS'S *TOPOGRAPHICAL DICTIONARY OF IRELAND*, 1837

RIGHT: 'Luggala's lake', wrote James Norris Brewer in 1825 'is here situated in a deep hollow, surrounded by stupendous and rugged mountains. The masses of rock, the succession of mountains on all sides, and the dearth of vegetation, would seem to indicate that this recess were beyond the limits of society.'

The name Luggala, often spelled Luggelaw in the 18th and 19th centuries, derives from the Irish Lug a' Lágha, meaning 'hollow in the ridge'. Luggala is located some 28 miles south-west of Dublin in the midst of the Wicklow Mountains. Created after the collision of two continents 445 million years ago and primarily composed of granite, the mountains run like a spine down the centre of County Wicklow. To the east lies the Irish Sea, to the west are the plains of the province of Leinster.

The area known as Luggala is found within a townland called Cloghoge. There is a river of the same name that flows from the north into Lough Tay before in turn draining into Lough Dan further south. To the east of the valley rises Djouce Mountain, its slopes densely forested, while the immediate west is occupied by Fancy Mountain (from the Irish, Fuinnse meaning ash tree), its steep and near barren cliffs of granite and quartzine rising to 595 metres.

The ancient history of this region, once heavily blanketed in native Irish oak and often inaccessible during the winter months, is little known. A scarcity of archaeological remains suggests Luggala was uninhabited by man during the pre-Christian period and possibly until much later. Oral legend proposes that in the 6th century St. Kevin, who founded one of Ireland's most important monastic settlements not far away in the valley of Glendalough, first came to Luggala. However, he was driven away from the place by the unwelcome attentions of a young woman called Kathleen who had 'eyes of most unholy blue'. She followed him to Glendalough where he dampened her ardour by beating her with nettles; Kathleen subsequently sought his forgiveness and became almost as holy as the former object of her lustful attention. In January 1829 a contributor to the Dublin periodical *The Kaleidoscope* wrote, 'If Luggelaw, in the time of St. Kieven, bore any resemblance to the present fairy scene, instead of imitating the saint by fleeing away from the beauteous Cathleen, and seeking an asylum in the gloomy caverns of Glendalough, I believe I should have wooed the lovely creature and, if possible, have filled up the only vacancy in this earthly paradise.' That same year, in an introduction to his short novel, *The Rivals*, Irish author Gerald Griffin included a poem called 'The Fate of Cathleen' which opens with the following lines:

'In Luggelaw's deep-wooded vale,
The summer eve was dying;
On lake and cliff and rock, and dale,
A lulling calm was lying;
And virgin saints and holy men
The vesper song were singing,
And sweetly down the rocky glen
The vesper bell was ringing.'

Whilst Glendalough became a major centre for monks and pilgrims until almost completely destroyed by English troops at the end of the 14th century, Luggala appears to have remained unoccupied, untended and largely unknown.
It is presumed that the lands were owned, if only nominally, by the Abbots of Glendalough, but after the latter diocese was united with that of Dublin in 1216 the whole area passed, more on paper rather than in practice, into the hands of the Archbishop of Dublin. Although located close to the centre of English government in Ireland, Wicklow remained stubbornly independent, and indeed insurgent, until the 17th century: it was the last part of the country to be shired in 1606. For a long time members of the O'Byrne family, then the dominant clan in the area, held actual control of the lands in which Luggala lies. They continued to do so up to the early 1600s, after which a succession of English military forces, first acting on the authority of the crown and then led by Oliver Cromwell, dispossessed them of almost all their holdings. This part of Wicklow was then once again deemed to belong to the Church of Ireland Archbishop of Dublin.

In a Report of the Irish Church Commissioners drawn up in 1868, when the Church of Ireland was disestablished, it was stated that one Thomas Hugo had been granted a lease in perpetuity from the Archbishop of Dublin, probably in the late 17th century, for the lands of Glendalough comprising 33,754 acres at an annual rent of £237, nine shillings and three

RIGHT: To the delight of dendrologists, large parts of the Luggala demesne remain as planted by the La Touches in the 18th century. It also continues to host a rich variety of animal and birdlife unlikely to discover such a nurturing environment elsewhere today.

pence. Luggala would have been included within this territory. The Hugo family lived at Drummin, later renamed Glendalough House, and while substantial landowners – still one of the greatest in Wicklow according to an 1837 survey – they enjoyed little pecuniary benefit from these areas of low-quality mountain and bog. It was only in the second half of the 17th century that the forests hitherto covering much of Wicklow began to be cleared, both to provide timber and to supply more land for farming. Even so, the more remote upland regions remained much as they had until then and no effort was made to open up the area. Luggala continued to be as secluded as had ever been the case.

This scenario began to change in the second half of the 18th century. Surviving documents show that in 1763 the Cloghoge townland was leased by another Thomas Hugo to James Sheil. Within a decade, Shiel had passed on the lease to William Bomford, originally of County Meath, who by 1785 was letting to John Ledsam, Public Notary of the City of Dublin, 'the house of Lake Tay, the meadows of Luggalow being part of Ballynastowe in the Barony of Ballynacor, Co Wicklow, at a rent of £51.' Sheil, Bomford and Ledsam: none of them was to enjoy possession of Luggala for long. Finally in 1788 the estate passed into the hands of a new owner under whose care it would become renowned and whose heirs would remain custodians of the place for the next seventy years. To these proprietors the value of Luggala lay not in its potential for cultivation but, on the contrary, in the valley's untamed beauty and seclusion. Other methods of appraisal than just monetary started to come into play when assessing a terrain's worth. As a result, for the first time Luggala's value as a place of exceptional beauty began to be appreciated.

In 1757 Irish author and future statesman Edmund Burke had published *A Philosophical Enquiry into the Origin of Our Ideas of the Sublime and Beautiful*, a key text in the emergence of the Romantic Movement and especially in changing public attitudes towards landscape. Whereas previously land had been regarded as something to tame and control, now it was feasible to consider the possibility that, on the contrary, nature was greater than man, not least because of its ability to induce extreme emotions, such as fear. In his text Burke argued, 'The passion caused by the great and sublime in nature ... is Astonishment; and astonishment is that state of the soul, in which all its motions are suspended, with some degree of horror.' Passion, astonishment and even a degree of horror – these are precisely the emotions visitors to Luggala were thrilled to experience from the late 18th century onwards. Isolation and apparent desolation were especially exhilarating, leading 'M' writing in *The Kaleidoscope* in January 1829 to exaggerate that in Luggala,

'Nor thicket, dell nor copse you spy
Where living thing concealed might lie
Nor point retiring hide a dell
Where swain, or woodman lone, might dwell.
There's nothing left to fancy's guess,
You see that all is loneliness.'

It is no coincidence that around the same time Burke was propounding his theory of the Sublime, Irish artists began to paint views of their country's most romantic landscapes, in particular those found in counties Kerry and Wicklow. In an age when Irish roads were notorious for their poor quality and facilities such as inns were few, Kerry was difficult to visit and remained beyond the reach of most travellers. Wicklow, on the other hand, was relatively accessible to anyone based in Dublin. Once Luggala became known it proved a favourite subject for romantically inclined painters looking for picturesque subject matter.

Writers, likewise, began to hymn the area's charms. Among them was Thomas Moore, Ireland's most celebrated poet during the early decades of the 19th century, as renowned for the charm of his verses as for the performances he gave of his own melodies, accompanying himself on the harp. Moore composed a number of poems about Wicklow, the best remembered being *The Meeting of the Waters*, but it is surely Luggala being described when, in telling the tale of St. Kevin's temptation, he wrote:

'By that lake, whose gloomy shore,
Sky-lark never warbles oe'r,
Where the cliff hangs high and steep,
Young Saint Kevin stole to sleep.'

Long before Moore, travellers of an elegiac disposition had taken to visiting various sites in Wicklow, a region that can claim to have been the cradle of the Romantic Movement in

Ireland. The Powerscourt Waterfall was one stop on a circuit that also took in a heavily wooded channel running over a mile between two mountain ranges called the Glen of the Downs, a ravine containing another water cascade and romantically named the Devil's Glen, and Glendalough, where the beauty of the setting was enhanced by the abundant monastic ruins. By the end of the 18th century, Luggala had been added to this itinerary and turned up with increasing frequency in guidebooks.

The language employed by writers when describing Luggala, with its inclination towards hyperbole and abundant use of superlatives, exhibits a desire to share with readers an overwhelming experience, one that had left them filled with awe and even dread. As Irish society, like elsewhere in Europe, grew steadily more urbanised, the countryside came to be seen as outside the norm, certainly not humdrum,

ABOVE: The unique charms of Luggala are revealed only by degrees. Nevertheless, 'the minute you start going down,' says poet and Nobel Laureate Seamus Heaney, 'you do cross a line into a slight otherwhere.' According to musician Paddy Moloney, while passing through the woods of Luggala, 'you can almost hear the trees playing music and whistling tunes.'

possibly almost exotic. Luggala was thus no prosaic place but a location liable to induce in visitors a heightened and unforgettable state of emotion. Observers were keen to emphasise the ferocious height of the surrounding mountains and the seemingly immeasurable depths of Lough Tay below them. George O'Malley Irwin's 1844 *Illustrated Handbook to the County of Wicklow* introduced just such an element of drama when he noted, 'The water obtains the resemblance of black slime, but when taken out of the lake, it looks clear and pure. So great is the rocky chasm occupied, that the centre of the lake is unfathomable and its acherontic tint is sufficiently accounted for by the enclosed situation, and the rising of dark slate rocks on the one side, directly above the water.'

Lough Tay, wrote the English topographer and novelist James Norris Brewer in *The Beauties of Ireland* (1825), 'is here situated in a deep hollow, surrounded by stupendous and rugged mountains. The masses of rock, the succession of mountains on all sides, and the dearth of vegetation, would seem to indicate that this recess were beyond the limits of society.' The author of a *Guide to the County of Wicklow* (1835) considered Luggala 'decidedly the most interesting object to the picturesque tourist in the whole county.' Having exclaimed over the 'lofty, inaccessible mountains,' he went on to enthuse about how, 'A line, or rather fairy path of golden lustre will, of course, extend across the rippled surface of the lake to the base of the dark and shadowy hill, looking like an allegorical representation of night and summer evening coming on hand from the west.'

Once Luggala's new owners had built a fine house, the disparity between civilized valley and untamed Wicklow landscape especially appealed to poets, who saw an opportunity to flatter the family responsible for bringing the benefits of progress to a hitherto savage spot. In 1807, Joseph Atkinson, an army officer-turned-playwright, published just such a poem on Luggala:

'In this sequester'd, wild, romantic dell
Where nature loves in solitude to dwell,
Who would expect 'midst such a lonely park
The charms of fancy and the plans of art,
Whilst the neat mansion, formed with simple taste,
Amidst a wilderness for comfort plac'd,
Adorns the scene and hospitably shews
The seat of pleasure and serene repose.'

This was an era when literature of the fantastic flourished, producing works of fiction like Mary Shelley's *Frankenstein* and, amongst Irish authors, Charles Maturin's *Melmoth the Wanderer*. Understandably, therefore, attempts were made to discover something supernatural in the terrain of Luggala. In *The Scenery and Antiquities of Ireland*, published in 1842, Joseph Stirling Coyne thrillingly proposed that in the outline of one of the site's rocks, 'is distinctly traced a gigantic resemblance of a human face, looking gloomily on the lake below. The eye-brows, broad and dilating, are marked by moss and heath, and the prominent cheeks and deep-sunk eyes perfectly formed by the clefts in the rock. The mouth appears open, but when you remove to some distance it closes, but without producing any alteration in the features.'

The desire to offer readers an enhanced experience also led several writers erroneously to propose that Luggala's original name was Lough Hela or the Lake of Death, the latter word having derived from the Hela (death) of Danish mythology and brought to Ireland by the Vikings in the 9th century. This notion was first proposed by Anne Plumptre, a prolific English author who in 1814 spent a summer travelling around Ireland, publishing an account of her journey three years later.

OPPOSITE AND ABOVE: Ancient dry-stone walls now covered in moss and lichen. Overlooked for millennia, the particular beauties of Luggala only began to be appreciated towards the close of the 18th century. 'Nature has been bountiful to this spot,' wrote John Ferrar in 1796, describing it as being 'diversified with rocks curiously shaped, wood and waterfalls. The mountains abound with grouse, and the lough with fish, which brings many visitors to the place. But what is most remarkable, frequent rumblings and roarings are heard in the bowels of the mountains, sometimes as loud as a cannon shot, probably occasioned by the firing of sulphurous and bituminous matter.'

Luggala in Song

Testifying to Luggala's fame, over the past centuries, several melodies have been associated with the place. The earliest reference to such music is believed to date from the 1780s, when the words to a song called 'Legalaw' were included in *The Lover's Jubilee. Being a Choice Collection of New Songs sung this and the last season at Ranelaugh, Vauxhall, Sadler's Wells, the Theatres, and in the politest companies.* Its verses feature the lines,

'There is hunting, fishing and fowling,
And salmon trowling as e're I saw,
There's quail and partridge the lake surrounding,
All in that island called Legalaw.'

The song also makes reference to 'a building, that's free from crack or flaw,' suggesting that either the present house is of an earlier date than hitherto proposed, or else more likely some structure already stood on the same spot. This song was also printed as a ballad sheet some time after 1819 by London publisher John Pitts.

In 1787 the lyrics to another popular song of the time, 'Hush Cat under the Table', were published in Monaghan and included were those of several other songs, the last being 'The Venus of Longford.' A note advises that the latter's air is 'Legalaw' but again no music is given.

Nor was it provided for the verses included in a collection of John Clare manuscripts now held by Peterborough Museum, England. The son of a farm labourer, Clare was born in 1793 and received little formal education after the age of 11. As a young man he began to write poetry and, having met John Keats' publisher, his own first volume, *Poems Descriptive of Rural Life and Scenery,* appeared in 1820. Several more followed as Clare enjoyed popular acclaim, but by 1837 he was in a lunatic asylum, suffering from delusions, and would spend the rest of his life in such institutions. Among the Peterborough papers is a poem entitled 'A senseless song with a most beautiful melody taken down from my mother's singing.' This is basically the same as the song included in *The Lover's Jubilee* although the last verse has been slightly changed to include reference to 'the fairest girl eyes ever saw.'

Some years earlier, in March 1815, poet Thomas Moore published his sixth selection of *Irish Melodies,* which included 'No, Not More Welcome.' This opens with the lines,

'No, not more welcome the fairy numbers
Of music fall on the sleeper's ear,
When half awaking from fearful slumbers,
He thinks the full quire of heaven is near...'

This is accompanied by the music to an air called 'Luggelaw' which may have been the tune John Clare heard sung by his mother, and indeed the same one accompanying the words featured in *The Lover's Jubilee.* An arrangement for piano of Moore's melody was created in 1963 by the Irish composer Frederick May. Claddagh Records recently issued the May arrangement performand by Irish pianist Veronica McSwiney accompanied on the uilleann pipes by Paddy Moloney.

It is possible that the original air used by Moore was given to him by an assiduous collector of Irish music, George Petrie. Born in Dublin in 1789, Petrie worked as an artist and antiquarian, achieving acclaim in both fields. But he was also intensely interested in Irish music and during his travels through the country would listen to singers and instrumentalists, noting down the tunes they performed. Some years after Petrie's death, poet Alfred Perceval Graves (father of the writer Robert Graves, who would visit Luggala in 1975) recorded a story told to him by another collector of Irish music, Patrick Weston Joyce: 'When Petrie was a boy he was a good player upon a little single-keyed flute. One day he and some young companions set out for a visit to Glendalough, then in its primitive state of solitude. While passing Luggelaw they heard a girl near at hand singing a beautiful air. Instantly out came paper and pencil, and Petrie took it down, and then played it on his little flute. His companions were charmed with it; and for the rest of the journey –

every couple of miles when they sat down to rest, they cried, "Here, Petrie, out with your flute and give us that lovely tune." That tune is now known as Luggelaw, and to it Thomas Moore, to whom Petrie gave it, wrote his words (as lovely as the music)...'

On the other hand, three tunes called 'Luggelaw', 'Luggelau' and 'Luggelain' respectively were included in *The Complete Collection of Irish Music* as noted by George Petrie. Compiled by composer Sir Charles Villiers Stanford in 1902-5, all three are different from that used by Moore to accompany 'No, Not More Welcome'. This suggests that either over time Luggala inspired more than one piece of music or the beauty of the place simply led to a number of tunes being given its name.

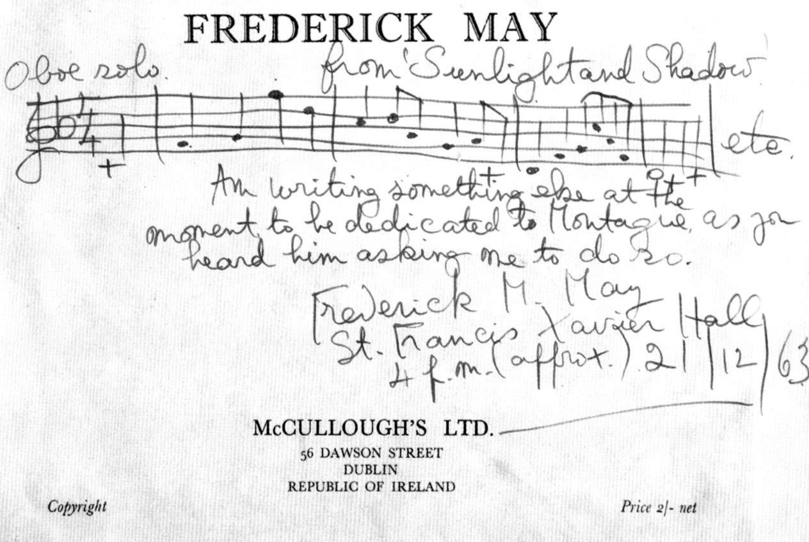

RIGHT: An arrangement of 'Luggelaw' by the composer Frederick May (1911-1985), a friend of the house's present owner the Hon. Garech Browne. Born in Dublin, where he studied at the Royal Irish Academy of Music, in 1935 May won a travelling scholarship to work in Vienna under Alban Berg; unfortunately the latter died before he arrived in the Austrian capital. Returning to Dublin the following year, he combined composing with the job of musical director at the Abbey Theatre, a position he held until 1948. The onset of tinnitus and increasing deafness hindered May's output, his finest work being the 'String Quartet in C Minor' (1935-36). This was subsequently described in the *Grove Dictionary of Music and Musicians* as 'one of the most individual statements from an Irish composer in the first half of the 20th century.' A recording of the quartet was released by Claddagh Records in 1974.

In this she argued that Luggala's original name was Lough Hela, 'though this derivation is lost in the corrupted name now so generally used.' Later writers followed her lead, not least because it added a frisson to their account of the place. Lough Hela, wrote Coyne more than two decades afterwards, 'must have been peculiarly appropriate to this dark lake before the hand of cultivation had softened the wild horrors of the valley, and it is not improbable, that it was bestowed upon it by that people while they possessed this part of the island, and handed down from them...'

During the same period Ireland's Gaelic past, which for political reasons had long been deemed imprudent to investigate, began to engage the attention of writers. In 1765 the Scottish poet James Macpherson had published *The Works of Ossian*, purportedly translated from ancient Gaelic with their eponymous hero based on the son of Fionn MacCumhaill, a character in Irish mythology. Enormously influential throughout Europe, Macpherson's book led to an interest within Ireland on the country's cultural history, manifested through such publications as Joseph Cooper Walker's *Historical Memoirs of the Irish Bards* (1786) and Charlotte Brooke's *Reliques of Irish Poetry*, which appeared three years later. In 1806 Sydney Owenson, later Lady Morgan, published her hugely successful novel, *The Wild Irish Girl*, which came with the subtitle 'A National Tale' and attempted to explain the history and folklore of old Ireland to contemporary readers. There was growing awareness of, and investigation into, the nation's earlier history. This was especially true of any period tinged with romanticism, such as the pre-Christian era when druids were the priestly caste. Writing of Luggala in 1822, the Rev. George Newenham Wright, who as an Anglican cleric might not be thought to have an interest in such matters, remarked that, 'On the eastern side of the valley was formerly one of those extraordinary druidical remains, called a "rocking stone" used by the artful arch-druid for oracular purposes. A large stone was placed on top of another, so balanced that the smallest effort would shake it, and was supposed to be self-moved in the presence of a guilty person. ...In the year 1800, a party of military, passing this mountain, dislodged the rocking stone from its pedestal, and it now lies some yards from its original position, but unfortunately deprived of its power of motion.'

But neither Wright nor any of the other writers who lauded the beauties of Luggala would have had the opportunity to do so had it not come into the hands of a benevolent owner possessed of both the wealth and sensibility to realise the place's hitherto dormant promise.

RIGHT: Calling Lough Tay 'this sad and gloomy, though sublime object,' in 1822, the Rev. George Newenham Wright went on to note how 'the waters of the lake appear perfectly dark' while the mountain rising from its shores offers 'the most complete representation of all that is wild, dreary and desolate in nature...'

OVERLEAF: Looking south across the valley of Luggala and towards Lough Tay. Close to the water's edge, in 1950 Oonagh Oranmore and Browne erected the small 18th-century domed temple that had once stood in the grounds of an estate close to Dublin but gives the impression of having been always destined for this spot.

CHAPTER TWO

The La Touche Family and Luggala

In the National Library of Ireland's archives is a document dated 24th December 1788. This leases the lands of 'Luggalow, Elikerivan and Cloghogue' to Peter La Touche for three lives at an annual rent of £39. Peter was a member of a wealthy Irish banking family of French Huguenot extraction. The second of three sons, he was born in November 1733 and since 1783 had been M.P. for County Leitrim where he owned extensive estates and where he had already acted as High Sheriff. In Dublin he lived splendidly in St. Stephen's Green, his residence there, decorated with superlative plasterwork by the Swiss-Italian Lafanchini brothers, today serving as the Stephen's Green Club. On his father's death in 1785 he inherited Bellevue, an estate of 300 acres some ten miles east of Luggala, with views across the Irish Sea. He was to add to Bellevue over a 40-year period, aided in the enterprise by his second wife Elizabeth.

Little is known of Peter's character; in 1805 John Carr mentions that his name 'has long been associated with every public and private virtue that can adorn human nature.' As a banker he was just as successful as had been his father and grandfather, and in politics, although not a notable public speaker, he was described as a 'Friend to Reform, but not against a Congress...' Like his forbears and siblings, he enjoyed a reputation for decency in business and contributed to many philanthropic enterprises; in 1811 he was a founder member of the Society for Promoting the Education of the Poor in Ireland. More than 20 years earlier he had paid for the building of a new church for the Church of Ireland in Delgany at the cost of some £5,000 and inside erected a monument in memory of his father sculpted by John Hickey. On his death in 1828 he left instructions that he should be buried in the Delgany churchyard, 'with as little expense as decency will allow.'

But he remains a relatively shadowy individual, unlike Elizabeth about whom a great deal was written during her lifetime. In 1787, a year after the death of his first wife Rebecca, Peter had married her cousin, 29-year-old Elizabeth Vicars; he was then aged 53. Neither marriage produced offspring, but Elizabeth La Touche was renowned for her good works on behalf of children. In an era not known for its religiosity or concern for decent behaviour, she appears to have been that rare creature: the embodiment of Christian virtue.

In 1796 *Walker's Hibernian Magazine* published an engraving of Mrs La Touche by John Whitaker, describing her as 'The Widow and Orphans' Friend.' Elsewhere in the same publication, it was reported that 'While dissipation, debauchery and infidelity to the marriage bed mark the manners of the higher circles of the female fashionable world, a conspicuous exception is to be found in the lady of Peter La Touche, Esq. The lady is eminently distinguished by her unbounded charities, her suavity of manner, her hospitality and all the virtue that the female breast can be susceptible of.'

When Joseph Atkinson wrote his poem on Luggala in 1807, he felt impelled to include the following lines regarding its chatelaine:

'Then who can envy fair La Touche a place
Which she, like Beauty's Queen, is form'd to grace?
Whether she here retires, or decks Bell'vue,
Her heart, to generous deeds and virtue true,
Is still the same – benevolent and bland –
To bless and ornament her native land,
And, like this sweet retreat, in modest pride,
From ostentation shrinks, her worth to hide.'

Soon after her marriage, Elizabeth La Touche established a boarding school for impoverished girls close to the main house at Bellevue. John Ferrar recorded seeing 24 of the school's pupils accompanying their benefactress from the church in Delgany; by the time John Carr visited in 1805 the number had risen to 28. Another contemporary observer, the Chevalier de la Tocnaye advised that when the girls came of age, Mrs La Touche 'gives them a dowry, and marries them to labourers of good character.'

In Dublin, Elizabeth was involved in the Female Orphan House, an establishment for Protestant girls; in 1792 she laid

RIGHT: The La Touche's house at Luggala nestles into a cleft at the northern end of the valley, its principal rooms looking south across a verdant sward towards Lough Tay. The white-washed exterior of the building serves as a counterpoint to the dense woodland that rises immediately behind and helps to make architectural details like the roofline crenellations all the more striking.

ABOVE: Painted in 1775 by Robert Hunter, this portrait of Peter La Touche explains his interest in acquiring Luggala as a centre for field sports at the end of the following decade. The artist has depicted his subject reclining against a tree in an idealised landscape and dressed for outdoor exercise. Peter's double-barrelled shot gun nestles in the crook of one arm while the other hand caresses a spaniel; by his side lie a brace of partridges.

the foundation stone for its new premises on the North Circular Road, wearing her husband's Freemason apron. The following year a Wicklow neighbour, Edward Tighe, adopting the pseudonym Melantius, published a volume of letters addressed to Elizabeth in which he considered the facilities available to orphans in a number of countries and praised her own efforts in this field. In 1800 the artist Hugh Douglas Hamilton, who was much patronised by the La Touche family, painted a view of the celebrated preacher Dean Walter Kirwan delivering his annual sermon on behalf of the Female Orphan House; the children on the pulpit's steps were said to have been members of the extended La Touche clan. When George IV came to Dublin in 1821, he visited the Orphan House accompanied by Elizabeth. That Peter and Elizabeth La Touche were deeply religious is further confirmed by their giving a home at Bellevue to the Irish theologian Alexander Knox, popularly known as the 'Sage of Bellevue' for 30 years before his death in 1831.

But if their piety and benevolence make them seem an unlikely couple to have created an earthly paradise at Luggala, it should be noted that they were perfectly capable of enjoying material pleasures. Bellevue was celebrated in Ireland and overseas for its opulence, and when not engaged in financial or charitable enterprises, the La Touches could be sociable. A family diarist recorded in November 1789: 'We remained at Bellevue till 21st...on the Monday a most splendid ball and supper – 100 persons at table – dancing till 5 in the morning.' Peter and Elizabeth may have been pious but they were not puritan.

There are many reasons why the La Touches should have decided to buy the lands of Luggala, not least the beauty of its setting and the opportunity it provided to escape from their many obligations. An interest in field sports, evident in a portrait of him painted by Robert Hunter in 1775, provided Peter with an additional motive. The woods around Luggala were replete with game while its lake was just as amply stocked with fish: an account of a fishing expedition in 1832 reported that Lough Tay was thick with trout and Arctic char, with some 80 catches being recorded for each fisherman on a single day.

Intended to serve as a hunting lodge, the house at Luggala was tucked for protection from the elements into a northerly point where the valley in which it lies comes to a close. Largely surrounded by sheltering belts of trees, only the building's south-facing entrance front is exposed and looks across open parkland to Lough Tay. While it cannot be described as distinctively Irish, the house's design was ancient in inspiration, romantic in spirit and perfectly suited to its location. In 1825 James Brewer remarked that this style of building 'is well adapted to the recluse parts of Ireland, where nature reigns in wild and mysterious majesty.' More recently Douglas Scott Richardson has observed how 'The concordance felt between much of the Irish landscape and Gothic Revival styles is a constantly recurring idea, virtually a cliché, through the late Georgian and Early Victorian periods.'

In the case of Luggala, the house, wrote the Knight of Glin in 1965, is an example of 'that special brand of eighteenth-century gothick that rejoices in little battlements, crochets, trefoil and quatrefoil windows and ogee mantelpieces: in fact, the gothick of pastrycooks and Rockingham china.' In England such a style came to be called Strawberry Hill Gothic, after Strawberry Hill, the Twickenham villa built between 1749 and 1776 by Horace Walpole, later 4th Earl of Orford, and incidentally also the author of what is regarded as the first Gothic novel in the English language, *The Castle of Otranto* (1764). Like Walpole's book, gothick, as this style is also named, is fanciful and decorative, a variant of rococo more concerned with deploying elements of mediaeval architecture for ornamental purpose than with demonstrating evidence of precise historicism. Several instances of the gothick and its variants had been used in Ireland before the construction of Luggala, with Castleward, County Down, dating from the 1760s, being the best-known example. Yet as was often the case at the time, Castleward's gothick aspects such as ogee windows and battlemented roof parapets, are largely superficial dressings on an orderly classical framework, and the same is also true of the only other extant large gothick house in Ireland, Moore Abbey, County Kildare, designed around 1767 by architect Christopher Myers for the 6th Earl and 1st Marquess of Drogheda. Here gothick is once more laid over the surface of classical construction and proportion, providing an opportunity to dress up facade and interiors with ornamental detail different from that customarily found in properties of similar size and date.

Aside from Castleward and Moore Abbey, the gothick style was most commonly used for lodges, pavilions and sometimes agricultural buildings, and intended to delight visitors to an estate as they wandered through the demesne. Gothic also became popular as a style for the hunting lodges beginning to be built around the country, not least that at Luggala. Patrick Bowe noted in 2004 that while game had once been plentiful throughout Ireland, 'As the country was settled gradually for agricultural use, the natural habitat of wild game was reduced. It was obliged to retreat to the more remote wilderness areas of mountain, bog, marsh or moorland. Sportsmen followed them to these regions and built lodgings nearby, especially as good sport often demanded rising early and staying out late.' But while roads were poor and means of transport limited, the 'remote wilderness' in which a lodge was constructed still had to be reasonably accessible and was preferably within a day's ride of the owner's principal residence: Bowe cites Mountain Lodge, built by the 2nd Earl of Kingston in 1785 in the Galtee Mountains within sight of his main house at Mitchelstown, County Cork. Similarly Luggala had all the attractions of remoteness while still being not far from Bellevue. Only after the advent of the railways in Ireland, and the simultaneous improvement of the country's roads, did it become commonplace for sportsmen to built hunting lodges far from their main estates.

Lord Kingston's Mountain Lodge was in the classical style, as was Sir William Chambers' unexecuted design of 1768 for a hunting lodge for the Earl of Charlemont. But as the century drew to a close and the notion of the picturesque in architecture became more popular, an alternative style for lodges was sought. Luggala encapsulates the expression of that desire and was followed by examples elsewhere in Ireland such as Hare Island Lodge, County Westmeath, and Glengarriff Lodge, County Cork. It can thus claim to be the original of a kind of hunting lodge that became familiar across Ireland over the following hundred years.

OPPOSITE: A 1797 engraving by Francesco Bartolozzi, an Italian artist who spent the greater part of his career in London. The picture is based on a now-lost painting, 'The Apotheosis of Female Beauty' by Matthew William Peters (1742–1814) who trained in Dublin. The work depicts an idealised Elizabeth La Touche being crowned by putti as she ascends into the heavens. Like her, Peters was extremely religious; in 1781 he became an Anglican clergyman and later served as chaplain to the future George IV.

However, none of its successors ever attracted as much attention, none of them being designed with such consistent attention to detail. Described around the time of its construction as a 'cottage mansion', the rendered exterior of the house, notes Patrick Bowe, 'boasts all the appurtenances of a grand castle' but on a miniature scale. There are battlements and crockets as well as a variety of pointed and quatrefoil windows together with other ornamentation such as the limestone obelisks embellishing the top of the main door and corners of the central, south-facing breakfront. 'Somehow,' declared the Knight of Glin, 'this whitewashed toy pavilion fits into its green-grey setting of old twisted oak-trees, beeches, mossy rocks and mountains in the most unnaturally natural way. Its very unlikelihood carries it off with a vivid panache.' The building's exterior design is elaborate and yet unified, and the same can be said for the interior where, once again, a composite sequence of elements work together to produce a coherent whole. Within an extremely limited space, Luggala somehow manages to contain three substantial reception rooms as well as a wealth of smaller chambers on both ground and first floors, with the latter's size not being externally apparent. From the start, as well as providing a base for hunting expeditions, the house also acted as a centre for entertaining. Luggala therefore needed to have ample public and private rooms, as well as to provide accommodation for the staff employed to look after owners and guests.

The presence of staff, even when its owners were not in residence, proved to be necessary owing to Luggala's ever-growing popularity as a destination for visitors to County Wicklow. Prior to Peter La Touche building his retreat, the place had already begun to be discovered by travellers, particularly those of a romantic disposition. In 1780 English agronomist and author Arthur Young published *A Tour of Ireland* based on extensive journeys around the country over the previous few years. Although primarily interested in economic and social affairs, Young was not immune to natural beauty and he described the area in which Luggala lies as being 'very noble scenery; a vast rocky glen; one side bare rocks to an immense height, hanging in a thousand whimsical yet frightful forms, with vast fragments tumbled from then, and lying in romantic confusion; the other a fine mountain side covered with shrubbery wood... Every feature of the

The La Touche Bank

One of the wealthiest families in 18th-century Ireland, the La Touches were of French Huguenot origin, their name derived from the demesne of la Touche near Blois. In 1685 Louis XIV of France revoked his grandfather Henri IV's Edict of Nantes, which had granted Protestants the right to practise their faith. As a result, some 400,000 French citizens left the country, among them a 14-year-old orphan called David Digues, who moved to Holland with the family bible and one hundred crowns from a pious aunt. Three years later he obtained a cavalry commission in a Huguenot regiment and in August 1689, as Monsieur David Digues de la Touche des Rompures, he arrived in Ireland with William of Orange's army. Following William's victory against his Catholic father-in-law James II at the Battle of the Boyne in July 1690, David Digues remained in Ireland. After being demobilised in 1694 at the age of 24, he set himself up in business in Dublin, like many other Huguenots manufacturing and trading in fabrics such as cambric and silk poplin. Joining the Guild of Weavers in 1701, two years later he became a naturalised citizen of Ireland. Once sufficiently prosperous, he not only acquired his own premises on High Street but also began loaning funds to former army colleagues, as well as looking after the money and valuables of members of the city's Huguenot community.

From these activities developed the La Touche bank and the family's subsequent affluence. In 1712 David Digues, by now using the surname La Touche, established a banking business with three partners, two of whom departed after a few years. Meanwhile, David La Touche had been using some of the profits he was making from his businesses to acquire property around Dublin, including a large site on Castle Street, where a new building was erected in 1722, possibly to the designs of Sir Edward Lovett Pearce. The latter was certainly the architect of Dublin's new parliament building which, following the 1800 Act of Union, became headquarters of the Bank of Ireland: this institution's founding Governor was David La Touche's grandson. The Castle Street bank premises was five bays wide and rose three storeys over a rusticated granite ground floor; wings, slightly lower in height, were added on each side in the early 19th century. Commercial activities took place on the lower levels while those above provided accommodation for David La Touche and his family. Although it had ceased to serve as a bank, the building survived until demolition in 1945: a 1750s stuccowork ceiling in the back boudoir depicting Venus and Cupid attributed to Barthelemy Cramillion was rescued from the property and installed in the directors' dining room of the Bank of Ireland.

In the year David La Touche moved to Castle Street, his bank's annual profits were £846; two decades later they had risen to £3,547. When he died in 1745, the bank was left to his older son, also called David La Touche, while the younger child, confusingly named James Digues (later anglicised to Digges) inherited the textile business. David II La Touche proved as adept at banking as his father and during the second half of the 18th century David La Touche & Sons, as the company came to be called following the involvement of his own offspring and the retirement of the final non-family partner, was considered the most trustworthy bank in Ireland. While many other private financial institutions failed, that run by the La Touches remained strong, consistently enjoying a reputation for probity and prudence. Unlike bankers in more recent times, the La Touches also enjoyed a reputation for philanthropy and civic mindedness. In 1778 the Irish government experienced financial difficulties and required a loan of £20,000: the full amount was advanced by the La Touche bank. As was written by C.M. Tenison in 1894, 'It had for its customers almost the entire Protestant community of Ireland, when the wealth and trade of the country was exclusively in Protestant hands.' The La Touche bank was particularly patronised by members of the landed classes, the clientele between 1765–90 including two dukes, six marquesses, 32 earls and 41 other peers, as well as many wealthy untitled individuals. It is noteworthy that no member of the family ever accepted a title although they soon began to acquire large tracts of land and fine country houses, and some of their children married the offspring of peers. They also became involved in politics through election to the Irish parliament; in its dying days there were five La Touches sitting in the House of Commons.

In Dublin, where most members of the family had left Castle

LEFT: An engraving of David III La Touche by David Fittler from a portrait by Hugh Douglas Hamilton. David was older brother of Peter La Touche and owned the Marlay estate on the outskirts of Dublin, its name deriving from his wife Elizabeth (née Marlay). Their second son Peter was left Luggala, along with Bellevue, by his uncle Peter on the latter's death in 1828. And it would be David and Elizabeth's grandson, David Charles La Touche, who bought Luggala from his cousins in the 1840s and then sold it on to Lord Powerscourt in 1857.

Street for new, splendidly decorated houses in St. Stephen's Green and Merrion Square, they were founder members in 1780 of the establishment Kildare Street Club, governors of the Rotunda Hospital, generous donors to sundry charities and treasurers of such worthy establishments as the Prussia St. Boys' Orphanage and the Lock Penitentiary. And they started to have their portraits painted and to collect works of art; David II commissioned a portrait from the Cork-born artist Philip Hussey in 1746 and a marble bust of him in old age was carved by John van Nost the younger. His eldest son, once more called David, was sent to Italy on a Grand Tour and had a portrait painted in Rome by Anton Raphael Mengs. When David III's own son, John David was likewise in Rome in 1789 he commissioned a marble sculpture of Amorino from Antonio Canova. The Irish artist Hugh Douglas Hamilton was much patronised by the extended La Touche family, producing portraits of many of them.

By the time of his death at the age of 82 in 1785, David II La Touche, Ireland's wealthiest commoner, was said to be drawing a rental income of £25,000 per annum from his lands, while the bank he had run produced annual profits of £20,000-£30,000. The next generation was to enjoy even greater affluence, but in the decades following the 1800 Act of Union the La Touche bank went into a slow, inexorable decline and so too did the family's fortunes.

ABOVE: A watercolour of Lough Tay by Cecilia M. Campbell (1791–1857). The daughter of a landscape artist by whom she was taught, she began to exhibit at the age of 18 and continued to do so for many years afterwards, principally views of Counties Kerry and Wicklow. Her husband, George Nairn, was a noted animal painter whose pictures were described as being 'in the style of Stubbs.'

whole view is great and unites to form a scene of natural magnificence.'

Young noted that nearby 'Mr La Touche has erected a banqueting room' in the grounds of Bellevue but as yet there was no reference to a house at Luggala. Nor indeed was there mention of it in the first edition of William Wilson's 500-page guide to Ireland, the *Post-Chaise Companion*, which appeared in 1786.

A decade later, however, John Ferrar published his *A View Of Ancient And Modern Dublin, With Its Latest Improvements: To Which Is Added A Tour To Bellevue, In The County Of Wicklow*, in which he gave the first known account of the lodge at Luggala. 'Mr La Touche,' he wrote, 'has another modern built house at Luggula [sic] about nine miles S.W. of Bellevue, agreeably situated between two mountains and extremely romantic. Fronting the house is a good piece of water, called Lough Tay, over a branch of which is a well executed rustic bridge. Nature has been bountiful to this spot, which is diversified with rocks curiously shaped, wood and waterfalls. The mountains abound with grouse, and the lough with fish, which brings many visitors to the place. But what is most remarkable, frequent rumblings and roarings are heard in the bowels of the mountains, sometimes as loud as a cannon shot, probably occasioned by the firing of sulphurous and bituminous matter.'

A year later Jacques Louis de Bougrenet, Chevalier de la Tocnaye, an aristocratic refugee from the revolution in his native country, published *A Frenchman's Walk through Ireland*, describing how he 'came to Loughilla, one of the houses of Mr Peter Latouche. One is surprised to find such a house in such a wild and lonely place. The next house to it is at a distance of five or six miles. There are not even peasants' cabins in the neighbourhood. It is seated on a little bit of fertile earth near a beautiful lake, a bit of earth as distinct from the rest of the country as an island is from the water that surrounds it.'

Increasing numbers of visitors travelled to Luggala in the early 1800s, their journey assisted by improved access. After the 1798 Rebellion, the British authorities realised that one reason why Irish insurgents had been able to hold out for so long in this part of Wicklow was because the roads were few and the terrain familiar only to local residents. Hence new routes were created through the mountains, not least the Military Road begun in 1800. An unexpected consequence of this road-building programme was that it made reachable previously out of the way places like Luggala and thus opened up the area to ever more visitors. In June 1822 *The Atheneum* magazine could report, 'The Glen of the Downs, the Dargle, the Devil's Glen, the vale of Obrea, Luggelaw, all the most charming scenery of Wicklow, is within a morning's drive of Dublin.'

Everyone coming upon Luggala was immediately enraptured. In 1829 Prince Herman von Pückler-Muskau, an impoverished German aristocrat then travelling through Britain and Ireland in search of a rich wife, visited the Wicklow countryside. While there, he reported, 'I reached the summit of the mountain above the magnificent valley and lake of Luggelaw, the sun gilded all the country beneath me, though the tops of the hills were yet shrouded in mist. This valley belongs to a wealthy proprietor, who has converted it into a delightful park...It is indeed a lovely spot of earth, lonely and secluded; the wood full of game, the lake full of fish and nature full of poetry.' In 1822 the Rev. George Newenham Wright devoted several pages of his *A Guide to the County of Wicklow* to Luggala. The author was awe-struck that the first view of the site 'is of a bold, awful and sublime character,' the sheer mass of mountainside that closes the prospect 'exhibiting a continued mass of naked granite to the very summit, forming the most complete representation of all that is wild, dreary and desolate in nature, and defying all attempts at innovation that the aspiring genius of man has ever dared to undertake.' Fortunately he was able to contrast this 'extremest degree of desolation' with the rest of Luggala's 'verdant lawns, waving woods, thriving plantations and mountains clad to the very summit with fir, larch, oak, hazel and ash trees...'

In the midst of this widespread ardour, an occasional dissenting voice can be found. In 1844 Dr James Johnson, who had been Physician Extraordinary to William IV, published *A Tour in Ireland* in which he displayed a more dyspeptic attitude towards Luggala than his contemporaries. 'Though the beauty of Luggelaw,' he wrote, 'like that of almost every place else, is exaggerated, yet I am not disposed to quarrel with Mr Latouche's taste, for his selection of this sequestered vale as his Tusculum. It is less over-praised than most other valleys in Wicklow; and that is saying a great deal. For my own part, I cannot say that I should like to pitch my suburban tent on the border of "a small dark lake in the midst of perpendicular mountains" – even should that be Lough Tay or Lough Dan.' Later in his text, Dr Johnson conceded that Luggala and other similar spots could serve as 'silent and solemn retreats for the merchant, the banker, the lawyer, and legislator, where meditation and devotion may usefully supersede, for a short time, the cares and perplexities of active and laborious avocations.'

Well before the middle of the 19th century, despite being privately owned and still relatively off the beaten track, Luggala had become a fixture on the Wicklow itinerary, together with more public sites such as nearby Glendalough. In part this was thanks to its increasing appearance in guidebooks, all of them equally enthusiastic about Luggala's inimitable appeal. In an entry on County Wicklow, the *London Encyclopedia* (1829) having reported 'The lake scenery is peculiarly interesting,' went on to advise, 'Mr Latouche's demesne of Luggelaw is generally preferred by tourists as the most delightful scene of this class.' James Fraser's 1845 *Handbook for Travellers in Ireland*, for example, called Luggala

Bellevue

ABOVE: Two photographs of Bellevue taken by Robert French, probably towards the close of the 19th century when the house and greenhouses were still intact. In 1796 John Ferrar wrote that the latter had been erected a few years earlier by 'Mr Michael Pennick, the gardener, to whom the author is indebted for much interesting and useful information. Bellevue is a striking proof that he is ingenious, laborious and extremely skilful in his profession.'

OPPOSITE: While most evidence of Bellevue's landscaped demesne has long since gone, a handful of ruins remain including the walls of the octagon room designed by Enoch Johnson in 1766.

In 1753 David II La Touche bought Ballydonagh, an estate of 300 acres, from the Rev. Doctor Francis Corbet, Dean of St. Patrick's Cathedral in Dublin. Located in Delgany, County Wicklow, the land offered splendid views towards the Irish Sea on one side and of the two Sugarloaf Mountains on the other. A year after his purchase, La Touche spent £30,000 building a house, which he named Bellevue. Facing east with a terrace looking towards Dublin Bay, the building was of two storeys, the central three bays being surmounted by a pediment. The surrounding grounds were duly landscaped and, as was the fashion for the period, a number of garden pavilions constructed, perhaps the earliest being an octagon room built in 1766 to the design of Enoch Johnson on the crest of the Glen of the Downs. In 1822 the Rev. George Newenham Wright noted 'the interior is hung with drapery and assumes the appearance of a bell tent; from the windows, which are glazed with plate glass, there are varied and extensive views...In the hall of the octagon building is a stuffed panther, so placed, that it scarcely ever fails of startling the stranger who enters unwarned of its presence.'

The stuffed panther, which was on a spring released when the door opened, was only one of many surprises discovered by visitors to Bellevue after it had been inherited by David La Touche's second son Peter in 1785. By 1790 he had greatly extended the size of the estate by buying the lands of Upper and Lower Rathdown, much of which is now covered by the coastal town of Greystones. The main house underwent some modifications, not least the addition of two-bay projections to each side of the central block and new stucco ceilings in the principal rooms done in the neo-classical style of Michael Stapleton. In 1803 a free-standing chapel was erected to the design of Richard Morrison.

Meanwhile, Peter La Touche and his second wife Elizabeth had done much to enhance the charms of Bellevue's demesne thanks to the addition of further buildings. A Gothic banqueting room was added below the octagon room in 1788 and five years later a 'Turkish Tent' with 'drapery and ornaments in the style of an eastern pavilion' was built southwest of the main house; both were designed by the architect Francis Sandys. In addition, a rustic habitation was constructed entirely of wooden stumps and roots with a heather-covered roof, and a thatched cottage orné built with an upper chamber in which Elizabeth would entertain her friends.

But by far the most remarkable of the La Touches' improvements was a sequence of interconnecting conservatories and greenhouses that ran some 500 feet from the back of the house and survived into the 20th century. Built by a Mr Shanley at the cost of £3,000, these glassworks were entered via Mrs La Touche's dressing room and consisted of a series of large spaces linked by glazed passages. The more notable sights included a square-shaped orangery, its centre filled with orange trees, a vinery measuring 42 by 24 feet and containing fifteen different varieties of grape, two peach houses each 60 feet long, a pinery in which much-prized pineapples were grown, and an immense oval conservatory rising 20 feet high. No wonder Edmund Burke, on a visit to Bellevue, exclaimed to his hostess, 'Oh, ma'am, this is absolutely the Arabian Nights Entertainments!'

In September 1803 the theologian Alexander Knox, who by then had taken up permanent residence at Bellevue, described it in a letter as 'one of the most charming places in the British empire...great wealth has enabled its owner, Mr Peter La Touche, to add to it every kind of decoration which good taste could approve, and some which visitors are surprised by.' Visitors there were aplenty. Like their lodge at Luggala, the La Touches' main residence soon became a popular destination for anyone passing through County Wicklow. In 1796 John Ferrar published *A View of Ancient and Modern Dublin With its Improvements...To which is added a Tour of Bellevue in the County of Wicklow*, its title page dedicated to Elizabeth La Touche. Three chapters of the book are devoted to Bellevue, which Ferrar described as being 'one of the best excursions near the capital.' So overwhelmed was the author by his own visit that he soon slipped from prose to verse:

'Here all the charms of chance and order meet,
The rude, the gay, the graceful and the great,
Here ev'ry tree with nature's music rings,
Here ev'ry breeze bears health upon its wings.'

Others had likewise waxed poetical about Bellevue, a writer in the June 1794 edition of the Dublin monthly *Walker's Hibernian Magazine* rhapsodising in a piece called 'To a Lady desiring a description of Bellevue Gardens',

'But ah! What language e'er can tell,
The blooming charms that always dwell,
On this enchanting spot!...
And, if on earth there can be found,
An Eden, or enchanted ground,
You'll own it is BELLEVUE'

Peter and Elizabeth La Touche had no children, so both Bellevue and Luggala were left to his nephew, also called Peter, second son of David III La Touche. Bellevue's last male heir, likewise called Peter, died childless in 1904 and his oldest sister Frances, who was married to the local doctor, Arthur Archer, moved into the house. Two years later, in May 1906, there was a three-day executors' auction disposing of Bellevue's contents. Along with an abundance of Chippendale and Sheraton furniture was a 104-piece Dresden dinner service originally purchased by a member of the family in Paris in 1788. It sold for £460, while £165 was paid for a portrait of a lady by Angelica Kauffmann and £800 for 'a reputed Velasquez.' The contents of the house's impressive library had gone to auction earlier in the month. In 1908 the Delgany Golf Club was established on part of the Bellevue demesne and a year later paying guests were being welcomed to stay in the house. However in 1913 the Archers moved out of Bellevue and after more than 150 years it ceased to be the La Touche family home. Rented for a few years, it was then left empty until inevitable demolition in the early 1950s. While most of the demesne has long since disappeared, the site of the house and some ruins, such as the octagon room and the gothic dining room, remain.

ABOVE: A highly romanticised watercolour of Luggala bathed in moonlight by Cecilia M. Campbell. To the left and to the north of the main house is clearly visible a dwelling. Parts of this were still extant when the house underwent its most recent restoration, thereby allowing the structure's recreation.

OPPOSITE: An oil painting of Luggala by Ireland's leading landscape artist during the second half of the 18th century, William Ashford (1746-1824). The picture may have been commissioned by Peter La Touche since it hung in Bellevue until Luggala was sold to Lord Powerscourt. Colonel David La Touche then said to the new owner 'as you have got the place you may as well have the picture too!' In the 1984 sale at Powerscourt, the painting was bought by the Hon. Garech Browne and now hangs in Luggala.

'one of the most romantic retreats in any country' and insisted that 'from no part is this sublime part of Wicklow scenery so finely displayed.'

Not surprisingly, when Sir Walter Scott, the most famous novelist of his generation, visited Ireland in July 1825, he included a stop at Luggala on his itinerary, writing afterwards to his son that it featured 'a very fine lake [on which he rowed], where Mr Latouche keeps a house *pro bono publico*; fine trees on one side, and a marvellously naked cliff on the other.'

It is to the credit of the La Touches that they were prepared to tolerate growing numbers of visitors to what had been originally created as a rural retreat for their personal use. In fact, in accordance with Sir Walter Scott's description of the house being kept '*pro bono publico*', the family appears to have gone beyond mere tolerance: as early as 1805 John Carr informed readers 'A part of the building is allotted for respectable strangers, where, in the spirit of Irish hospitality, beds and attendants are provided.' When writing of Luggala in 1822, the Rev. Wright speculated that 'the chief object of its erection appears to have been public accommodation, and a spirit of improvement; for the politeness of the proprietor induces him to give tickets to persons of respectability, allowing them to make use of the accommodations which his house at Luggelaw affords, for several days at a time.' No wonder Wright concluded, 'This is another instance of consideration for the public convenience and benefit, which has marked the character of this distinguished family, and rendered them so deservedly popular from the period of their arrival in this country to the present moment.'

In case the Rev. Wright's remarks on the La Touches' hospitality to strangers seem barely credible, it is worth quoting *The Angling Excursions of Gregory Greendrake, Esq. in Ireland* which appeared two years later and which observed that 'In summer, scarcely a day passes without Luggelaw visited by parties of pleasure, which, on presenting a ticket from any member of the La Touche family, are accommodated with beds, and receive every other attention which the lodge can afford.' According to Greendrake, an album was kept inside the house, 'for the purpose of the visitor recording any observation arising out of the conduct of the domestics, who are instructed to be very attentive, or the impressions made upon him by the scene.' He went on to quote some lines of verse written in this album. These requested,

'Reader, obey the grateful muse,
With thanks enjoy, and not abuse,
This little book, in which we trace,
The transient inmates of this place;
Let no rude thought deform its page,
To shock the eye, and shame the age;
But pure its every line appear,
As that pure hand which placed it here...'

In the 25th January 1834 edition of the *Dublin Penny Journal*, its editor Philip Dixon Hardy reported on a three-day expedition he and a group of friends made from the capital to County Wicklow. Their itinerary had, inevitably, included a stop at Luggala: 'We reached Mr Latouche's cottage late in the evening, and in consideration of our benighted state, and because there was a lady of the party, we were accommodated there for the night. The evening was fine, and there was a brightness over the whole scene, never to be erased from my memory.'

Perhaps the sheer number of visitors taking advantage of the La Touches' generosity proved too much: by the time the *Guide to the County of Wicklow* appeared in 1835, access had become more limited and 'strangers are allowed to see the place on Wednesdays and Thursdays'. On the other hand, even as late as 1853, the *Tourist's Illustrated Handbook for Ireland* could report that admission to Luggala 'is most freely

Who designed Luggala?

Who was responsible for this sophisticated piece of architecture? Who managed to conceive a building that looks so effortless and is yet as complex a piece of design as can be imagined? The answer remains unknown, along with the precise date of Luggala's construction and even whether it was entirely new-built or instead developed on the site of an existing structure. The last of these seems possible; given the sheltered nature of the site it is likely there would already have been some sort of dwelling house there when it was first 'discovered' by Peter La Touche around 1788, perhaps a tenant farmer's residence or a more primitive hunting lodge than that afterwards constructed. Remains of a sod house have been found near the north shore of Lough Tay; once the La Touches started to improve the valley of Luggala, it is probably this building would have been taken down in order to provide an unimpeded view of the lake from the house.

Extant documents relating to the leasing of the land shortly before it passed into La Touche hands suggest there was a decent property already on the site where the present house now stands: a lease drawn up by William Bomford refers to 'the house of Lake Tay and the lands of Luggallow.' This house would have provided the basis for the subsequent building, as well as somewhere for the La Touches to rest on visits while more superior accommodation was being built.

In 1802 the Waterford-born artist Thomas Sautelle Roberts exhibited 40 Irish landscapes in watercolour at the former Parliament House in Dublin's College Green. These were intended for a work he hoped to publish, *Illustrations of the Chief Sites, Rivers and Picturesque Scenery of the Kingdom of Ireland.* Some of the pictures were subsequently issued as coloured aquatints by the engraver Frederick Christian Lewis, including one dated 1803 showing the Lake of Luggelaw, County of Wicklow. The most interesting feature of this particular work is the inclusion of the La Touche property as it then stood. The accompanying text comments, 'A neat Banqueting house erected in the Glen speaks of the chaste Taste of its Proprietor, Peter La Touche Esq.' This can be clearly seen in the picture and has none of the Gothic features that now distinguish Luggala. Instead, it looks a plainly constructed building backed by a series of outhouses, successors of which exist to the present time.

It is worth noting that no early commentators on the house refer to its appearance or Gothic ornamentation, John Ferrar in 1796 calling it simply a 'modern built house.' In her *Narrative of a Residence in Ireland during the Summer of 1814, and that of 1815* (published 1817), Anne Plumptre states that at Luggala, Peter La Touche had 'made a very pretty shooting-box.' Only in 1822 did the Rev. George Newenham Wright note that the structure 'is but one storey in height, built with excellent taste, and in the pointed style...' It may therefore be the case that the house as seen today was developed in stages, especially if there was an existing structure on the spot when the land was bought by Peter La Touche. This building could have been gradually augmented over a number of years before being given its final coherent decoration.

The question of who was responsible for that decorative scheme has exercised many writers but nobody has yet come up with a convincing argument in favour of any one individual. In the mid-1960s the Knight of Glin first proposed Francis Sandys junior, usually believed to be the son of another architect of the same name who worked for Peter La Touche at Bellevue, there designing both the Gothic banqueting room and the Turkish tent, and lauded for these buildings by John Ferrar in 1796: 'The design and execution of his various works will remain a lasting honour to his name and to his country.' The older Sandys died at Bellevue in 1795, and, given his connection with Peter and Elizabeth La Touche, he might therefore have had a hand in the creation of Luggala, although if this were the case it seems strange the fact passed unrecorded by Ferrar. Sandys fils, on the other hand, is not known to have had any direct ties with the La Touche family but did work for the wealthy and unconventional Frederick Hervey, Bishop of Derry and 4th Earl of Bristol, overseeing construction of the clerical peer's immense new neo-classical house at Ickworth in Suffolk.

More recently, Sir Richard Morrison has been proposed as the man behind Luggala's design. This industrious Irish architect, who produced buildings in whatever style took his patrons' fancy, carried out work for a number of members of the extended La Touche clan, specifically for Peter and Elizabeth La Touche he designed a chapel in the classical manner at Bellevue, as well as a number of cottages

on the estate. The former building was constructed in 1803 and likewise his other La Touche commissions date from the early years of the 19th century. If, therefore, the Lewis engraving of Luggala in 1803 accurately represents its state at that date, it is feasible Morrison designed the final building. On the other hand, while there are stylistic similarities between the design of the house and other Morrison work in the Gothic manner, many of these details found at Luggala were common architectural currency at the time and cannot be regarded as exclusive to him.

There is yet another possibility. James Gandon, the most distinguished member of that profession working in Ireland in the closing decades of the 18th century, once complained that the country's gentry were 'almost always their own architects.' Could this be true of Luggala? Might it be that the La Touches did not employ someone to design their lodge but instead personally directed the builders to employ Gothic elements?

The architect of Luggala continues to be unknown. So, too, is the architect of Castleward, a much more substantial building, together with the names of those responsible for many other notable houses constructed during this period. Unless autographed drawings should turn up, or other equally convincing evidence be produced, it is likely the person responsible for designing Luggala as it now exists must remain the subject of speculation.

ABOVE: In 1803 the engraver Frederick Christian Lewis produced a series of coloured aquatints based on Irish landscape watercolours exhibited the previous year by Thomas Sautelle Roberts. One of these pictures was of Luggala and featured the La Touche house and outbuildings as they then appeared. The structures all look free of any Gothic ornamentation and the accompanying text comments 'A neat Banqueting house erected in the Glen speaks of the chaste Taste of its Proprietor, Peter La Touche Esq.'

LEFT: Another watercolour of Luggala painted by Cecilia M. Campbell. As well as showing the house in daylight, the work also displays a more realistic approach to its subject than its nocturnal companion. Luggala's popularity as a destination for visitors to Wicklow in the first half of the 19th century meant the house was readily identifiable, in turn ensuring a market for pictures such as this one.

extended by the esteemed proprietor, Mr Latouche, whose lodge is justly regarded as one of the sweetest summer villas in Wicklow.'

Keeping an eye on those strangers for much of the period was boatman Charley (or Charlie) Carr, notable for his stature and storytelling alike. The indefatigable Mr and Mrs Samuel Hall, who produced a three-volume *Tour of Ireland* in 1841–43, recommended, 'Let no one who visits Luggelaw leave without striving to make the acquaintance of Charley Carr, the guide, whose cottage is at the entrance to the domain. Charley is, of course, very jealous for the honour and glory of Luggelaw, and very envious of the superior attractions of Glendalough – which he abuses with a right good will, affirming that it is unnatural not to love nature better than ould stone and mountain, and at times he cannot conceal his anger at the holy saint – St. Kevin – for not having carried out his intention of building his churches around Lough Tay.'

Charley Carr acted as the guardian of Luggala for several decades: an unnamed writer in *The Irish Monthly Magazine of Politics and Literature* of October 1832, referring to the Greek mythical hero, described Carr as 'the Evander of Wicklow'. Meanwhile *The Kaleidoscope*'s 'M' in 1829 had called him 'the famous Luggelaw boatman' and observed, 'Parties coming out from Dublin, and bringing with them provisions, may, at Charlie's, be accommodated with everything to enable them to partake their meal in comfort.' The fullest description of Luggala's guardian is provided in *The Angling Excursions of Gregory Greendrake, Esq*. The author informed readers that Carr had previously been a grenadier in the Antrim militia and though excessively fond of whiskey, 'retains much of his military air and, as we witnessed, almost to our inconvenience, during a walk across the mountain, his strength and activity very little impaired.' Carr's fame was sufficient for him to be commemorated in an undated, hand-coloured print by the artist William Brocas (1794–1868). Carr's cottage, mentioned by the Halls, still stands overlooking Lough Tay, although today unroofed.

Although he retired from active public life soon after the turn of the new century, Peter La Touche lived to the age of 95, dying in 1828. In his final years he seems to have suffered from physical and possibly mental infirmities. In 1827 the Chief Secretary for Ireland William Lamb, later second Viscount Melbourne and Prime Minister of Great Britain, visited Bellevue and dined with its aged owner. Afterwards

Lamb wrote to his estranged wife Caroline (notorious for her affair with Lord Byron fifteen years before) that the household at Bellevue kept Peter La Touche 'upon a strict regimen of sherry and water, but if he can get a bottle of wine now, he drinks it off in a crack. There's a fine old cod for you.' At the time, Lamb, whose extra-marital relationships were as recurrent as those of his spouse, was in the throes of an affair with Peter La Touche's great-niece Elizabeth. More than a decade earlier she had married an older cousin, the Rev. William Crosbie, Baron Branden. The relationship between Lamb and Lady Branden soon became such common knowledge that her husband sued the Chief Secretary for 'criminal conversation' as a legal wrong arising from adultery was then known. Gossipy English diarist Thomas Creevey recorded that Lord Braden, who was an Anglican cleric as well as a peer, had advised his erring wife that 'if she will exert her interest with Mr Lamb to procure him a bishopric, he will overlook her offence'. The bishopric not being forthcoming, Lord Braden was instead paid off with £2,000, which he insisted on receiving in cash. When he died in 1832, he left one shilling to his 'very base and vicious wife whose infidelity to me is the least of her crimes'.

Peter La Touche's own will was a less unpleasant document. He left his wife Elizabeth an annuity of £1,200 and in addition a long list of items from the couple's house in Dublin, and the Bellevue property. She died in 1844 at the age of 86, long before which, as had been arranged by her husband, the Wicklow estates, including Luggala, passed to his nephew Peter, second son of David III La Touche. The older Peter's will directed that his heir was not free to dispose of anything he had been left but had to pass it on to his son. He also instructed that whoever inherited Bellevue in future would have to live in Ireland for at least six months each year or else forfeit the property. This may have been a way of ensuring Bellevue – and the extensive Leitrim estates – did not suffer from the curse of an absentee landlord, indifferent to his holdings except as a source of income.

In 1828, Peter II La Touche had received his uncle's stock in the family bank and also the house on St Stephen's Green, Dublin. Born in 1777, he only outlived his older relative by a year and three months, dying in February 1830; his widow was to live for another 44 years. The heir was the couple's eldest son, another Peter, who died unmarried in 1856, after

TOP: Charley Carr, the boatman of Luggala, as seen in an undated engraving by William Brocas (1794–1868). This shows him standing on the shore of Lough Tay, while behind a party of visitors can be seen out on the water. Evident in the picture is the most distinctive aspect of Carr's appearance, as mentioned by angler Gregory Greendrake in 1826: 'black whiskers of unusual magnitude, of which he seems vain, and suffers to meet in a sort of ruff that covers his throat and the under part of his chin.'

ABOVE: Also mentioned by writers of the period, Carr's house above the lake still stands. Although without a roof, its external walls have been partly rebuilt.

Luggala and the 1798 Rebellion

Less than a decade after being acquired by Peter La Touche, Luggala risked being destroyed during a period of national unrest. Led by the Society of United Irishmen, an outlawed political organisation, uprisings against British rule broke out across Ireland in May 1798. The rebellion was quickly suppressed in Dublin but proved more enduring elsewhere, not least in neighbouring County Wicklow, where the revolutionaries found an inspirational leader in Joseph Holt. His memoirs, edited by Thomas Crofton Croker, were posthumously published in 1838.

Born in 1756, Holt was the son of a Protestant farmer and builder. As a young man he spent some time in the British army and in 1782 he married Hester Long who, like him, came from Protestant farming stock. The couple had a son and daughter, and Holt worked both as both a farmer and a wool buyer in Roundwood, less than five miles from Luggala.

When trouble broke out in 1798, Thomas Hugo, a local landlord who lived nearby at Drummin House and seemingly owed Holt a sum of money, made public the latter's involvement with the United Irishmen. As a result, a group of yeomanry burnt down the Holt family home, driving him to take up arms. With his military background he was soon leading a large band of fellow insurgents.

Memories of the atrocities committed in County Wicklow by both sides during this period survived long after the rebellion had come to an end. In October 1832 the *Irish Monthly Magazine of Politics and Literature* described a recent visit to Luggala by a party of pleasure-seekers and reported that 'Charley Carr, the boatman of Luggelaw, accompanied them to the top of a small cliff that overhangs the larger lake, and having told them a legend of the cave that ran under the rock they stood on, where in '98 two refugees found a shelter in, until a detachment of Highlanders on the opposite bank perceived smoke creeping through the bushes that stopped up the entrance, and compelling an old fisherman to row them over, burst in on them and shot the wretches on their knees, while they begged for mercy (Carr himself being one of the number who buried them that night where they died).' Many large houses in Wicklow were ransacked and burnt by the insurgents during this period. Luggala might have suffered such a fate but for being protected by Holt. In fact, for most of his time as a rebel leader, he based himself in the Cloghoge townland, in other words only a short distance from Luggala.

By September 1798, aware there was a price of £300 on his head and that the uprising had been crushed across much of the country, Holt began considering surrender. Alhough the British authorities had hitherto not shown leniency to the rebels, he was fortunate to find his cause championed by the La Touches. Seemingly, his wife Hester proposed initiating contact with Elizabeth La Touche. 'I told her it would be well done,' he wrote many years later, 'but I feared they knew nothing of me, and that they were not aware I had saved Luggelaw House from being burned.' However, one of Hester's relations was then employed by the family and so they were asked to help. Elizabeth La Touche advised Holt to write her a letter stating his willingness to surrender to Viscount Powerscourt, head of the local militia. This she promised to deliver to Lord Powerscourt in person 'and try what could be done for me.'

She duly did so. On reading Holt's letter, Lord Powerscourt 'was much gratified, and with humane and generous kindness, said my life should be spared, and I should be protected from further pursuit.' Thanks to the intervention of Elizabeth La Touche, Holt was sentenced not to death but to exile in Australia. Further assistance from the La Touches meant he did not have to endure life there alone. Once more he wrote to his protectress – whom he described as 'the concentration, the accumulation, the very essence of benevolence' – asking whether she could provide 'some small assistance to enable me to pay the passage of my wife and family, to the far distant land of my exile.' Holt received the reply that the La Touches would not only pay for his wife and son to accompany

him but also provide funds for the whole group to sail together in comfort. The couple's daughter Marianne, then aged seven, remained in Ireland as a pupil at the La Touche school in Bellevue.

The rest of the family travelled to Australia, arriving in Sydney in January 1800. There Joseph Holt initially managed a farm for the English soldier William Cox before acquiring land of his own. Following several setbacks, he was finally pardoned in 1811 and after many adventures, including shipwreck on the Falkland Islands, returned to Ireland with his wife and a younger son in 1814. He died eight years later in Kingstown, now called Dún Laoghaire, but never forgot the kindness shown to him by Peter and Elizabeth La Touche. 'The particulars which I mention occurred so many years ago,' he wrote in his memoirs, 'that it may be supposed the extreme warmth of my gratitude has in some measure subsided...but if it was in my power to do so, I would hand down the names of Mr and Mrs Peter Latouche in the annals of history, for admiration and imitation, as illustrious patterns of excellence, to the remotest posterity.'

ABOVE: Until a road-building programme was initiated after the 1798 Rebellion, much of the Wicklow Mountains' upper reaches were inaccessible and unknown to government authorities. This made them an ideal refuge for Joseph Holt and his forces. They were thus able to hold out against the British army for longer than did the Irish rebels elsewhere in the country.

which Bellevue was inherited in succession by three more brothers before passing in 1897 to the next generation, Peter IV, who would be the estate's last male heir.

However, over half a century before that date, the Bellevue La Touches had sold Luggala to the senior branch of their family whose main residence was at Marlay in Rathfarnham, County Dublin. Born in 1800, David Charles La Touche of Marlay was a descendant of David III, older brother of Peter La Touche, who had first bought Luggala around 1788. David Charles was evidently familiar with the place, his father writing in March 1832 that 'David...is just returned from the Co. Wicklow. He shot 4½ brace of cocks at Luggala.' Involved in the family bank, like his forebears he was also much involved in Dublin charities such as the Royal Hospital for Incurables at Donnybrook. Neither the exact date nor the reason for his acquisition of Luggala is known, but it may be that as head of the extended family he wished to help a branch experiencing financial difficulties, as were they all soon enough.

There are many explanations for the decline of the La Touche Bank – and a corresponding deterioration in the family's fortunes – during the 19th century. At least in part it must have been due to the establishment in 1783 of a national bank, the Bank of Ireland. Unlike a private financial institution such as the La Touche Bank, this benefitted from state support. The 1800 Act of Union also played a part in the weakening of Irish private banks. This legislation dissolved the Irish Houses of Parliament and transferred their responsibilities to Westminster. Thereafter London rather than Dublin was the centre to which both politicians and peers – many of whom would have been clients of the La Touche Bank – gravitated. Dublin, which had experienced almost unbroken growth throughout the 18th century, began a long descent into provincialism and poverty.

In the economic depression following the end of the Napoleonic Wars, 16 of Ireland's 31 private banks collapsed and this damaged the entire financial sector. During the following decade, legislative changes permitted the creation of a new form of competition, the joint stock bank. Some of these were set up specifically to look after the business interests of Catholics, a growing sector of the market, whereas the La Touche Bank had always been known for its Protestant clientele. Unlike the new institutions, the La Touche Bank failed to open branches elsewhere in the country and this also proved a handicap. Problems became acute from 1850 onwards, with members of the family having to bolster the bank's resources from their own assets and through growing indebtedness to the Bank of Ireland. Ultimately it proved impossible to sustain a private bank and in January 1870 the La Touche Bank merged with the joint stock Munster Bank, which had been set up six years earlier and wanted to open a branch in Dublin. The Munster Bank only survived until 1885 when its assets and liabilities were taken over by the newly formed Munster and Leinster Bank. In 1966 this in turn merged with the Provincial and the Royal Banks to form Allied Irish Banks; as of December 2010 the Irish government has been the majority stakeholder in Allied Irish Banks and is thus heir to Ireland's greatest 18th-century bank. Meanwhile, the Castle Street premises were sold to the government in 1870 and occupied by the Veterinary Department, the Privy Council and the Loan Fund Board before being demolished in the mid-1940s.

The disintegration of their family business inevitably had consequences for the La Touches, not least the Marlay branch. Unlike his cousins based in Bellevue and Harristown, David Charles did not own large estates elsewhere in the country but only the demesne around Marlay. The greater part of his income derived from the bank's profits, and once these started to drop, he needed to find an alternative source of funds. It could be that he bought Luggala because he believed the estate offered an opportunity to make money. This rationale would explain why, following his acquisition, he began to engage in land drainage and clearance, moving small tenant farmers off the property so that it could be used for intensive sheep farming. It had long been recognised the terrain in this part of Wicklow could be put to more efficient use were certain improvements first carried out. An unsigned article in the *Quarterly Journal of Agriculture* in 1835–6 observed that the area's extensive tracts of heath and bog 'only require draining, paring and burning, to become

RIGHT: An early 19th-century oil painting of Luggala, not dissimilar to the watercolours of Cecilia M. Campbell. The figures to the right of the picture suggest an almost arcadian world, reflecting contemporary attitudes towards Luggala as being the romantic landscape incarnate.

LEFT: Luggala and Lough Tay painted in 1839 by Henry O'Neill (1798–1880). Originally from Clonmel, County Tipperary, O'Neill was a watercolourist and engraver, often producing quiet pastoral scenes such as that shown here. Here he shows the original entrance to the demesne, to the north of the house.

OPPOSITE: A drawing from an undated and unsigned album of Wicklow landscapes, presumably by a 19th-century artist. This picture carries the caption 'The Lake at Luggala from the Lane before the Cottage.'

meadows or sheep pastures, and yet there is no attempt made to reclaim these tracts.'

What the writer failed to appreciate was that ever since acquiring Luggala, the La Touche family had treated the place not as an agricultural estate expected to generate income but as a country retreat to be shared with likeminded visitors to the area. That laissez-faire approach changed once David Charles acquired the property. For many years, at least some of the land had been leased to small tenant farmers; the 1841 census reveals the townland of Cloghoge to have had a population of 148 divided between 19 dwellings. Ireland's Great Famine of 1845–8 made an impact here, as it did throughout the country, and by 1851 the population had dropped to 95 people living in 15 houses. But thereafter it fell sharply so that by 1861 there were only 14 people in two houses. The reason for this steep decline in numbers is that David Charles La Touche had cleared out his tenants and then set about draining the land so as to engage in large-scale sheep farming. An 1852 report by the government's Board of Public Works noted that the operations 'already extend to 1,400 statute acres, and upwards of 50,000 perches of open drains have been cut...Previous to draining, the surface of this mountain was very wet, and the herbage consisted of heath, rushes, coarse sedgy grass, and bog moss. The surface is now comparatively firm to the tread, and the herbage is gradually improving, and will eventually, as in Scotland, produce sweet succulent pasture grasses.'

Meanwhile, the main house on the Luggala estate was offered for rental. No more a place of pleasure, from now on it was expected to produce a profit. This might eventually have been the case for David Charles had other family circumstances – including persistent demands for money from an impecunious younger brother – not obliged him to realise the value of his assets.

Writing to his brother in January 1860, David Charles advised, 'I forget whether I told you that Luggala is no longer mine. I was sentimentally ridiculous in that affair. Also I ought to have sold it better and had a little surplus instead of the other.' Luggala's new owner was Mervyn Wingfield, 7th Viscount Powerscourt (1836-1904). As he was a minor at the time of his father's death in 1844, for the next 13 years the Powerscourt estate was administered by his mother, who had not long remained a widow but subsequently married her lover, the 4th Marquess of Londonderry. On reaching the age of 21 in 1857, Lord Powerscourt sold a parcel of land he owned in England on the outskirts of Portsmouth and used the money realised to buy land adjacent to his own estate. His acquisitions comprised the townlands of Glasnamullen

and Ballinastoe, both hitherto owned by Conservative politician Major William Beresford, and Luggala.

In *A Description and History of Powerscourt*, which he published in 1903, the year before his death, Lord Powerscourt discussed the problems of land ownership in the Wicklow Mountains over the course of several centuries. By buying what had previously been the cause of dispute, he 'thereby obliterated the disputed boundaries and the law suits...Thus all arguments by gentlemen of the long robe over these mountains ceased, and the only voices now heard upon them are those of the beaters driving the grouse, and the only money now spent there goes into their pockets instead of into the denizens of the Four Courts in Dublin – a much happier state of things – and now there is a lasting peace on the former scenes of strife on the old Wicklow Hills!' Having added to his holdings, by 1883 Lord Powerscourt's total land holdings extended to 53,641 acres, the greater part of them in County Wicklow.

Photographs present him as the very model of Victorian rectitude and high mindedness, and indeed he held many public offices such as Lord Justice of Ireland and president of the Royal Dublin Society. However, like his forebears, he was an extravagant man and inclined to overspend, especially on further enhancing the house and grounds at Powerscourt.

Family legend has it the explanation for Lord Powerscourt's profligacy was that, not having a son, he did not want anything to pass to a despised younger brother Lewis; the reason for this dislike may be that the sibling in question was widely believed to be the child of his mother's lover (and second husband), Lord Londonderry. The Hon. Lewis Wingfield's unusual choice of pursuits would also most likely not have met with his older brother's approval; at various times he acted on the stage of London's Haymarket Theatre (and later designed costumes for plays in which the likes of Lily Langtry appeared), studied singing in Antwerp, and took painting classes in Paris, where he was forced to remain during the Prussian siege of 1870–71, writing about the experience for both the *Daily Telegraph* and *The Times*.

In 1864 the 7th Viscount had married Lady Julia Coke, daughter of the 2nd Earl of Leicester, but the couple remained childless. That is until 1880 when an heir was born, followed over the next few years by a further four offspring. Lord Powerscourt's lack of thrift, and belated fecundity, would have consequences for his successor.

During this time, Luggala largely disappeared from public view, reverting back to the obscurity it had known prior to being discovered by Peter and Elizabeth La Touche. The estate and house were no longer freely accessible to visitors, fishing expeditions to Lough Tay seem to have ceased, there

The Wingfields of Powerscourt

Descended from an old Suffolk family, Richard Wingfield (1550-1634) came to Ireland as a young man while his uncle Sir William Fitzwilliam was serving as the country's Lord Deputy. A member of the English army, Wingfield fought against the rebellious Earl of Desmond and Viscount Baltinglass before seeing further action in Flanders, France and Portugal, rising to the rank of Lieutenant Colonel. Back in Ireland, he was knighted in Dublin's Christchurch Cathedral in 1595 and five years later was advanced to the office of Marshal of Ireland with a retinue of 50 horses and a company of foot-soldiers. In 1601 he led a force at the conflict in Kinsale, County Cork, during which the English army decisively beat an Irish force assisted by Spain; Wingfield was afterwards among the signatories of the articles of capitulation made between the Lord Deputy of Ireland and Don Juan d'Aguila, Commander of the Spanish troops. Further military success in Ulster in 1608 led to his being granted an estate in County Wicklow, its extent described in the Down Survey of 1653–57 as being 'five miles in length by four miles in breadth.' This land had once been the property of the Norman de la Poer, or Power, family but they had long since lost control of it to the indigenous O'Tooles, who remained in possession until the estate was granted to Wingfield in 1609. He also acquired 800 acres in County Wexford, and the castle and 2,000 acres in Benburb, County Tyrone. In 1618 he was created Viscount Powerscourt.

Powerscourt House, Dublin

Dying without issue in 1635, Lord Powerscourt left his estates to a cousin whose grandson was created a viscount in 1665. He, too, died childless and once more the Wingfield estates passed to a cousin, Edward Wingfield, for whose son the title of Viscount Powerscourt was revived a third time. When Richard Wingfield had first been granted his land in Wicklow, it was described as being 'mostly mountainous and stony, and with a ruinous castle.' Now the remains of that castle were incorporated into a superb Palladian house designed by Ireland's leading architect of the era, the German-born Richard Cassells. Built in pale granite from the nearby Glencree quarries and completed in 1741, Powerscourt is agreed to have been Cassell's masterpiece, the beauty of the house enhanced by its setting on a ridge from whence the land drops into a valley and then rises on the other side to close with the Sugarloaf Mountain. The interior of the building was likewise renowned for its splendour, not least the first floor saloon, described by the Hon. Desmond Guinness as 'possibly the grandest room in any Irish house.' 80 foot long, 40 foot wide and 40 foot high, it had fluted marble columns, a compartmented and part-gilded ceiling and a walnut parquet floor.

Richard Wingfield, 3rd Viscount (1730-1788), was known as 'the French Lord' owing to his long residence at the court of Louis XV. In 1771 he commissioned architect Robert Mack to design a townhouse on Dublin's South William Street, an immense structure once more constructed of Wicklow granite with interiors containing elaborate plasterwork by James McCullagh and Michael Stapleton. This building was sold by the 4th Viscount in 1807 for £7,500, £500 less than it had cost; today it is a shopping centre.

The 4th Viscount is best remembered for his opposition to the 1800 Act of Union. He was one of only five Irish peers to vote against the legislation abolishing Ireland's parliament. When a government representative arrived at Powerscourt with the offer of an earldom if he would change his mind, the 4th Viscount, although suffering from gout, came downstairs and threw the man out of the house, saying 'You are not going to bribe me.'

His son, the 5th Viscount, entertained George IV at Powerscourt during the monarch's visit to Ireland in August 1821. Lord Powerscourt arranged for the famous waterfall on his estate to be damned ahead of the occasion and the construction of a special viewing bridge on which it was intended the king would stand when the water was finally released. George IV was delayed in the house and did not go to see the waterfall, which was probably as well since the damn broke and the torrent of water swept away the newly installed bridge.

Both the 6th and 7th Viscounts greatly enhanced Powerscourt internally and externally, between them creating the Italianate terraced gardens at the back of the house to the designs of Daniel Robertson. Like his patron's grandfather, Robertson suffered from gout and is said to have directed operations from a wheelbarrow in which he sat with a bottle of sherry; once the bottle was empty, the day was deemed over. Although work on the grounds temporarily ceased on the 6th Viscount's death in 1844, they resumed towards the end of the following decade and were finished around 1880 with the completion of the Triton Lake. Further garden works were undertaken in the first half of the 20th century, but, owing both to the extravagance of previous generations and sales of land enforced by the Irish government, in 1961 the 9th Viscount was forced to sell the estate to the Slazenger family. The latter undertook a thorough restoration of the house and it looked as though Powerscourt, which still retained the greater part of its original contents, would survive for another couple of centuries. In November 1974 the house was gutted by fire which had broken out in the morning room chimney. Since 1996 Powerscourt has been partially restored; sections of it can now be hired for events, such as weddings, while the greater part is occupied by retail units. The formal gardens are open to the public but much of the rest of the parkland has been developed as a golf course and hotel.

OPPOSITE: A view of Powerscourt House in central Dublin. Designed by Robert Mack for the 3rd Viscount in 1771, a generation later it was sold for £500 less than the original cost of construction. Here it is seen in an engraving by James Malton, one of the 25 views of the city he produced between 1792 and 1799

ABOVE: Powerscourt, County Wicklow seen from beyond the Triton Basin that lies at the bottom of the Italianate terraced gardens. The splendid mid-19th century Palladian house designed by Richard Cassells survived intact until seriously damaged by fire in 1974. It has since been re-roofed and the main block is now mostly given over to retail units.

TOP: A drawing of the west elevation of Luggala by Anne La Touche dated 1825 and showing an original upstairs quatrefoil window. A member of the Marlay branch of the family, Anne was a gifted amateur artist who produced a number of drawings of her own home and its interior. This is the only picture of Luggala produced by one of the La Touches.

ABOVE: A photograph of the 7th Viscount Powerscourt, which acted as a frontispiece for his 1903 history of the family estate. The many improvements and embellishments he made to house and gardens, while unquestionably superb, left his heirs greatly impoverished and were at least partly responsible for the sale of Powerscourt less than 60 years after his death.

was no equivalent of Charley Carr to act as cicerone and recount local legends. An *Official Railway Handbook to County Wicklow* published in 1860 makes reference to the house – 'a solitary mansion is seen surrounded by a fine plantation' – but does not suggest visitors are permitted to enter the grounds. Likewise Ward & Lock's 1886 *Illustrated Guide to Dublin and its Neighbourhood*, while it describes the scenery of Luggala and makes reference to the house as belonging to Lord Powerscourt, in no way suggests the estate was open to the public. Powerscourt Estate records indicate that although David Charles La Touche sold the land to the Viscount around 1857, he continued to rent it back for some time afterwards for hunting, and received a 50 per cent rent rebate due to damage caused by a trespasser in 1860/61. Even before his eventual death in 1872, the La Touche link with the estate had come to an end.

It would appear that from the early 1860s onwards the greater part of the Luggala terrain served two purposes, the first being pasturage for sheep. In September 1872, a David Stiell who was then giving up his lease on the land, sold 4,267 sheep at auction, the flock described as having been founded five years before with hoggets from Scotland. Thereafter auctions of Luggala sheep, as well as lambs and cattle from the estate, were an annual event until the early years of the 20th century, some 650–1,000 animals being sold each year.

In addition, the land was used for shooting game birds during the autumn and winter season, an activity that had taken place there since the time of Peter La Touche. An advertisement in the *Irish Times* in May 1887 offered 'Extensive Shooting to be let at Luggala, Co. Wicklow, with a good lodge' and advised interested parties to contact the Powerscourt Estate office. Whether Lord Powerscourt ever used the house at Luggala as a residence is unknown but this advertisement and the fact that the only reference to the place in his 1903 book comes in an appendix and concerns the purchase of land suggests minimal interest, especially since he writes at length about building improvements he carried out elsewhere. However, some work certainly was done on the property during his lifetime. A very early photograph dating from the 1860s and believed to have been taken by the Hon. Lewis Wingfield (the Viscount's despised younger brother) shows the house much as it looks today, with the ground floor windows' glazing rising to the top of each arch. On the other hand, photographs from the close of the 19th century indicate that the house had undergone alterations, since the windows were now squared off; they were to remain like this until the start of the present century. The reason for the modification in the building's appearance might be that window frames required renewal and it was simpler and presumably less expensive to insert regular rectangular glazing than go to the trouble of having windows made to the house's specifications. Since it remained in structurally good condition, the likelihood is that the house continued to be occupied after coming into Lord Powerscourt's ownership, perhaps by one of the estate managers, perhaps by a lessee.

Yet as it became, once again, less accessible, Luggala began to be celebrated in verse, the greater part being of poor quality. In *The Pretty Girl of Lough Dan* of 1865, Samuel Ferguson refers to Luggala, writing,

'For such another smile; I vow,
Though loudly beats the midnight rain,
I'd take the mountain-side e'en now,
And walk to Luggelaw again.'

Eight years later, in Volume 1 of the *Irish Monthly Magazine*, the Rev. Michael O'Ferrall, a Jesuit priest, published a poem called *Luggelaw*, the first lines of which run:

'Fare ye well, of rural glory,
Brightest scenes mine eyes e're saw!
Scenes surpassing song or story,
Mount and vale of Luggelaw!
Lake and lawn, and circling highland,
Wooded slope, and heath-clad hill,
Fairest spot of this fair island,
Luggelaw! I love thee still.'

And in 1891, another verse of the same name was written by journalist and poet John Francis O'Donnell, opening as follows:

'By thy dim wave, O Luggelaw!
The mountain fir, dismantled, towers,
And spring with winter dallying,
Has garlands sparse of buds and flowers.
Above thee rolls the ruling cloud,
Around thee creeps the sliding mist...'

Even if rarely seen, the beauties of Luggala had not been forgotten.

ABOVE: Two early photographs of Luggala, believed to have been taken in the 1860s by the Hon. Lewis Wingfield, brother of the 7th Viscount Powerscourt who bought the estate towards the close of the previous decade. These pictures were restored by George Morrison for Garech Browne from the original glass negatives. They are important because they show the ground-floor windows still rising to the top of the Gothic arches, whereas in photographs from the late 19th/early 20th century the windows have been squared off. Lewis Wingfield was not just a gifted photographer but also a painter, actor, playwright and novelist. According to family tradition, he had a bad relationship with his older brother who, prior to having children, spent as much money as possible to ensure it was not inherited by Lewis.

Sika Deer

A native of East Asia, Sika (*Cervus nippon*) are small-sized wild deer today found in abundance in Luggala. The animals have a chestnut coat with white spots in the summer months, a short white tail and white rump; the male of the species has four pointed antlers, which are shed during April and May. During the mating season, around September, the males can be heard uttering a sequence of short, high-pitched screams, which sound as though they could have come from a human in torment.

Sika are not indigenous to Ireland. Prior to their arrival, Luggala, like the rest of Wicklow, had been home only to Red and Fallow Deer. But this scenario changed in the 1860s thanks to the 7th Viscount Powerscourt among whose many interests was a fascination with deer, both living and dead. Renowned as an avid collector of antler and game horn, he assembled a significant number of these trophies, including a number of prehistoric examples, such as those of Irish elk. Displayed on the walls of Powerscourt's entrance hall, the entire collection was lost when the house was wasted by fire in 1974.

Lord Powerscourt's passion for deer – he devotes several pages to the subject in his 1903 book *A Description and History of Powerscourt* – led him to introduce new species into the demesne. 'Soon after I came of age in 1857,' he wrote, 'I had a fancy to try to acclimatise various kinds of deer and other animals, and enclosed a small park by a 6-ft. wire fence, embracing about 100 acres...In this enclosure I turned out Wapiti deer, Indian Sampur deer, red-deer and also the South African Eland...'

Lord Powerscourt admitted that his efforts at acclimatisation failed, and he was forced to sell on the animals to other collectors, except in the case of Sika deer. Around 1860 he bought a hind and three females from a well-known London animal dealer, Charles Jamrach. 'They are nice little deer,' he observed, 'very handsome, and they get very fat and the venison is very good, and a handy size, rather smaller than fallow deer.' These were the first Sika to arrive in Ireland and it soon transpired that the country's conditions suited them admirably: within 24 years of their introduction, the Powerscourt herd already exceeded over a hundred animals. Soon Lord Powerscourt was giving some of them away to other land owners, not just in Ireland but also England and Scotland. 'I also gave some of them to the Zoological Society in London,' he wrote, 'and I believe they have bred and sold a good many from my original stock, so that from here the whole United Kingdom is overspread, and my having introduced them is recorded in the Transactions of the Society.' France's Société impériale zoologique d'acclimatation also presented Lord Powerscourt with a gold medal for his work in acclimatising the Sika deer in Europe.

It appears the deer at Powerscourt were contained within the demesne until the early 1920s when, during a time of widespread political and civil disturbance throughout Ireland, some of them escaped and spread across the Wicklow Mountains and beyond. Preferring areas that combine open glades with dense thickets, and readily adapting to sparse conditions, such as those found in conifer plantations, Sika soon found themselves at home in Luggala where they have flourished ever since.

OPPOSITE AND ABOVE: Deer were among the 7th Viscount Powerscourt's many enthusiasms and he was responsible for introducing the Asian Sika breed into Europe around 1860 when he bought a hind and three females from a London dealer. Quickly acclimatising, within 24 years the herd had grown to over a hundred animals and Lord Powerscourt was giving away deer to other landowners both in Ireland and overseas. Those retained seem to have been contained within the grounds of the estate until the 1920s but have since spread throughout the country and today are found in abundance within the safe confines of Luggala.

CHAPTER THREE

Oonagh Guinness: 'Luggala has been given to me by my kind father'

The 7th Viscount Powerscourt died in June 1904 and was succeeded by his son, a decent man given to public service who, like many other Irish landowners of the time, would find himself overwhelmed by events. Shortly before his father's death, decades of campaigning by nationalist politicians and their followers for large estates to be broken up and the land distributed among tenants had finally led to the introduction of relevant legislation by the British government. As a result of what became known as the Wyndham Act, and of subsequent acts by both British and Irish Free State governments, landlords were effectively obliged to relinquish the greater part of their estates, and thus lose their principal source of revenue. The consequence was that they could no longer afford to sustain their large houses and so these were frequently let go.

In the case of the 8th Lord Powerscourt, already difficult financial circumstances were exacerbated by the improvidence of his father who had lavished money on beautifying the estate without making due preparation for its future maintenance. Before long, therefore, Lord Powerscourt had to find ways of making his land holdings pay, and one option was to rent out parts of the estate, not least Luggala. At some date around 1912, the house was let for the first time to the Hon. Arthur Ernest Guinness (1876–1949), along with Lough Bray, another Wicklow shooting lodge also owned by the Powerscourts and dating from the second half of the 19th century.

Ernest Guinness, as he was always known, was the second son of Edward Guinness, created 1st Earl of Iveagh in 1919. An astute businessman, by the age of 29 Edward Guinness had taken over the family's Dublin brewery after buying out his older brother's half-share. In 1886 he became the richest man in Ireland, having floated two-thirds of the company on the London Stock Exchange for £6 million; he remained chairman of the company and chief shareholder, retaining about 35 per cent of the stock. When he died in 1927, the shares were left equally to his three sons. Of these, the eldest, Rupert, had been a politician and a successful farmer on the family's English estate, Elvedon which straddles the Norfolk/Suffolk border, before assuming the chairmanship of Guinness on his father's death. The youngest, Walter, was a Conservative politician who in 1932 was created Baron Moyne; in 1944, when serving as British Minister of State in the Middle East, he was assassinated in Cairo by members of a militant Zionist group.

Ernest Guinness lived up to his name by being solid and dependable, even if, owing to the cosseting of great wealth, his behaviour was sometimes inclined to appear mildly peculiar. Once when sailing through the Caribbean in his yacht, he decided to stop by a rum distillery on a small island. When the ship's tender reached shore, Ernest's valet Hallam was sent ahead to make necessary arrangements. Coming across a slumbering beachcomber, the valet duly instructed, 'Kindly conduct these gentlemen to the First Class Waiting Room.' On another occasion Ernest, whose crew on the yacht included three cooks, was persuaded by friends to go ashore at Cadiz for lunch at a restaurant. A bottle of Guinness, his only drink, was sent ahead and when the party arrived, it was discovered the bottle had been placed in a tureen of ice. 'I will not drink iced Guinness,' declared Ernest, turning on his heel and leading his reluctant paarty back to the yacht.

Unlike his siblings, Ernest took no part in public life but of the three he was most closely involved with the brewery from which they all derived their wealth. After attending Eton, he went up to Trinity College, Cambridge, leaving there with a degree in engineering. While his brothers participated in the Boer War, he was sent to Dublin where he trained as a brewer before becoming assistant managing director at Guinness in 1902 and vice-chairman in 1913. His professional life was spent at the brewery in St James's Gate where he always wore around his waist an enormous bunch of keys to the company's safes. According to his great-nephew, the Hon.

OPPOSITE: Oonagh Guinness painted in April 1931 by Philip de László. The picture, commissioned by Oonagh's husband Philip Kindersley, cost £1,575 and was exhibited later that year in a retrospective of the artist's work held in Paris. From 1950 until Oonagh's death in 1995 it hung in the drawing room at Luggala; the painting's present whereabouts are unknown.

Desmond Guinness, Ernest 'was the only one of the family in his generation who really knew the brewery well. He understood and cared about every valve and every pipe, much more so than any of his brothers.'

Stockily built and moustachioed, throughout his life Ernest was fascinated by machines and their operation. In Glenmaroon, his Dublin residence, he installed a coal scuttle with a small button that, when pushed, caused an automatic pipe organ to rise up and begin playing *Cherry Ripe*, a popular song of the period. One of the first young men of his generation to acquire a motor car, he was later one of the oldest to be issued a British pilot's licence and came to own four aeroplanes, the only private individual in Ireland to do so. When the autogyro, a precursor of the helicopter, was manufactured in 1923, he bought one and kept it in his garage. In his fifties he bought a three-engined biplane flying boat to carry family and friends between England and the west of Ireland. There was widespread press coverage of the first occasion on which he made the trip, in September 1928, since it was broken by an overnight stay in Kingston (now Dún Laoghaire) Harbour. In February 1932, Tom Driberg in the *Daily Express's* Dragoman gossip column reported that Ernest's flying boat had been given wheels, 'so he can land it anywhere and is called "Amo" from the initials of his three daughters, Aileen, Maureen and Oonagh.'

Two years earlier at the Vickers' Supermarine Aviation Works, Ernest had supervised the construction of a three-engined monoplane with a wing span of 92 feet. Described as 'an air yacht', in addition to the cockpits, this had accommodation

There was a young lady called Russell
Who left Elveden's fine hall in a bustle
'Cos a disolute peer
Whispered things in her ear
Which alarmed that poor girl Chloe Russell
S.

LEFT TOP AND BOTTOM: In 1894 Edward Guinness, 1st Earl of Iveagh bought the Elveden estate on the Norfolk/Suffolk borders where he often entertained large shooting parties that included the Prince of Wales, future Edward VII; it remains in the family. Among the guests at Elveden in the early years of the 20th century was Marie Clothilde Russell, known as Chloe, who in 1903 married Lord Iveagh's second son Ernest. One such visit by Chloe is the subject of a limerick by an unknown admirer.

OPPOSITE: The mother of Oonagh Guinness's second husband, Dominick Oranmore and Browne, was Lady Olwen Ponsonby, daughter of Edward Ponsonby, 8th Earl of Bessborough. Here in a page from her visiting book is the Ponsonby family home, Bessborough in County Kilkenny, which was burnt by the IRA in 1923. Lord Duncannon, seen in one of the photographs on this page, was Lady Olwen's brother, future 9th Earl of Bessborough.

Bessborough
Louise Margaret.
BESSBOROUGH
The Courtyard, Bessborough.
Bessborough, Piltown.
H. S. Goodhart-Rendel
B. Bessborough. Sept 23–28 1909.
H.R.H. Princess Patricia of Connaught.
Patricia
Walter Guinness
Myles Ponsonby
Irene Congreve
Gweneth Ponsonby
Duncannon
John Congreve
Bertie B. Ponsonby
Mr. J. J. Stafford, 6 George's St., Waterford.
The Fox.
Lord Duncannon.
Lady Gweneth Ponsonby
Tuesday, Sept. 14th, 1909.
Iverk Farming Society.

Daily Graphic

The bridegroom.
(Photographed by Werner and Son, Dublin.)

The bride.

THE HON. ERNEST GUINNESS AND MISS RUSSELL, MARRIED AT ST. MARGARET'S, WESTMINSTER.

WEDDINGS.

GUINNESS—RUSSELL.

Yesterday, at St. Margaret's Church, Westminster, there was a large gathering to witness the marriage of the Hon. Arthur Ernest Guinness, son of Lord Iveagh, and Miss Marie Clotilde Russell, daughter of the late Sir George Russell, Bart., of Swallowfield Park, Reading. The Bishop of London officiated, assisted by the Rev. R. J. Maunsell Bacon, vicar of Swallowfield, and the Hon. Rupert Edward Guinness supported his brother as best man. The bride was given away by her brother, Mr. Arthur E. Russell, and wore a dress of soft white mousseline de soie and silver lace, with lace train, embroidered at the Dublin School of Art Needlework, in design of silver true lovers' knots, and wreaths of white roses. The Brussels lace veil had been worn by Lady Russell at her own wedding, and covered a tiara of orange-blossoms. The bridesmaids were Miss Elspeth Campbell (niece to the Duke of Argyll) and Miss Mary Dawson-Greene (the bride's cousins), Miss Victoria Campbell and Miss Ogilvie Grant (cousins of both bride and bridegroom), Lady Marjorie Erskine, Miss Florence Foster, Miss Elinor Hankey, Miss Cope, Miss Violet Corry, and Miss Aileen Pachell. They were attired in very pretty dresses of white satin, voiled in sunray-pleated chiffon, with angel sleeves, and Medici collars of silver, and instead of hats, wore wreaths of white lilies in the hair. The bridegroom gave the bridesmaids diamond and jewelled pendants, with initials and date, and sheaves of white lilies in fresh green foliage. After the ceremony Lady Russell held a reception at Claridge's Hotel, among those present being Princess Christian and the Duke of Argyll, and subsequently the bride and bridegroom left for Swallowfield Park, lent by the bride's eldest brother, Sir Charles Russell, Bart. The presents were exceptionally handsome and costly.

Hearth and Home

GUINNESS—RUSSELL.

At St. Margaret's Church, Westminster, on the 15th inst., the wedding took place of Miss Cloë Russell, daughter of Lady Russell, of Swallowfield Park, Reading, and the Hon. Ernest Guinness, son of Lord Iveagh, of Farmleigh, Co. Dublin. The Bishop of London officiated, assisted by the Rev. M. Bacon, Vicar of Swallowfield. The bride wore a gown of white chiffon and silver, the train from the shoulders being of embroidered lace with true lovers' knots in silver, and a wreath of orange blossoms covered by a veil of Brussels lace worn by her mother at her marriage. There were ten bridesmaids, who wore pretty dresses of white chiffon over satin, and sleeves and collars of silver, and they carried bunches of white lilies. The bride was given away by her brother, Mr. Arthur Russell, while the Hon. Rupert Guinness was best man. After the ceremony a reception was held at Claridge's Hotel, among those present being the Prince and Princess Christian

THE HON. E. GUINNESS. MISS CLOE RUSSELL.

of Schleswig-Holstein and the Duke of Argyll. Later in the afternoon the Hon. Ernest and Mrs. Guinness left for their honeymoon tour. The presents were numerous and costly.

A POPULAR HOSTESS IN LONDON & DUBLIN

THE HON. MRS. ERNEST GUINNESS

Lord Iveagh's sister-in-law is well known for her intense love of yachting. She is presenting her youngest daughter Miss Oonagh Guinness this season

ABOVE LEFT: The wedding of Ernest Guinness and Marie Clothilde Russell at St. Margaret's, Westminster on 15th July 1903 was widely reported in newspapers at the time. Wearing a dress of white chiffon embroidered in silver, Chloe, like her daughter Oonagh 26 years later, had no less than ten bridesmaids.

ABOVE RIGHT: Following her marriage to Ernest Guinness, Chloe's life was divided between London, where the couple had a house in Grosvenor Place, and Dublin where her husband had been appointed assistant managing director at Guinness's in 1902 and became vice-chairman of the company in 1913. In both cities Chloe was responsible for the running of large houses, as well as the couple's country estate Ashford Castle, County Mayo. She spent many months in France every year.

for six passengers including a saloon and several cabins equipped with electric lighting and a ventilation system.

More than half a century after Ernest Guinness's death, his former son-in-law, Dominick, Lord Oranmore and Browne, remembered the two of them taking a flight in a seaplane from Ashford Castle, County Galway. Initially it had been proposed they travel as far as Dublin, but an outbreak of bad weather meant returning back to the house after a tour of Lough Corrib: 'As we got off the plane, I could hear awful curses coming from above us. Looking up I saw it was the mechanic who was climbing down from the wing simply furious. He had been forgotten on take-off and had been there clinging to the plane all the way round the Loch. "You must be more careful next time," Ernest said severely as we walked off.'

But Ernest Guinness's greatest passion was for boats. All three brothers were ardent sailors, members of the Royal Yacht Squadron and regular participants in Cowes Week. All of them also owned a number of superlative sailing vessels, the best known of Ernest's being the *Fântome II* on which he travelled around the world with his family in 1923-24.

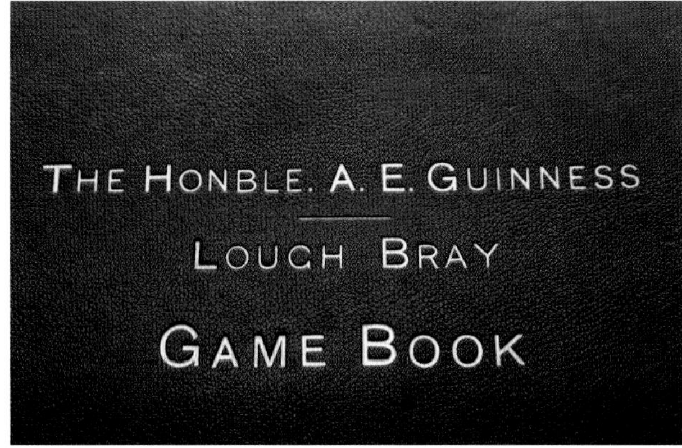

Date 1923	GUNS	BEAT	Grouse	Woodcock	Snipe	Hares	Rabbits	Wild Duck	Various		TOTAL	REMARKS
Brought forward												
August 13	Mr Brinsley Plunket: Mr A.E. Guinness	Kippure	5								5	Wet
14	"	Luggala	6			6			1		13	Fine
15	"	Luggala	6								6	Wet
16	"	Sheep Bank	10		2		4				16	Fine
17	"	Lough Bray	10	1							11	
19	Mr M. Russell	Kippure	7								7	Showery
24	"	"	10								10	Fine
25	"	On the road	1				2				3	
26	"	Sheep Bank				1					1	Showery
27	Mr A.E. Guinness	Luggala	5			1	2				8	Fine
29	Mr C Hamilton: Mr A.E. Guinness	Maulin	3								3	Wet
31	Mr A.E. Guinness	Lough Bray	6				1				7	Showery
Sept 1	"	Luggala	12			1	1				14	Fine
3	"		4								4	
~~Carried forward~~			85	1	2	9	10		1		108	

ABOVE: From 1912 onwards Ernest Guinness rented both Lough Bray and Luggala, two properties in County Wicklow owned by Viscount Powerscourt. Here Ernest hosted regular shooting parties, the number of birds killed on each day meticulously recorded in a game book kept for this purpose.

Even with boats, his interest was most often of a mechanical bent. On one occasion he ordered a yacht from the firm of Camper and Nicholsons but then requested that the vessel be cut in half to insert a 12-foot section in the middle with a diesel engine. When it was pointed out that this procedure would be more expensive than the simple purchase of an intact new boat, he retorted, 'Never mind the money. That is how I want it done.' Another instance of his singularity was recorded by a member of the Guinness staff who, during the early 1920s, when Ireland was engaged first in the War of Independence and then in a civil war, was taken on a trip down the river Liffey on board one of Ernest's boats. He recalled sitting on a deck chair, 'being offered drinks by Ernest's butler when shooting broke out between buildings on the bank and he could see men firing at each other with great danger to life and limb, which did not affect the life on board though there was a separation of no more than 400 yards.'

In 1903 Ernest married Chloe (Marie Clothilde) Russell, only daughter of Sir Charles Russell, 4th Bt. Her mother was the granddaughter of the fourth Duke of Richmond, making Chloe a direct descendant of Charles II and his French mistress Louise de Kérouaille. The couple had three daughters, Aileen Sibell (b.1904), Maureen Constance (1907) and Oonagh (1910), who would later be known collectively as the Golden Guinness Girls. All three were given Irish names, as if in premonition of the central role Ireland would play in their lives. This may be because Ernest spent more time in Ireland than did his two brothers. Like them, he had a large house in central London at 17 Grosvenor Place (now occupied by the Irish Embassy) and also a house outside the capital, Holmbury in Surrey – chosen for its proximity to an airfield – in which a system of concealed loudspeakers piped music into every room. But owing to his involvement with the family brewery, he was perceived as being domiciled in Ireland, when in Dublin staying at Glenmaroon on the edge of Dublin's Phoenix Park; from here he walked to his office every day. Around the time of his death in 1949, Ernest's granddaughter Neelia Plunket described Glenmaroon as 'A fascinating but hideous house. Fascinating, because each time we go there, there is some new electrical device or mechanical gadget that makes an organ play, panels in the wall open or something unusual happens.'

Around the time of his marriage in 1903, Ernest bought an existing property at Glenmaroon and then enlarged it in Tudor-esque style to the designs of a minor Dublin architect, Laurence McDonnell. In 1911 Glenmaroon's size was further increased by the addition of an indoor swimming pool – one of the first private pools in Ireland – and a smoking room, which

Fantôme II

Although Ernest Guinness owned many sailing vessels during his lifetime, the best-known, and best-preserved, is a three-masted barque from France. In December 1895 Fernand Crouan, head of a family firm of ship owners based in Nantes, ordered a new cargo vessel from the Dubigeon shipyard in nearby Chantenay-sur-Loire. Launched the following June, the ship made its maiden voyage in July 1896 and was named the *Belem* after the Brazilian port, which was one of her destinations on that occasion.

Over the next 18 years, the *Belem* crossed the Atlantic 33 times, transporting sugar from the West Indies and cocoa and coffee from Brazil and French Guiana to France. In May 1902 she narrowly escaped destruction at St Pierre de la Martinique. A bureaucratic muddle meant the *Belem*'s berth had been assigned to another ship and she was forced to anchor several miles away: the following morning, the volcanic Mont Pelée erupted, destroying the entire town and all the ships in the harbour, and killing 30,000 people.

Less than twenty years after her construction, the *Belem* was no longer deemed fit for purpose as a cargo vessel, with sailing ships unable to compete with speedier new models powered by steam. Unlike many comparable boats, however, she escaped being sent to the breaker's yard. Instead in February 1914 the boat was bought for £3,000 by one of the richest men in Britain, Hugh Grosvenor, Duke of Westminster. Over the next four years the firm of Summers & Payne converted the former cargo ship into an exquisitely appointed yacht holding 14 cabins and five bathrooms, a galley, dining room, smoking room, drawing room and semi-circular library as well as a Cuban mahogany double-revolutionary staircase; all furnishings were provided by the London firm of Maple & Co. The result was described by English novelist Arnold Bennett as 'One of the finest yachts afloat; but for all the fantastic luxury there was real taste.' The refurbished ship doubled its crew numbers to 31, including three cooks and four stewards.

In addition to being equipped with electricity, water and sanitation, the *Belem* was now fitted with twin 480 HP Swedish Bolinder engines and two propellers, and her wooden masts replaced by steel-based ones. By the time all this work had been completed and the *Belem* welcomed her new crew under British Captain William Henry Simmonds on New Year's Day 1919, the cost to the Duke of Westminster was in the region of £100,000.

Yet within a couple of years, the Duke had whimsically decided to sell the *Belem* and buy another boat, a four-masted schooner called *Flying Cloud*. This would also later be bought by the man who in 1921 became the *Belem*'s new owner, Ernest Guinness. Despite all the money spent on her refurbishment, the yacht was offered for sale for £60,000 and finally sold in September 1921 for just £25,000, less than a quarter of what she had cost the Duke of Westminster. Ernest Guinness would, in turn, spend £20,000 on further alterations to the vessel, but first he changed her name to *Fantôme II*, having previously owned another yacht called *Fantôme*.

The main changes made to the yacht were internal and designed to prepare her for long-distance travel. The library was converted into a sanatorium-cum-office, the main deckhouse attached to the smoking room and made into a dining room, an additional deckhouse provided to serve as a ladies' boudoir. A telegraph set, long-range wireless and gyrocompass were installed, and, among other improvements, an electric piano placed in the saloon. The crew numbers now rose to 33 and included a doctor.

'The yacht is just too wonderful,' wrote Brian Howard in 1925. 'Black and white outside, with three masts with square-rigged sails...and is one of the biggest yachts on Lloyds' register – 700 tons. Marvellous food, twenty sailors or so – bathrooms, electric piano,

electric heaters, and three motor boats on board, one big launch, one racing launch and a small one.' When not berthed during the winter at Cowes or in Glangarriff, Co Cork, *Fantôme II* was constantly in use by Ernest and his family and friends, during the summer often sailing across the Mediterranean as well as around the coasts of Britain and Ireland.

But *Fantôme II*'s greatest voyage began on 29th March 1923 when she departed from Cowes for a year spent cruising 40,000 miles around the world. In addition to a full crew on board were Ernest and Chloe Guinness, their three daughters, a cousin Algernon Guinness and three family friends, 18-year old Nancy Tennant, Ian Murray and J.A. Fane, known as 'Pop.' Travelling first to Gibraltar, the ship then crossed the Atlantic via Las Palmas to the Caribbean before proceeding down the coasts of Venezuela and Colombia. Passing through the Panama Canal, *Fantôme II* visited the South Sea

OPPOSITE: A passionate yachtsman, prior to his purchase of the *Fantôme II* from the Duke of Westminster, Ernest Guinness owned another three-masted vessel called the *Fantôme*. This was sold in 1921 and later went down in a hurricane in the Pacific Ocean, off South America.

ABOVE: In September 1921 Ernest Guinness paid £25,000 for a three-masted barque made in France 25 years earlier and called the *Belem*. Having spent a further £20,000 on refurbishments, Ernest renamed the vessel the *Fantôme II*. It remained in the family's possession until after his death in 1949.

Japan. September

propellers were foul. another message said "Mrs – has just died with 2 broken legs" and lots of other messages. We decided to go to Shimisu which is 80 miles, only oil for one more day.

Monday Sept 3rd

Sea calm. In the afternoon we heard that Tokyo was on fire. Got into harbour about 10.15 with difficulty as rain showers obscured the lights.

Tuesday Sept 4th

Tidal wave reported at Odawara. In the afternoon we went ashore and I was thrilled at everything I saw. The colours of all the womens kimonos and parasols were lovely, the babies slung on their backs were very sweet. The men wore frightfully mixed sort of clothes.

We went into several tiny wooden shops and I bought some japanese note paper and tiny envelopes. Refugees were pouring in in hundreds by all sorts of boats and by train.

Crowds were watching at the quay. Some of the refugees looked too pathetic with just a few belongings in a handkerchief on their backs. Pip and I after walking about for some time got into two rickshaws and went to see a temple, we went through rice fields to the base of a hill where the temple was. There was a lovely garden and we took our shoes off and went inside the temple. Afterwards we went up millions of steps to a shrine at the top of the hill, there was a very good view of Shimisu. Returned to the yacht at 6.30 pm. After dinner

Betty Lord Altrincham Phil.

A.E.G.

O.K. issues a challenge to Mercedes Gleitz.

O.K.

O.K

P.K. O.K.

LEFT: While on a round-the-world voyage on the *Fantôme II* in 1923, Ernest and Chloe Guinness's eldest daughter Aileen, then aged 18, kept a daily diary. Here in the first days of September she records her impressions after the yacht's arrival in Japan which had just been devastated by a massive earthquake.

BELOW LEFT: The Guinnesses and their daughters never embarked on as long a voyage as that undertaken in 1923 but they regularly took the *Fantôme II* on trips along the coast of North Africa and around the Mediterranean. On such occasions, they would bring friends with them for extended holidays, all recorded in the family photograph albums.

BELOW RIGHT: The *Fantôme II* had originally been built as a cargo vessel and used to transport sugar, cocoa and coffee from the West Indies and South America to France. Even after conversion into a private yacht, it was well able to withstand long voyages such as that undertaken by Ernest Guinness and his family around the world in 1923.

OPPOSITE: As well as being luxuriously appointed, the *Fantôme II* boasted a crew of 33, including two chefs and a doctor. Many of them can be seen in this 1933 photograph which also features, seated front centre, Ernest and Chloe Guinness, their daughter Aileen, and Dominick, Lord Oranmore and Browne with his first wife, Mildred.

FANTÔME R.Y.S. 1933

Islands, a two-month journey inspired by the writings of Robert Louis Stevenson. The yacht next headed for the Japanese port of Yokohama but fortuitous delays meant the party had not reached their intended destination when it was devastated by earthquake on 1st September 1923; for a second time the boat had narrowly avoided catastrophe. Reaching Japan, *Fantôme II* berthed at Shimizu, with Algernon Guinness and the resident doctor travelling north to bring medical supplies to the afflicted region. The vessel moved on to China, with a visit to Peking by train, before heading south for Borneo, Singapore, Sarawak and Malaysia and reaching Ceylon in time for Christmas. The homeward journey took *Fantôme II* through the Red Sea and the Suez Canal into the Mediterranean, where there were various sight-seeing stops before most of the passengers disembarked in Naples and made their way to London by land. The yacht once more reached Cowes on 2nd March 1924, 338 days after her initial departure.

Ernest Guinness continued to own and sail *Fantôme II* until the outbreak of war in September 1939, when the yacht was taken out of commission and laid up in Cowes Harbour where she temporarily served as headquarters to the Free French Force. Although the area was subject to German bombing in 1942, *Fantôme II* survived undamaged, only her yards and sails being destroyed. In 1947 she left Cowes for Belfast and made a number of journeys between Britain and Ireland before Ernest Guinness's death two years later. *Fantôme II* was inherited by his youngest daughter Oonagh. In February 1951 she sold the vessel to Count Vittorio Cini, who had established a charitable foundation on the Venetian island of San Giorgio Maggiore in memory of his son Giorgio, killed in a plane crash in August 1949. Brought to Venice and once more structurally altered, the yacht, now renamed the *Giorgio Cini*, became a training ship for young sailors. In 1965 it was decided the vessel had become too old and dangerous to be used for this purpose and she was moored at San Giorgio Maggiore for seven years until the Italian carabinieri began a programme of restoration. When this undertaking proved too expensive, she became the property of the Venice shipyards, which completed the project. Finally, in January 1979, she returned to France and reverted to her original name, the *Belem*. Since then the vessel, which was classified as a French historical monument in 1984, has been used as a sail training ship.

ABOVE: A page from one of Chloe Guinness's photograph albums showing a house party at Lough Bray in April 1914, during which time the group also visited Luggala; notice her spelling of the place as 'Laggala.' Amateur theatricals were much in vogue at the time, and the page shows some of the guests dressed in character for a performance.

together cost in the region of £5,000. The house's distinctive features included not just the indoor pool and automatic organ operated by coal scuttle button, but also a covered bridge that linked one section of the building with another across a public road. During the Civil War, Oonagh watched the burning of the Four Courts in Dublin from Glenmaroon's water tower.

Ernest and his family also spent some time each year at Ashford Castle in County Mayo. Situated on the shores of Ireland's second largest lake, Lough Corrib, Ashford had originally been owned by the Browne family, into which Ernest's youngest daughter would marry in 1937. The estate was bought by Sir Benjamin Lee Guinness in 1852 and then left to Ernest's uncle Arthur Edward Guinness, created Lord Ardilaun in 1880. Between them, the two men had not only greatly enlarged the old Browne house but also extended the estate to some 33,000 acres, much of which benefited from judicious tree planting. By the end of the 19th century, at a time when many landlords were struggling to find the funds needed to sustain their family property, Ashford was one of the best-maintained estates in Ireland. Recalling a visit

ABOVE: In Dublin, Ernest Guinness and his family lived in Glenmaroon, a large house immediately to the west of Phoenix Park that he bought around the time of his marriage in 1903. During the First World War it served as a convalescent home for wounded soldiers. Sold by the family in the 1950s, today Glenmaroon is a centre for persons with intellectual disability run by the Daughters of Charity.

he made there in the 1880s, Irish novelist George Moore would later write, 'Below us, falling in sweet inclining plain, a sea of green turf flows in and out of stone walls and occasional clumps of trees down to the rocky promontories, the reedy reaches and the long curved woods which sweep about the castle – such a castle as Gautier would have loved to describe – that Lord Ardilaun has built on this beautiful Irish land. There it stands on that green headland with the billows of a tideless sea, lashing about its base; and oh! the towers and battlements rising out of the bending foliage of ten thousand trees.'

Lord Ardilaun regularly held shooting parties at Ashford, in January 1905 entertaining the future George V, then Prince of Wales. Since he had no children, on his death in 1915 the estate reverted to the family trust, which passed it on to Ernest Guinness for his personal use. He spent as much time at Ashford as his uncle had done, particularly for woodcock shooting. Dominick Oranmore and Browne would later recall, 'It was very luxurious staying at Ashford, and chefs were brought into the house from the yacht.' In addition, 'When we went shooting there were usually

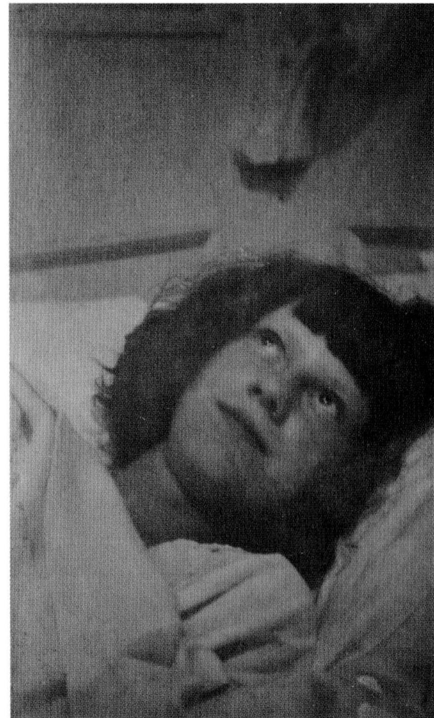

ABOVE: Oonagh Guinness as a girl. The youngest of three sisters, she was born in February 1910 and spent her early years between Dublin and London, like her siblings receiving a somewhat perfunctory education; Oonagh later told her grandson Dorian Browne that the girls' governesses would take care of any required homework.

OPPOSITE: Known in the 1920s as the Golden Guinness Girls, the three sisters Aileen, Maureen and Oonagh were each born three years apart in 1904, 1907 and 1910 respectively. As children they were close but in adulthood, while Aileen and Oonagh continued to spend a great amount of time together, Maureen saw less of her siblings.

100 beaters, many more than were required, and they continually went on strike for more money.' Ernest Guinness had often joked that he employed far too many people at Ashford, 'Every one of whom might fall over if you removed his (sweeping) brush.' Relations with workers on the estate deteriorated, and in the summer of 1938 they went on strike once more, this time seeking a wage increase of two shillings a week, which equated to a rise of 7.5 per cent. Their behaviour finally proved too much for Ernest, who left Ashford in his private plane and did not return. That autumn the Iveagh Trust placed Ashford on the market and in spring 1939, shortly before the estate went to public auction, 22,000 acres were bought by the Irish State for £20,000. The castle and immediate 170 acres were leased by hotelier Noel Huggard; Ashford Castle has operated as a hotel under a succession of managements ever since.

Ernest and Chloe Guinness were conscientious, if somewhat aloof, parents. Oonagh would later recall being brought by a nanny to see her mother and father for half an hour in the morning and late afternoon, but otherwise having little contact with them. Maureen, who in turn would prove a poor parent, claimed her father showed his children no affection, being less concerned about their welfare than that of the brewery. The three girls received adequate rather than ample education; Oonagh told her grandson Dorian Browne that governesses would take care of any required homework. They were all sent to Paris in their teens to improve their French and acquire additional social graces. But if nominal attention was paid to their formal education, their material comfort was amply secured, not least thanks to Ernest's various well-furnished and staffed houses

Notwithstanding an abundance of residences from which to choose, by 1912 he found it necessary to rent Luggala, together with Lough Bray, from Lord Powerscourt. A photograph album originally belonging to Chloe Guinness and covering the years immediately before and during the First World War has several pages devoted to time spent at Luggala, which she misspells Laggala. These pictures show not just shooting parties in the surrounding Wicklow countryside but also the three Guinness daughters playing outside the house and swimming in Lough Tay.

During the difficult years from 1916 onwards when Ireland was often in a state of near or actual war, Ernest preferred that his family remain primarily in England. Once a degree of peace was restored to the country, however, the family once again spent time in their various Irish houses, including Luggala. Ernest's three daughters were now old enough to use the estate as a place of entertainment for their own friends. In August 1925 the aesthete and aspiring poet Brian Howard, then a 20-year-old Oxford undergraduate (and later a model for Anthony Blanche in Evelyn Waugh's *Brideshead Revisited*) was invited to stay at Luggala by Aileen Guinness. From there he wrote to his mother, 'This is one of Ernest Guinness' shooting lodges, twenty miles from Dublin and really *the most beautiful place I've ever seen*. A tiny little house on the edge of a great lake with huge feathery mountains towering all around... What a life to lead – so perfect. Meals when you like. Everything when and where

ABOVE: The Guinness sisters and their friends on board the *Fantôme II* during Cowes Week 1928. Oonagh is shown in the photograph to the top right of the album page. Then aged 18, within a year she would have shed her puppy fat and be married to her first husband, Philip Kindersley.

OPPOSITE: The three Guinness sisters as drawn by Aileen's brother-in-law Terence, Lord Plunket, who was always known as Teddy. Married to Dorothé Mabel Lewis, illegitimate daughter of the 7th Marquess of Londonderry and American actress Fannie Ward, he was a gifted caricaturist who would later paint accomplished portraits including a fine one of Aileen's husband Brinny. Both Teddy and Dorothé died in a plane crash in California in February 1938.

you like. Plain nursery food, which I love, and the nicest play fellows in the world. We draw one another, photograph one another, write things about one another, and adore one another, realising the indisputable fact that WE are the nicest young things in the world!'

Another member of the same house party was future writer Daphne Fielding (née the Hon. Daphne Vivian) who was to become Oonagh Guinness's closest friend and an habitué of Luggala. In her 1954 memoirs *Mercury Presides* (of which Waugh wrote, 'Contrary to what one would have expected they are marred by discretion and good taste'), Fielding recalled that 1925 visit to Luggala: 'High up in the craggy rocks surrounding the house was a cave where, after creeping out of the girls' dormitory and meeting the others at midnight, we would spend the rest of the night telling ghost stories round a fire in which we baked potatoes. Most of the day we spent by the lake in dressing-gowns and pyjamas, fancying that we looked like the photographs we had seen in *The Tatler* of smart people at the Lido.'

In fact, before long Daphne Fielding and her friends did start to feature in the pages of *Tatler*, and every other society magazine. This was especially true of the

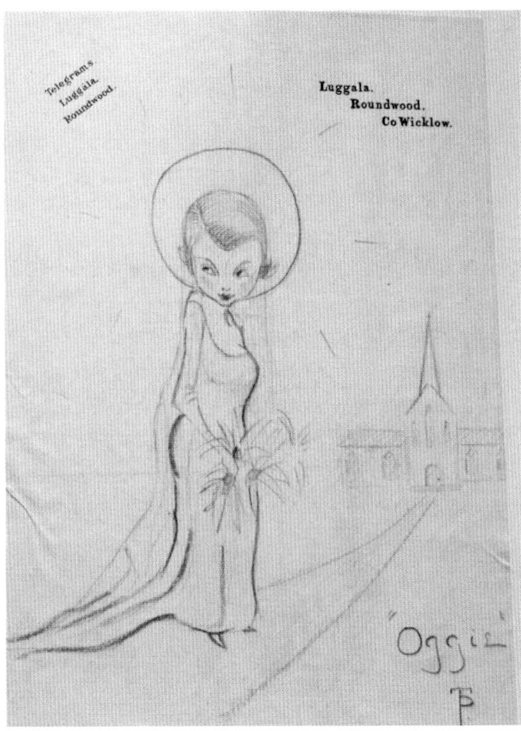

three Guinness sisters, who were blessed with good looks, sociability and sizeable fortunes – a combination that made them, individually and collectively, irresistible for the next half century. In his 1980 memoir *An Open Book*, film director John Huston famously described the Guinness sisters as witches: 'lovely ones to be sure, but witches nonetheless. They are all transparent-skinned, with pale hair and light blue eyes. You can very nearly see through them. They are quite capable of turning swinish folk into swine before your very eyes, and turning them back again without their even knowing it.' The Bulgarian-born writer Stephane Groueff, who at one point was engaged to Aileen's eldest daughter Neelia, in 2002 described the sisters, by then all dead, as having been, 'each one more spoiled, helpless and charmingly irresponsible than the other...Extravagant spenders, they lived way beyond the generous revenues from their trusts.'

Attractive, charming and free-spending, the trio were not averse to having their activities recorded and imparted. Aileen, Maureen and Oonagh seemed to relish being the recipients of public attention, all of it scrupulously cut out and preserved in hefty photograph albums and scrapbooks. This was especially the case once they married and left the restraint of their parents behind, something all three did at relatively young ages.

The first wedding was that of the eldest. A conspicuous nose denying her true beauty, Aileen would always be the most chic of the sisters, impeccably groomed and a loyal client of French couturiers; a social flutter was stirred in June 1966 when she and her friend the Duchess of Windsor were photographed by the Earl of Lichfield wearing the same dress from Givenchy at a party in Paris. Almost 40 years earlier, in November 1927, Aileen had married the Hon. Brinsley Plunket to whom she was related: his grandmother Anne Guinness had been a sister of her grandfather, the 1st Earl of Iveagh. Curiously, the groom's great-great aunt, the Hon. Katherine Plunket, who only died in 1932 at the age of 112, had met Sir Walter Scott when he visited Ireland – and Luggala – in July 1825. Brinsley Plunket was always known as Brinny and his older brother Terence, 6th Lord Plunket, as Teddy. The latter was a talented cartoonist who later turned to painting portraits. In 1922 Teddy had married Dorothé Mabel Lewis, illegitimate daughter of the 7th Marquess of Londonderry and American actress Fannie Ward. Teddy and Dorothé were intimate friends of the Duke of York (later George VI) and his wife Elizabeth; the latter was godmother to the couple's second son Robin in 1925, whilst the Duke was godfather to their third child, Shaun, six years later. Both Teddy and Dorothé would be killed in a plane crash in California in February 1938.

As a younger son, Brinny had no estate and little money, but his wife's father was able to provide both. Not long after

ABOVE: In June 1929 Oonagh married Philip Kindersley at St Margaret's, Westminster. Her dress, of parchment-tinted satin sewn with pearls and bordered with a design of lilies in gold and silver, was designed by Norman Hartnell, later to be favourite designer of George VI's wife, Elizabeth. Hartnell subsequently recalled that Oonagh had had 'the looks and manner – although perhaps not the personality – of a Raphael cherub.'

the Plunkets' marriage, Ernest bought Aileen Luttrellstown Castle, an 18th-century house Gothicized in the early 19th century and set in 560 acres some seven miles north-west of Dublin. Here Aileen would hold court in notable style for more than 55 years. (Aileen sold the estate in 1983 to a private consortium; in July 1999 it was the venue for the wedding of David and Victoria Beckham.) As late as 1966, when many other Irish house owners had been forced to cut back on hospitality, Mark Bence-Jones could report, 'Mrs Plunket entertains in the grand manner, giving large dinner parties, dances and balls; she invites people from all walks of life in Ireland together with many friends from abroad.' He also noted that 'what seems like an army of footmen, something very rare in Ireland, adds to the splendour.'

Racehorses were Brinny Plunket's chief interest and, as a result, during the early years of her first marriage Aileen came to own a number of thoroughbreds, including Millennium, which she regularly led into the winner's enclosure. One contemporary later recalled bumping into Brinny, who drove a Delage sports car painted in his racing colours of black and gold, and being persuaded to come to dinner at Luttrellstown that night. Once seated at table, 'my neighbour turned to me, "I understand you are not interested in horses. Then what *are* you interested in?" – a difficult question to answer in a company whose sole interest was horses.' After having had three daughters, Neelia (which is Aileen spelt backwards), Doon and Marcia (who died at the age of three), Aileen began to seek alternative amusement to that provided by her husband. Her lovers in the pre-war years included impoverished Austrian playboy Baron Hubert von Pantz, who also had an affair with Coco Chanel; he would later marry Terry McConnell, a rich widow whose former father-in-law had founded Avon cosmetics, and create the ski resort Club Mittersill in New Hampshire.

The Plunkets finally divorced in 1940; Brinny was killed in aerial combat over Sudan in November 1941 while serving as a flight-lieutenant in the RAF.

Maureen, the second of the three Guinness sisters, was the last to marry in July 1930, her husband being Basil Sheridan Hamilton-Temple-Blackwood. Heir to the 3rd Marquess of Dufferin and Ava, as well as being related to his wife he was also a first-cousin of her sister Aileen's husband, Brinsley Plunket. Barely a fortnight after the wedding, he inherited his

title and the family estate of Clandeboye in County Down when his father was killed in an aeroplane crash. During the 1930s, Basil Dufferin and Ava pursued a career in politics, acting as Parliamentary Private Secretary first to the Marquess of Lothian, who was Under-Secretary of State for India, and then to Viscount Halifax (later 1st Earl of Halifax), who was successively President of the Board of Education from 1932 to 1935, Secretary of State for War in 1935, and Lord Privy Seal from 1935 to 1937. Basil Dufferin was himself appointed Under-Secretary of State for the Colonies in 1937 before refusing a post in the wartime coalition government of Winston Churchill to join the British Army in 1940. He was serving as a staff officer when killed in an ambush by Japanese soldiers during a covert mission in Burma in March 1945; ironically, his grandfather, the 1st Marquess, had been responsible for annexing Upper Burma

ABOVE: The young Kindersleys a year after their wedding and a month after the birth of their first child, a boy named Gay. Oonagh was then aged 20 but looked much younger; she retained her childlike appearance into old age.

Camera Portrait by Bertram Park.

MADAME RÉCAMIER—OF THE BALL: MRS. PHILIP KINDERSLEY.

It was arranged that Mrs. Philip Kindersley should take the part of Madame Récamier (1777-1849), the beautiful wife of the Parisian banker and queen of one of the most interesting salons of a thrilling period in French history, at the Famous Beauties Ball on June 25. Mrs. Kindersley was formerly Miss Oonagh Guinness.

LEFT AND OPPOSITE: Following marriage to Philip Kindersley, Oonagh became one of the most photographed women in London, her frenetic social life meticulously covered by magazines and newspapers. Neither she nor her sisters were averse to publicity, and each of them preserved all such coverage in a series of large, leather-bound scrap albums.

The BYSTANDER

Dorothy Wilding

MRS. PHILIP KINDERSLEY

Mrs. Philip Kindersley is the third of the lovely Guinness sisters, daughters of the Hon. Ernest and Mrs. Guinness. She married Sir Robert and Lady Kindersley's son in 1929 and has a two-year-old boy, Gay, and a baby daughter, Tessa

The Bystander, August 17, 1932 303

Photographs: Dorothy Wilding, (inset) Lenare

The "Young Marrieds"

No. 12. Mr. and Mrs. Philip Kindersley

Mr. Philip Kindersley, Sir Robert and Lady Kindersley's son, married Miss Oonagh Guinness, youngest daughter of the Hon. Ernest and Mrs. Guinness, in 1929. They have spent most of this summer down in the country, with Gay and Tessa, their two-year-old son and baby daughter, at the attractive house they took in Kent

E

Arthur Owen

AT THE CARLTON: LORD DONEGALL AND MRS. PHILIP KINDERSLEY

On the "Dubarry" dinner night last week in connection with the big success now running at His Majesty's. Lord Donegall is a most industrious society journalist, and Mrs. Philip Kindersley was Miss Oonagh Guinness, and is a daughter of the Hon. Arthur and Mrs. Guinness and a niece of Lord Iveagh

The TATLER

Vol. CXXXI. No. 1704. London, February 21, 1934 POSTAGE: Inland, 2d.; Canada and Newfoundland, 1½d.; Foreign, 4d. Price One Shilling

Poole, Dublin

THE HUNT BALL SEASON

MR. EDWARD LINDSAY-HOGG AND MRS. PHILIP KINDERSLEY

At the Meath Hunt Ball. There may be some hunting countries in the world as good as Meath, but no Irishman and no Sassenach either (who has ever crossed it) will admit that there is a better one. The Hunt Ball, which was held at Abbotstown House, was as good a party as any that an Irish hunt has ever flung. Mr. Edward Lindsay-Hogg, a brother of Sir Anthony, is training at the Curragh and gets up and rides some of his own horses. Mrs. Philip Kindersley was Miss Oonagh Guinness, and is a daughter of the Hon. Ernest and Mrs. Guinness

RIGHT AND OPPOSITE: While weekdays were spent in London where they had a house at Rutland Gate, for several years the Kindersleys passed weekends at Great Tangley Manor, a moated mediaeval house near Guildford rented from Sir Frederick Ponsonby. A distant cousin of Oonagh's second husband, Ponsonby, who was raised to the peerage as Baron Sysonby in 1935, served as a courtier during the reigns of Queen Victoria and her successors, Edward VII and George VI. He wrote frankly about these monarchs in his posthumously published autobiography *Recollections of Three Reigns*.

A NOTABLE CHRISTENING

Mr. and Mrs. Philip Kindersley's little daughter was christened at St. Margaret's, Westminster, last week, and the above photograph shows the baby with her parents, her little brother Gay, and the godparents, after the ceremony

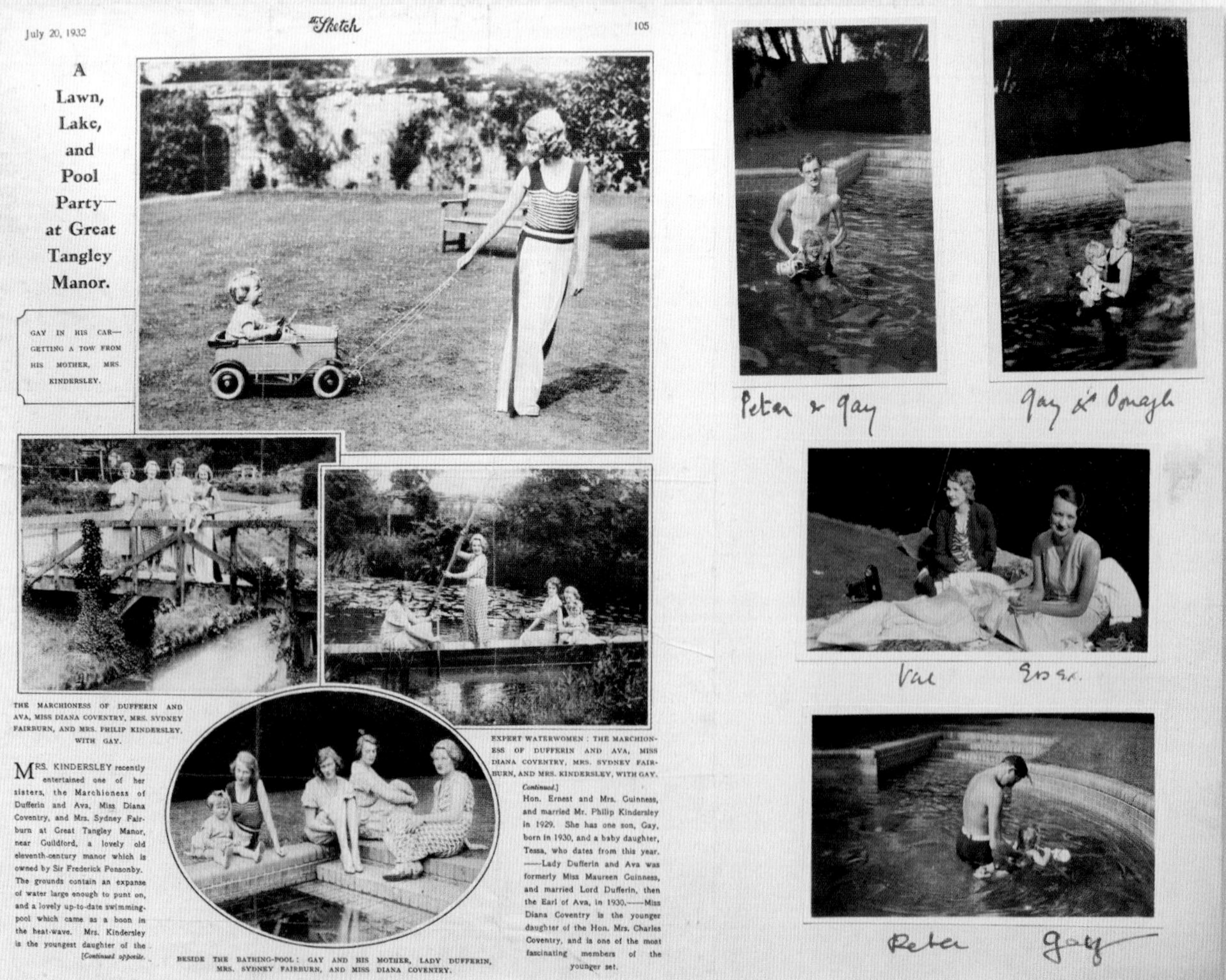

July 20, 1932 — The Sketch — 105

A Lawn, Lake, and Pool Party—at Great Tangley Manor.

GAY IN HIS CAR—GETTING A TOW FROM HIS MOTHER, MRS. KINDERSLEY.

THE MARCHIONESS OF DUFFERIN AND AVA, MISS DIANA COVENTRY, MRS. SYDNEY FAIRBURN, AND MRS. PHILIP KINDERSLEY, WITH GAY.

EXPERT WATERWOMEN: THE MARCHIONESS OF DUFFERIN AND AVA, MISS DIANA COVENTRY, MRS. SYDNEY FAIRBURN, AND MRS. KINDERSLEY, WITH GAY.

MRS. KINDERSLEY recently entertained one of her sisters, the Marchioness of Dufferin and Ava, Miss Diana Coventry, and Mrs. Sydney Fairburn at Great Tangley Manor, near Guildford, a lovely old eleventh-century manor which is owned by Sir Frederick Ponsonby. The grounds contain an expanse of water large enough to punt on, and a lovely up-to-date swimming-pool which came as a boon in the heat-wave. Mrs. Kindersley is the youngest daughter of the [*Continued opposite.*

BESIDE THE BATHING-POOL: GAY AND HIS MOTHER, LADY DUFFERIN, MRS. SYDNEY FAIRBURN, AND MISS DIANA COVENTRY.

Continued.] Hon. Ernest and Mrs. Guinness, and married Mr. Philip Kindersley in 1929. She has one son, Gay, born in 1930, and a baby daughter, Tessa, who dates from this year.——Lady Dufferin and Ava was formerly Miss Maureen Guinness, and married Lord Dufferin, then the Earl of Ava, in 1930.——Miss Diana Coventry is the younger daughter of the Hon. Mrs. Charles Coventry, and is one of the most fascinating members of the younger set.

No. 1618, June 29, 1932 THE TATLER

ENTERTAINED AND ENTERTAINING

Dates in the Social Diary

Arthur Owen

STAYING WITH MR. AND MRS. PHILIP KINDERSLEY IN SURREY: MISS DIANA COVENTRY AND MR. JIM LAWRENCE

Arthur Owen

MRS. PHILIP KINDERSLEY, HER SISTER LADY DUFFERIN, AND HER SON GAY KINDERSLEY

Arthur Owen

ALSO AT GREAT TANGLEY MANOR: MR. REX COLCLOUGH AND MRS. FAIRBURN

When Mr. and Mrs. Philip Kindersley entertain week-end parties guests always enjoy themselves exceedingly, a fact which is suggested by these smiling snapshots taken at Great Tangley Manor, Wonersh. Miss Diana Coventry is Mrs. Jim Dugdale's sister

NEWS FROM TANGLEY

THE Hindlips, on the other hand, are in London, but have not yet had a house-warming. As for the Philip Kindersleys—it seems very strange not to see them at cocktail-parties and so on as much as we did: but every week-end now they are entertaining at Tangley, and their friends have as much news of them—more, indeed; for how much, of any value, gets said at a party?—there as ever they did in London.

The Anthony Jenkinsons were among the first people to go down to them.

ALL this week people with country houses near London have been inundated with friends whose thoughts have turned eagerly to the delights of swimming-baths and gardens.

Except for Wednesday, when they came up to Town for the Pearson wedding, the Philip Kindersleys have had relays of guests, and have been spending the warm days in bathing-dresses and loose wide trousers. The babies have had the time of their lives, little Gay tumbling round the garden of Tangley like an infant Pan, in and out of the bathing pool with his mother and father, and made much of by all their friends.

Mrs. Philip Kindersley

MRS. DROGO MONTAGU is, perhaps, the loveliest of the Guinness collection. She has a repose which Lady Dufferin lacks, a perfect skin, and, of course, that wonderful corn-coloured hair. Mrs. Brinsley Plunket has refused to cut hers, which is wise, but, oh, so troublesome for milliners! Mrs. Kindersley is the tiniest and perhaps the sweetest Guinness.

Mrs. Philip Kindersley, formerly Miss Oonagh Guinness, had a light dress trimmed with silver fox,

Deserters from Mayfair

Mr. and Mrs. Philip Kindersley have not waited this year till the Season is over before going to the country; they are seen here, with their two children, at Great Tangley Manor, which they have taken for the summer

Miranda Angie Bunny Benita Hume Penelope Anne Phil
Noelin
Oonagh Jacques D'Arcy Gay

Great Tangley Manor

June 1934

Jacques D'Arcy Gay Kit Angie

Benita Hume Jacques D'Arcy

Tangley
June 1934

Oonagh

into the British Empire almost sixty years earlier. He and Maureen had three children, Caroline, Perdita and Sheridan. Although she continued to use the title from her first marriage, Maureen had two further husbands. While her two sisters were close to each other, shared many of the same friends and often stayed in each other's houses, Maureen remained aloof from their worlds. Once married to Basil Dufferin, she ceased visiting Luggala regularly, or indeed spending time in the Republic of Ireland; her life centred on London and Clandeboye.

Of the three sisters, it was always agreed that Oonagh, future chateleine of Luggala, in addition to being the youngest was also the prettiest and nicest. Furthermore, she was the least given to airs, or to the kind of infantile humour relished by her siblings: in later years, Maureen became well known in London for opening the door to her dinner guests 'disguised' as an Irish maid called Mabel who would leer and ask ribald questions. Similarly at Luttrellstown, Aileen's guests could find a bowl of artificial vomit placed beside their bed, or a stuffed dummy seemingly asleep between their sheets. Although forever childlike, Oonagh was not childish. She was the smallest of the sisters, standing little more than five foot tall and as a girl her lack of stature combined with a round face and quantities of untamed blonde hair inclined her to look dumpy. But having tamed the hair and shed adolescent fat, Oonagh emerged as slim and sleek as her older sisters. Barely launched into society, she met her first husband Philip Kindersley at a ball in London and five months after turning 19 she married him at St Margaret's, Westminster, in June 1929. For the occasion the bride wore a dress designed by Norman Hartnell of parchment-tinted satin sewn with pearls and bordered with a design of lilies in gold and silver. Her pearl-embroidered tulle veil was held in place with a 'halo' coronet of gold tissue. In August 1940 Hartnell recalled that Oonagh had had 'the looks and manner – although perhaps not the personality – of a Raphael cherub.' The wedding was zealously and effusively covered by all British and Irish newspapers, a single sour note being struck by the *Sunday Worker,* which warned readers 'Every time you stand the missus a Guinness in future you'll think of that golden halo and feel quite happy as you push your seven-pence over the bar counter.'

As tall and dark as his young wife was petite and fair, Philip Kindersley was born in 1907, youngest son of Sir

Robert Kindersley, a businessman who became partner in the merchant bank Lazard Frères & Co in 1905 and its chairman in 1919. A director of the Bank of England, he served as chairman of Britain's National Savings Committee from 1916–20, then president until 1946. For these and other public services he was knighted in 1917 and raised to the peerage as Baron Kindersley in 1941. He and his wife had four sons, the eldest of whom, Lionel, was killed in the First World War. The second son, Richard, appears not to have shared his father's high-minded industriousness. Moving to Hollywood, he tried acting, wrote poetry for children and painted before travelling on to Canada, where, inspired by film stunts, he took up the unusual hobby of hopping from one railway carriage to another while the train was moving. After his return to England, this had unfortunate consequences. In November 1932, at the age of 27, he was killed at Farnham

OPPOSITE: Published in *The Tatler* on August 6th 1930, this picture is captioned 'Our cartoonist – in savage mood – at a Bright Young Party.' Philip and Oonagh Kindersley are the two figures to the extreme left. The work is by Tony Wysard, an old Harrovian who produced similar drawings for many society magazines and would later become editor of *Harper's Bazaar*.

ABOVE: A series of cartoons drawn in 1933 by one of the Kindersleys' friends, Richard Sutton, imagining what members of their family would look like ten years later. In fact, long before that date, Philip and Oonagh had divorced and both remarried, he to Valerie Brougham and Vaux, who is seen in the picture on the upper right sitting on the sofa beside Oonagh.

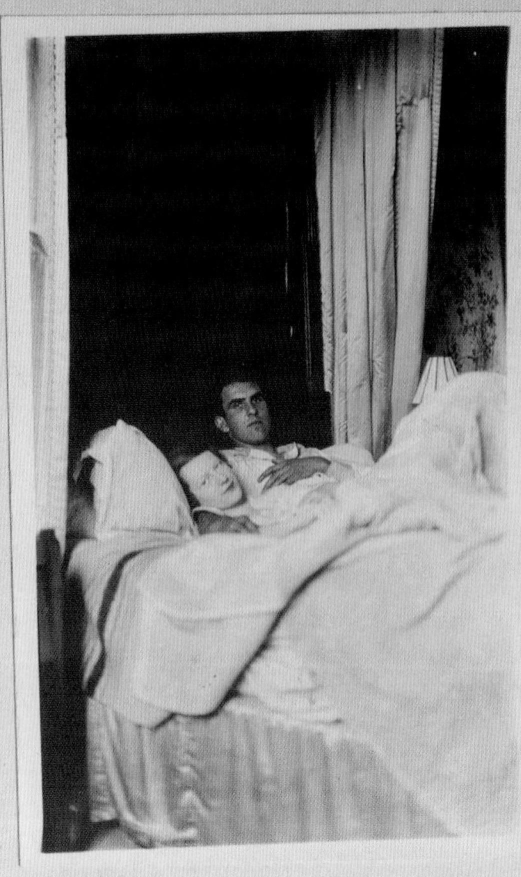

Station, his head coming into collision with an unyielding railway bridge: the body was identified by his name on a sock. The third Kindersley son, Hugh, proved to be steadier, following his father into Lazard Frères and the Bank of England as well as taking up positions on the boards of other major organisations.

After Eton and Oxford, Philip Kindersley had likewise gone into Lazards. For a period during his first marriage he served on the Guinness board and following divorce from Oonagh he set up his own stockbroking firm in 1936. When war broke out, he joined the Coldstream Guards and took part in the Dunkirk evacuation before going to Africa with the First Army; he was then captured and spent the next couple of years as a prisoner of war. On the conclusion of hostilities, he returned to the Stock Exchange until his retirement in 1976. A keen golfer and horseman, when young he harboured ambitions to be a gentleman steeplechase rider but was precluded by his weight and height; he stood at least a foot taller than his wife. In an effort to please her husband, Oonagh also tried to show an interest in horses, gamely hunting with the Whaddon Chase to show wifely solidarity. 'They were obviously ill-suited,' says Margaret, Lady Brinckman, who in 1956 married the couple's son Gay.

ABOVE: Oonagh and Philip Kindersley staying at Luggala in the early 1930s. At this date, the house had yet to be given to her by Ernest Guinness, who continued to rent it mostly for his daughter Aileen's use.

OPPOSITE: Although Oonagh sometimes came to stay at Luggala while married to Philip Kindersley, his dislike of Ireland made her visits infrequent. On the other hand, while her sister Aileen owned Luttrellstown Castle on the other side of Dublin, she and her then-husband the Hon. Brinsley Plunket regularly entertained house parties at Luggala, where guests included film actor Douglas Fairbanks and his mistress (and subsequently wife) Sylvia Ashley-Cooper, together with her then-husband Lord Ashley.

Brinny Dorothea

Daily Express

ENORMOUS crowds, I learn from a correspondent, were attracted to the Irish St. Leger at the Curragh by the presence of the Derby and St. Leger hero, Trigo.

MR. COSGRAVE was among those watching the races, and an attractive girl whom my correspondent noticed was the Hon. Angela Pearson.

Sir Anthony Weldon and the Hon. Brinsley Plunket and his wife, who are now to be seen at every Irish race meeting, were there, too; and so was General Sir Bryan Mahon, who is now completely recovered from his recent illness.

Irish Times

THE CURRAGH RACES.
Lady Weldon and the Hon. Mrs. Brinsley Plunket.

Luggala

Teddy Brinny

Terence Weldon, Nancy Pearson, Sophie Burton, Brin, Tony Weldon, Tommy Weldon, Joan Pearson.

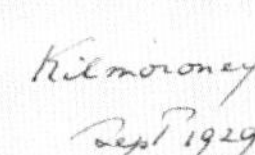

Tommy Weldon, Nancy Pearson, Joan Pearson, Sophie Burton.

Tony, Douglas, Sylvia, me, Billy

The Irish Press

MR. FAIRBANKS' VISIT

Mr. Douglas Fairbanks, the film star, who is at present the guest of the Hon. Brinsley Plunket and Mrs. Plunket at Luttrellstown Castle, Clonsilla, had a round of golf over the Portmarnock course yesterday. He afterwards paid a visit to the Wicklow Mountains.

Luggala.

Windy Brinny Sylvia Tony

Billy Sylvia Douglas Tony Brinny

NOTED FILM STAR LEAVES

Mr. "Doug" Fairbanks left for England yesterday by the Mail boat from Dun Laoghaire. He was seen off by the Hon. Brinsley Plunkett, Luttrelstown Lodge, Clonsilla, whose guest he had been during his stay in Ireland.

THE IRISH FIELD.

MR. BRINSLEY PLUNKET'S Buckup Bryant won the Glencairn Selling T.Y.O. Plate as easily as his jockey, B. Curran, cared to allow him, and this quite useful son of Buckler was bought in for 150 sovs. His lines next season are, we think, likely to be cast on a higher plane than contesting "sellers."

DUBLIN, SATURDAY, NOV. 18, 1933.

3.45—GLENCAIRN PLATE of £50; 2nd £5. A selling race for two-year-olds, maidens at starting. 5 furlongs.

Hon Brinsley Plunket's BUCKUP BRYANT, by Buckler—England's Match, 8-7 B Curran 1
Mr J J Cooney's Buckbasket, 9-0 Jos Canty 2
Lord Milton's Coollattin, 9-0 ...... J Moylan 3
Miss Phil Ryan's Copper Patch, 9-0 W Howard 0
Mr E J Byrne's Repent, 8-11 .. E Gardner 0
Mr J J Parkinson's Swift Guard, 8-7 M Barrett 0
Col Clarke's Miss Kapper, 8-4 ..... P Maher 0
Capt Brench Davis's Ya Ya, 8-4 G A Christie 0
Mrs E Fetherstonhaugh's Happy Vale, 8-4 Jas Doyle 0
Mr N Kelly's Royal Tribute, 8-4 (car 8-6) M Wing 0
Col J McLaughlin's Rockbois, 8-4 W Barrett 0

(Winner trained by E. More O'Ferrall.)

Betting—6 to 4 on BUCKUP BRYANT, 7 to 2 agst Swift Guard, 5 to 1 Repent, 100 to 14 Rockbois, 20 to 1 each Buckbasket, Coollattin, or any other.

Tote (2/-)—Win, [illegible]. Places, 3/-, 15/-, 4/6. Won by two lengths, three-quarters of a length.

1st – 8th.

MONTE CARLO

crossing the channel.

Oonagh and Coocles

Oonagh & Phil

Lord Scarsdale – Phyllis Allen – Phil

Phil

Hubert Pantz & Oonagh

Phil

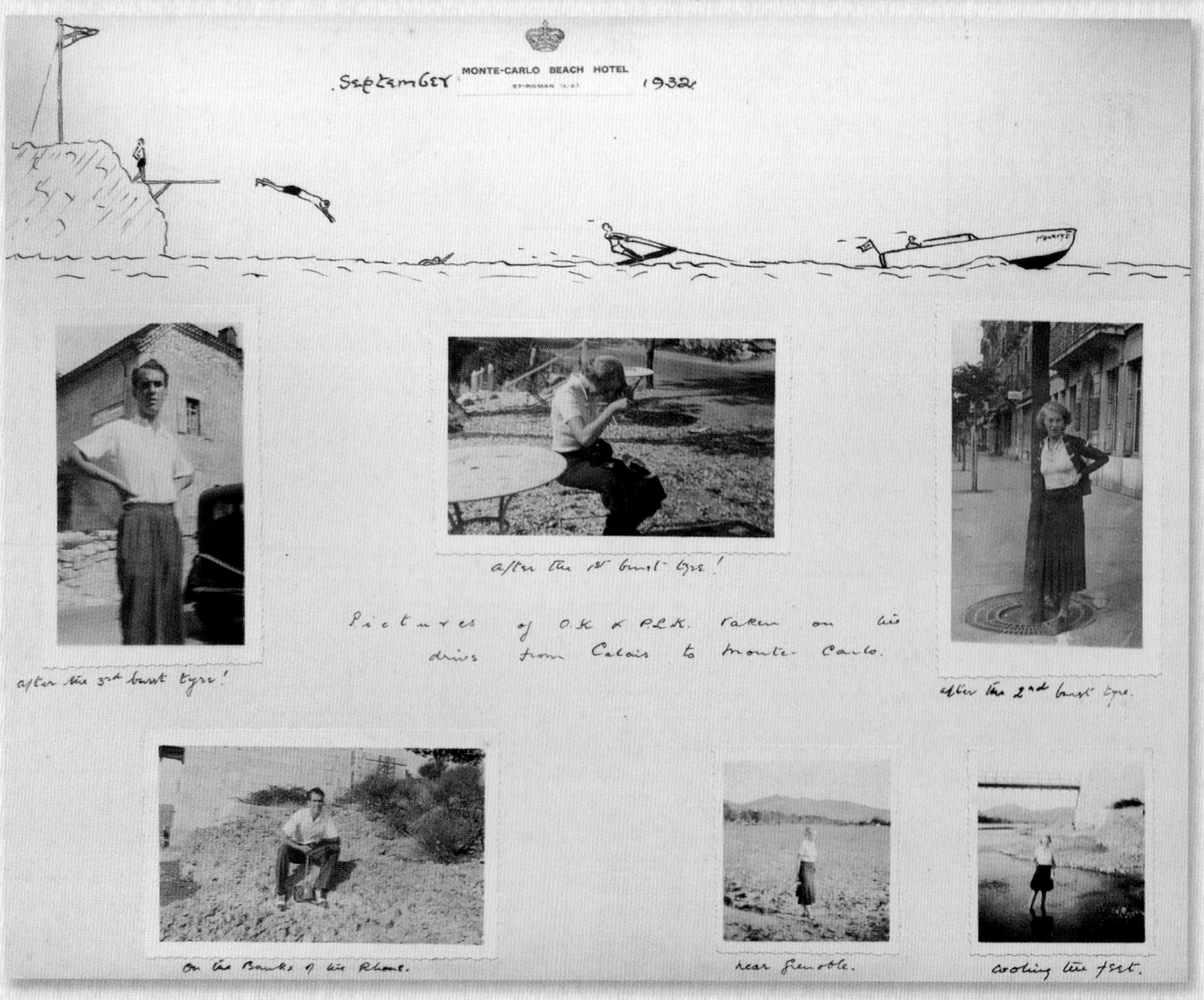

'I adored Philip, but he certainly wasn't well-read. He was very much a hunting man, he wouldn't have understood her at all. It seemed to me that the marriage was doomed to failure.'

Difference of interests between the couple soon became apparent, especially when they spent weekends with Philip's parents at their home, Plaw Hatch Hall in Sussex. Lady Kindersley was as devoted to public service as her husband, later acting as chair of two hospitals during the Second World War. Never an early riser, Oonagh's belated appearances at the breakfast table would be greeted by her mother-in-law with the cutting observation 'You look seedy this morning.' Philip Kindersley apparently was just as ill at ease with his wife's family as she with his. He never cared for Ireland, mistrusted the Irish and when first taken to Luggala declared it to be 'a god-forsaken place'. This dislike of Ireland would be a problem later when the question of their son's education became an issue between Philip and Oonagh.

That son, her first child, was born in June 1930 and given the unusual first name of Gay; seemingly Philip had come across someone called Gaylord in the South of France and decided a variation of this would suit his heir. The name was later the cause of some merriment, even gaiety. In 1985, for example, Gay Kindersley, who in adulthood became a

OPPOSITE: Within a couple of years of marrying Oonagh, Philip Kindersley had begun an affair with one of her bridesmaids, Valerie, Lady Brougham and Vaux. But in an effort to ensure their marriage survived, the Kindsleys embarked on an extended trip driving across France to Monte Carlo. The attempt was unsuccessful and in 1935 the couple divorced, Philip subsequently marrying Valerie Brougham and Vaux.

ABOVE: By the mid-1930s Oonagh's was not the only marriage in trouble; so too was that of her sister Aileen. Here Oonagh is seen with Aileen's then-lover, impoverished Austrian playboy Baron Hubert von Pantz. He would later marry the wealthy Terry McConnell, whose deceased husband had been heir to the Avon cosmetics fortune.

successful amateur jockey and horse breeder, found himself and Graham Lord, literary editor of the *Sunday Express*, in the company of the Australian national cricket team at the Savoy Hotel. 'Hello,' he said, extending a hand to the Australian captain Allan Border, 'I'm Gay and this is my friend Graham.' A silence followed, eventually broken by one of the cricketers declaring, 'Strewth; hang onto your strides, mate. The bastard's a poofter.'

In January 1932 the Kindersleys had a second child, a daughter to whom they gave the more conventional name of Tessa. By then their marriage was beginning to register faultlines, although in public they remained united and were regularly photographed both attending parties in London, where they had a house in Rutland Gate, and hosting weekends at the ravishing, moated Great Tangley Manor near Guildford, which they rented from that consummate courtier Sir Frederick Ponsonby (whose posthumously published memoirs, *Recollections of Three Reigns*, were described by Nancy Mitford as containing 'a shriek on every page'). Sir Frederick's daughter Loelia was then married to the Duke of Westminster, from whom Ernest Guinness had bought *Fântome II*.

In fact, within a couple of years of marrying Oonagh, Philip had begun an affair with the woman who would become his second wife, Valerie French, granddaughter of the 1st Earl of Ypres. One of the most attractive women of her generation, in April 1931 Valerie, known as Valsie, had married Victor, 4th Lord Brougham and Vaux, but the relationship was even more short-lived than that of the Kindersleys, ending in divorce after just three years. It did not help that Victor Brougham was a chronic gambler. A year after the wedding, debts he had run up in Monte Carlo forced the sale of valuable items from Brougham Hall in Cumbria; in 1934 the house itself was sold. Eventually in 1950 Victor Brougham would be declared bankrupt, having lost more than £125,000 in gambling, stock market speculation and an abortive attempt at farming.

Despite attempts at discretion, it is evident that the affair between Philip Kindersley and Valerie Brougham and Vaux did not go unnoticed. A *Tatler* column in May 1933, having remarked that Lady Brougham could not 'possibly in any way be regarded as being in the bluestocking class,' nevertheless noted that this handicap in no way meant she lacked admirers, thereby 'showing that beauty and girlish charms are a woman's best weapons.' The same piece then continued by describing Valsie as Oonagh Kindersley's 'erstwhile' friend, and commenting how Oonagh, 'despite her lack of inches,

OPPOSITE: To the left is a mid-18th-century portrait of Dominick Browne of Castle MacGarrett. In 1754 he conformed to the Church of Ireland, the first member of the family to abandon the Catholic faith, presumably in order to preserve the Browne estates, which would otherwise have been at risk under the Penal Laws of the period. Centre and right are representations of a later Dominick Browne, who in 1836 was raised to the peerage as Lord Oranmore and Browne, indicated by the ermine-edged robes he wears in his portrait. To his chagrin, it was only an Irish peerage, owing to British government fears that he faced bankruptcy; these concerns were proven correct in the 1850s when the greater part of the Browne estates had to be sold to pay his debts.

RIGHT: In the early 1920s, the third Lord Oranmore and Browne and his wife had moved to England where they lived at Mereworth Castle, Kent. In June 1927 the car in which they were travelling collided with a bus. While Lady Oranmore died instantly, her husband survived for three weeks. His high position in both Ireland and England meant that both deaths attracted considerable notice, with telegrams of condolence being sent by a number of members of the royal family, including George V.

POST OFFICE TELEGRAPHS.

This Form must accompany any inquiry respecting this Telegram.

O H M S Buckingham Palace

TO The Lord Oranmore & Browne Mereworth Castle Maidstone

The Queen and I have heard with much regret of the grievous loss which you have sustained by the fatal accident on Tuesday last and assure you and your family of our heartfelt sympathy in your sorrow we trust that you are recovering from your injuries George R I

On Tuesday June 7th 1927 the motor car in which Geoffrey, Lord Oranmore and his wife Olwen were driving collided with a motor bus. Lady Oranmore was killed instantaneously. The funeral took place on Saturday June 11th at 11.30 at Mereworth Church. The Service was performed by the Bishop of Rochester assisted by the Rev. W. Moore and the Rev. Montagu Alderson. A memorial Service was held at the same time at St Anselm's Davies Street, the Vicar, the Rev A Sinclair, performing the Service. The following came back to lunch at Mereworth.

Dominick Browne.
Hildred Browne.
Thomas Egerton.
W. H. Cooper
Geoffrey Browne
Henry H. C. Moore
Bessborough

On Thursday June 30th 1927. Geoffrey, Lord Oranmore died at Mereworth Castle as a result of injuries received in a motor car accident on June 7th. The funeral service took place at Mereworth Church on July 4th at 11.30. The Service was performed by the Bishop of Rochester assisted by the Rev. W. Moore, vicar of Mereworth. A memorial service performed by the Rev A Sinclair, was held at the same time at St. Anselm's, Davies Street. The following came back to lunch at Mereworth after the funeral.

Dominick Browne
Hildred Browne.
Charles des Graz
Geoffrey Browne
Henry H. C. Moore
Bessborough
Thomas Egerton
W. H. Cooper
Richard Nevill

Castle MacGarrett

Lying two miles south of the town of Claremorris, County Mayo, Castle MacGarrett today shows little evidence of its ancient history. The original mediaeval castle was built by the Prendergasts in the 13th century on the banks of the river Robe: in 1169 Maurice de Prendergast, a Norman knight, came to Ireland with Richard de Clare, Earl of Pembroke, popularly known as Strongbow. In the 16th century, Geoffrey Browne of Galway married the heiress Mary Prendergast, and thus came into possession of Castle MacGarrett, but may not have lived there since his main estate at Carrabrowne was in neighbouring County Galway.

It was probably only towards the end of the following century that the Brownes began to spend more time on their Mayo property. Family tradition states that in 1694 another Geoffrey Browne found that the old castle had grown unsafe and therefore abandoned it for a new house further from the river. Both he and his father planted many trees in the demesne, some of which remain.

The new Castle MacGarrett was occupied by successive generations until largely destroyed by fire in 1811. When the present house was being rebuilt at the start of the last century, a stone was discovered in the foundations inscribed 'By Geoff Browne 1719.' And now embedded in the wall of the building is another stone with the initials G and E separated by the date 1738 and surmounted by the letter B; this is believed to refer to Geoffrey Browne and his wife Elizabeth, although the significance of 1738 is not known.

Castle MacGarrett, c. 1846

Following the fire of 1811, the house's stables were converted for use as a residence. The architect Sir Richard Morrison drew up various plans for a new, elaborately gothic castle, but none of these was executed, presumably because Dominick Browne was too busy spending his fortune on elections and then on efforts to gain first an Irish and afterwards an English peerage. The sale of the greater part of his lands through the Encumbered Estates office between 1852 and 1855 ensured nothing further was done until the time of his grandson, the third Lord Oranmore and Browne, who, after coming into his inheritance, decided to remodel and extend the old stables in order to create a more comfortable house.

The architect engaged for this task was Richard Caulfield Orpen, older brother of the painter Sir William Orpen, who carried out work on many other Irish country houses and also has the questionable credit of being 'the originator of the bungalow in Ireland.' Orpen's revamped Castle MacGarrett is not a thing of beauty, its lumpen, cement-rendered exterior lacking grace, the two irregular wings that jut out to create a forecourt each featuring a small crenellated tower as though to justify the building's use of the title castle. The interior is rather more successful, beginning with the staircase hall that rises to a first-floor gallery, the walls carrying plaster swags in which the Browne arms are quartered with those of heiresses the family had married. The drawing room and dining room both have elaborate neoclassical stucco ceilings copied from those designed by James Wyatt for Leinster House, Dublin. The drawing room contained a notable collection of Meissen porcelain, the hall a large number of miniatures by Anne Mee. The library, previously the billiard room, had a beamed ceiling and walls lined with mahogany bookcases. Hicks of Dublin made the chimneypieces, while the panelling came from Crowthers of London. The cost of the refurbishment was £21,422.7s.6d.

In the early 1920s Castle MacGarrett survived the War of Independence and the Civil War, although the house was raided by armed men one night in May 1922. The following year it was occupied by Free State troops who only left in June 1924. A feature

Castle MacGarrett, c. 1857

on the property in the *Irish Times* of 18th September 1937 noted that one of the reasons for the third Lord Oranmore's purchase of Mereworth Castle in England in the early 1920s had been the excessive cost of making Castle MacGarrett habitable following its military occupation. In February 1923, after visiting the house and seeing the damage done to it by the occupying soldiers, he wrote in his journal, 'I don't think it will ever be possible to go back and live at home.' However, following Lord Oranmore's death and the sale of Mereworth, his son and heir Dominick did return to live in the house, remaining there for more than thirty years.

During the time Dom was married to Oonagh Guinness, there were ample funds to maintain Castle MacGarrett, but after the couple divorced in 1950 it became a struggle to make the place economically viable. The walled kitchen gardens produced vegetables and fruit, including more than 80 varieties of apple, which were then sold, while much of the rest of the land was stocked with cattle and sheep. Commercial shoots were run and architect Michael Scott designed new stables with twenty boxes and an exercise yard for the Castle MacGarrett stud. Dom offered guided tours around the house, which he led, for the price of five shillings. It was all to no avail. Writer Eamon Delaney, many of whose family worked on the estate, recalls that when his uncle PJ sought to be paid for his labour, Dom Oranmore lamented he was broke; eventually PJ Delaney received four fields in lieu of money.

OPPOSITE AND ABOVE: Situated on the banks of the river Robe in County Mayo and dating from the 13th century, the original Castle MacGarrett was abandoned by the Brownes in the 1690s for a new house. Unfortunately, this was destroyed by fire in 1811; a report at the time in *The Gentleman's Magazine* noted that the blaze had 'originated in the kitchen and the Cook perished.' Thereafter a number of plans were drawn up by Irish architect Sir Richard Morrison for an elaborately gothic castle to replace the destroyed house. None of these was executed, presumably because Dominick Browne was too busy, first spending his fortune on elections and then seeking a peerage. As a result, until the beginning of the 20th century, the family lived in what had once been the old house's stable block.

In July 1960 the contents of Castle MacGarrett – everything from a pair of old Waterford glass decanters to a Chippendale mahogany side table – were dispersed in a four-day auction held on the premises, after which Dom Oranmore and his third wife, Sally, moved to London. The empty house was then used for 'armchair farming', which involved rearing pigs in the main rooms, the notion being that a sow reared in this environment would sell for about 90 guineas, thereby yielding a profit of some £55 per animal. 'Not a bad investment,' commented Dom's nephew, Michael Mordaunt-Smith, who was in charge of the enterprise and whose previous jobs had included acting as London bureau chief for the Hollywood scandal magazine *Confidential*; he had been a star witness at the publication's August 1957 libel trial.

The pig scheme proved no more successful than any others. Since the beginning of the century there had been intermittent pressure, official and informal, to encourage the Brownes to sell their land so that it could be broken up and divided between local

ABOVE: At the start of the last century the third Lord Oranmore and Browne decided to remodel and extend the old stables at Castle MacGarrett in order to create a more comfortable house, employing the architect Richard Caulfield Orpen for this purpose. Although with the advent of Ireland's war of Independence the Brownes preferred to spend more time in England, following Lord Oranmore's death in 1927 his heir Dominick returned to Castle MacGarrett which remained his home until he was forced to sell the estate in the early 1960s.

farmers. In 1964 this finally came to pass when the 1,750 acre estate was bought for £95,000 by the Irish Land Commission, so ending the family's association with the area going back more than 350 years. The Land Commission, having parcelled out most of the land, then offered the house and 125 acres for sale, the buyer being an order of nuns, the Sisters of Our Lady of Apostles, who tacked on a utilitarian extension and from 1967 ran the place as a retirement home. In 2005, at the height of Ireland's economic boom, the Sisters sold the house and 120 acres for some €5 million to a business consortium, the members of which intended to convert the place into a hotel and spa. That plan never came to fruition and Castle MacGarrett now sits empty and in need of major repair.

ABOVE: For some forty years until 2005 Castle MacGarrett was run as a retirement home by an order of nuns. It was then sold to a group of property developers who planned to redevelop the house and grounds into a hotel. This did not happen and today Castle MacGarrett stands empty and in poor condition.

has only to enter a room to be the cynosure of all eyes, which always seems to embarrass her acutely.'

In fact, Valsie had been one of Oonagh's closest friends, and a bridesmaid at her wedding, so the affair with Philip must have seemed something of a betrayal. On the other hand, it was not long before Oonagh had found consolation elsewhere, with a man who was at the time also married.

After his death in August 2002 at the age of 100, obituaries of Dominick, 4th Baron Oranmore and Browne, focused on the fact that although the longest-serving member ever of the British House of Lords, from 1927 when his father died until 1999 when hereditary peers were abolished, he never once spoke in the chamber. It is true that Dom, as he was universally known, did not lead a very active public life, certainly not when it is compared with those of his ancestors.

Born in October 1901, Dom was the youngest page at the coronation of George V nine years later. Sent to Eton, his return from Ireland for the summer half of 1916 was delayed because of the Easter Rising. Leaving school, he went to Christ Church, Oxford and then briefly served in the Grenadier Guards, where he earned a reputation as a fine shot. Indeed his shooting prowess might be claimed as Dom's greatest skill; as a boy he got into the habit of firing his airgun at the Castle MacGarrett dairymaid, on the basis that she had an ample figure. He was said to have been the best shot in Ireland with a particular fondness for shooting snipe 'because it was the most difficult'.

Dom's more visibly industrious father, the 3rd Lord Oranmore and Browne – who in 1926 had been raised to the Peerage of the United Kingdom as Baron Mereworth, hence his son's right to sit in the House of Lords – wrote a detailed account of the Browne family's origins, published in

OPPOSITE: Two cartoons by Teddy Plunket. That on the left, showing Dominick Oranmore and Browne, is on paper from his own property, Castle MacGarrett.That on the right showing his brother the Hon. Brinsley Plunket and Dominick, 4th Lord Oranmore and Browne is drawn on notepaper from Luttrellstown Castle, owned by the former's wife, Aileen Guinness.

RIGHT: Two pages from Oonagh's photograph albums indicate the complexity of her personal life by this time. She and her husband, Philip Kindersley, both spent a weekend in August 1934 at the races in Tramore, County Waterford, but so too did Dominick Oranmore and Browne, her future second husband, and Valerie Brougham and Vaux, Philip's future second wife. Despite efforts to keep their private lives out of the public arena, inevitably Oonagh's public profile meant her divorce from Philip Kindersley in November 1935 and marriage to Dominick Oranmore and Browne the following April received widespread press coverage.

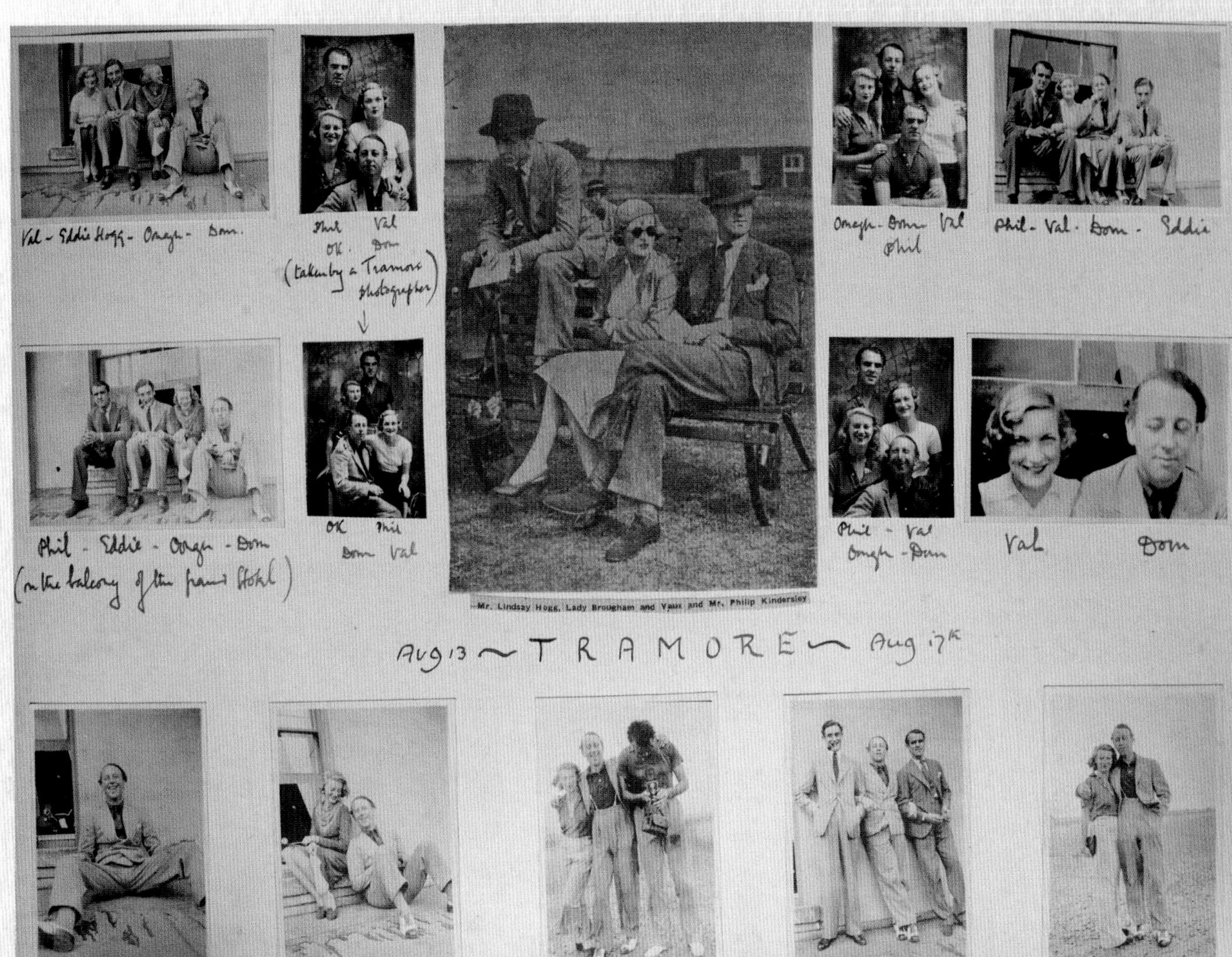

Daily Sketch

Lord Oranmore's Surprise Register Office Wedding

Lord Oranmore and Browne and Mrs Oonagh Kindersley, formerly Miss Oonagh Guinness, after their marriage at Marylebone register office yesterday.

Daily Express

CAR CHASE BEFORE THEY POSED

LORD ORANMORE AND BROWNE and Mrs. Oonagh Kindersley made three unsuccessful attempts to leave Marylebone (London) Register Office after their marriage yesterday. This picture was only taken after stern car chase. Mrs. Kindersley, who is twenty-six, is former wife of Mr. Philip Kindersley.

The Scotsman

PEER'S WEDDING

Register Office Ceremony

BARON ORANMORE AND BROWNE was married yesterday at Marylebone Register Office, London, to Mrs Oonagh Kindersley, of Grosvenor Place, London. He is 34, and she is 26.

They stepped from their cars and hurried to the steps of the register office, trying to avoid photographers. The bridegroom wore a navy pin striped suit, with a red carnation in his buttonhole. The bride wore a mauve blue ensemble, with hat to match. About half-a-dozen guests were present.

Baron Oranmore and Browne is the owner of the historic MacGarrett Castle, County Mayo. Two years ago part of the castle was burned, and many art treasures were destroyed. The Baron also owns Mereworth Castle, Maidstone.

Daily Record and Mail

The Irish Partners

THE quiet register office marriage of Lord Oranmore and Browne and Mrs. Oonagh Kindersley recalls to a great many minds the lovely and lavish weddings of the three Guinness sisters, Aileen, Maureen, and Oonagh, all in the fashionable setting of St. Margaret's, Westminster.

Miss Aileen Guinness, eldest of the Hon. Arthur Guinness's lovely daughters, married the Hon. Brinsley Plunket, Lord Plunket's brother. Her sister Maureen married an Irishman, too, and is Lady Dufferin and Ava. Oonagh, at nineteen, married an English bridegroom in Mr. Philip Kindersley, but now, following her divorce, she follows the family custom in taking an Irish husband.

Lord Oranmore and Browne, eight years older than his twenty-six-year-old bride, has also been married before, to a niece of Lord Ellesmere, and of that marriage there are five children.

PEER'S BRIDE

Daily Mirror

Married yesterday at Marylebone Register Office: Lord Oranmore and Browne and Mrs. Oonagh Kindersley, formerly Miss Oonagh Guinness.

Morning Post

MARRIAGE ANNOUNCEMENTS

Lord Oranmore and Browne and Mrs. Oonagh Kindersley

The marriage will shortly take place between Lord Oranmore and Browne and Mrs. Oonagh Kindersley.

Daily Mirror

TO MARRY MRS. OONAGH KINDERSLEY

Mrs. Oonagh Kindersley (left) and Lord Oranmore and Browne (above), the Irish peer, notice of whose intended marriage has been given at a London register office.

Mrs. Kindersley, who is twenty-six, was formerly Miss Oonagh Guinness. She is a niece of the Earl of Iveagh.

Lord Oranmore and Browne is thirty-four years of age.

Daily Express

TO MARRY PEER

MRS. OONAGH KINDERSLEY, formerly Miss Oonagh Guinness, is to marry Lord Oranmore and Browne, the Irish peer. The bridegroom's age is given as thirty-four, and his address as Quebec Mews, London, W.; the bride's age as twenty-six.

Evening Standard

Lord Oranmore to Marry Again

Notice has been given at a London register office of the forthcoming wedding of Lord Oranmore and Browne and Mrs. Oonah Kindersley, formerly Miss Oonah Guinness.

The bridegroom's age is given as 34, and his address as Quebec-mews, W. [illegible] and the bride's age as 26, and her address as Grosvenor-place, S.W.

successive issues of the *Journal of the Galway Archaeological and Historical Society*. Unlike other Irish landowners who shared the same name and who arrived as part of the 16th- and 17th-century settlements, it is believed that these particular Brownes came to Ireland with the Normans and soon settled in the region of Galway where they built the castle of Carrabrowne at Oranmore. However, details of their early history must remain something of a mystery, since the family papers were lost in a fire that destroyed the main Browne residence, Castle MacGarrett, County Mayo, in 1811; a report in *The Gentleman's Magazine* noted that the blaze had 'originated in the kitchen and the Cook perished'.

Certainly it is possible to trace a clear line from one Stephen Browne who lived in the mid-15th century. By then his family had become one of the Tribes of Galway, the fourteen merchant clans who dominated the political, commercial and social life of Galway city. Stephen's direct descendant, Dominick Browne, was Mayor of Galway in

ABOVE AND OPPOSITE: As a peer of the realm, Dominick, together with Oonagh, attended the coronation of George VI in Westminster Abbey on 12th May 1937. Oonagh's brother-in-law, Teddy Plunket and his wife, Dorothé, were intimate friends of the new King and Queen; when still Duchess of York the latter became godmother to the Plunket's second son, Robin, in 1925 whilst her husband was godfather to the couple's third child, Shaun, six years later. Yet it is clear that Oonagh remained in contact with the Duke of Windsor, who had abdicated the previous December, as is indicated by the telegram sent to her by the Duke and his future wife two days before their wedding on 3rd June 1937.

The MARCHIONESS OF DUFFERIN AND AVA, *wife of the fourth Marquess of Dufferin and Ava, posed holding her coronet. She is the eldest daughter of the Hon. Ernest Guinness.*

C. or B.

Telegrafa an Puist.

13

Ní mór an fuirm seo do chur le h-aon fiafraí a dhéantar mar gheall ar an telegram so.

Jul 10

XC 1915 1 Tours 17

The Lady Oranmore
and Browne Claremorris
Ireland

We both appreciate so
much your kind wishes

Edward Wallis

Wt. 1798—220. 5,500,000. 10/35.

LORD ORANMORE AND BROWNE (RIGHT) AND LADY ORANMORE AND BROWNE

Lord and Lady Oranmore, who are with some more weary waiters, were married last year. She is the former Miss G[illegible]h Guinness

Right: LORD *and* LADY ORANMORE AND BROWNE *waiting for their car after the service.*

ABOVE: Architecturally attuned to the environment, the lodge at Luggala nestles into the top of its own valley. As Douglas Scott Richardson has observed, 'The concordance felt between much of the Irish landscape and Gothic Revival styles is a constantly recurring idea, virtually a cliché, through the late Georgian and Early Victorian periods'.

1575 and at the time of his death was described as 'the richest merchant in Ireland'. This wealth was enhanced by his eldest son Geoffrey's judicious marriage to an heiress, Mary Prendergast, who brought with her thousands of acres in counties Mayo, Longford and Westmeath. Their son, another Dominick (all eldest sons in the Browne family have been christened either Dominick or Geoffrey), led an exceedingly colourful life that saw him elected both a Member of Parliament and Mayor of Galway, as well as receive a knighthood, but also see his Galway estates confiscated by the government of Oliver Cromwell. These lands were subsequently returned to his son, and later Brownes opted to be more circumspect in their behaviour. In 1754, for example, Colonel Dominick Browne conformed to the Church of Ireland, presumably to avoid any loss of lands under the Penal Laws operating against Roman Catholics. By that time there was a lot to lose, the Brownes being the 22nd largest landlords in Ireland with 13 estates spread across several counties. In 1807 the 13th Viscount Dillon, who was to marry a Browne,

ABOVE: The west front of Luggala, with an archway leading into the yard. The building's gleaming white exterior makes it almost glow in this verdant setting. It was Desmond Fitzgerald, 29th Knight of Glin, who proposed painting architectural details like the brackets beneath the building's castellation so that they imitated the granite used on the window sills and arches.

wrote that his future father-in-law 'has 23,000 acres in Connaught so that his son has £20,000 a year'.

The son to whom he referred, again called Dominick, harboured political ambitions, representing County Mayo for the Whig interest in seven Parliaments between 1814 and 1836 (with a break in 1826–30). This enterprise was his undoing since he was obliged to spend a fortune on each election to ensure success; one of them cost him £40,000 of which £600 alone went on lemons for whiskey punch. As a reward for his diligence, he was made a Privy Councillor of Ireland in 1834 and two years later was created an Irish peer as Baron Oranmore of Carrabrowne Castle and Baron Browne of Castle MacGarrett. But an Irish title did not automatically carry the right to sit in the House of Lords at Westminster and he therefore energetically lobbied for an English peerage. Three British Prime Ministers turned down his requests, the reason being they had heard that the newly ennobled Lord Oranmore and Browne was on the verge of bankruptcy. This he denied, even though his debts

ABOVE: A quatrefoil window on the main building. Although obviously intended to be decorative, and to emphasise the house's Gothic character, at the same time these windows serve a practical purpose, providing light to a series of bedrooms cunningly tucked into the first floor.

OPPOSITE: The house's main entrance, today looking much as it must have done when Luggala was first constructed sometime around 1790, especially since the ground floor window arches were reinstated. The only recent addition is the double-headed eagle temporarily placed atop the door: a feature of the Browne coat of arms, the eagle was bought by Garech Browne and installed during the building's most recent restoration by David Mlinaric.

amounted to an astonishing £199,320. The Irish Great Famine of 1845–8 completed his ruin, and in a series of sales during the first half of the following decade, the majority of the Browne lands, including a large portion of Galway city, were sold through the Encumbered Estates Court. It was at this time that Sir Benjamin Lee Guinness bought Ashford Castle, where the first Lord Oranmore's great-grandson would later stay as guest of Ernest Guinness.

The only part of the old estates to be saved was some 7,000 acres around Castle MacGarrett (later reduced to 2,000 acres as a result of the 1903 Wyndham Land Act). This was thanks to the intervention of the 1st Lord Oranmore's older son, who had regained some measure of wealth following marriage to a Scottish heiress. Both the 2nd and 3rd Lords Oranmore sat in the Westminster House of Lords as a Representative Peer for Ireland, and in 1921 the latter, a Southern Unionist who in 1917 was invited to participate in the Irish Convention, also became a Senator for the new Irish State. It was he who, in addition to being made a Knight of the Order of St. Patrick in 1918 eight years later received the English peerage for which his grandfather had so longed and the denial of which, as he noted in his journal, 'has always been a grievance in the family'.

The title of Baron Mereworth was chosen because some years before the 3rd Lord Oranmore had bought Mereworth Castle, Kent, one of the finest 18th-century Palladian houses in England. Mereworth was designed by Colen Campbell in 1723 for the Hon. John Fane, who, in a neat reversal, had first become an Irish peer, Baron Catherlough, before inheriting his brother's title, Earl of Westmorland. Lord Oranmore and his wife Olwen, a daughter of the 8th Earl of Bessborough, were living at Mereworth at the time of their deaths in June 1927 when the car in which they were travelling collided with a bus; Lady Oranmore died instantly, her husband three weeks later. Both their funerals were attended by bizarre incidents. The motor hearse carrying Lady Oranmore's coffin caught fire on its way to the church and another had to be ordered. Meanwhile, the lead coffin in which her husband had been placed (deceased peers of the realm being customarily buried in lead coffins) proved too heavy to carry downstairs; it was therefore placed in the service lift at Mereworth but the ropes broke and the casket plunged into the basement.

In January 1928 Dom moved to Ireland after selling Mereworth, which was subsequently owned by press magnate Esmond Harmsworth, 2nd Viscount Rothermere. Three years

earlier, in 1925, Dom had married Mildred Egerton, granddaughter of the 3rd Earl of Ellesmere. Over the next seven years the couple had five children: three daughters (one of whom would die young) and two sons. Dom had known the Guinness family for most of his life; Castle MacGarrett was just twenty miles from Ashford Castle, where he was often invited to shoot. In the early 1930s he and Mildred more frequently socialised with Aileen and Brinny Plunket than with the Kindersleys; Philip's dislike of Ireland meant he rarely visited the country. In May/June 1933 the Oranmore and Brownes and Plunkets undertook an extended cruise in *Fantôme II* with Ernest and Chloe Guinness, travelling along the coast of Morocco and around the Mediterranean; among the other passengers was a friend of both young couples, Ulick Browne, future Marquess of Sligo, who, because of his generous girth, was always known as 'Lump' Sligo.

Photographs from this trip suggest all was well between Dom and Mildred Oranmore, but an album from the following year tells another story. Here are pictures of a weekend at the races in Tramore, County Waterford, followed by several days at the Lake Hotel, Killarney, County Kerry, in which, tellingly, the participants were Dom – without his wife – the now-divorced Valerie Brougham, Philip and Oonagh Kindersley. The only other member of this party was aspiring author and song-writer Edward Lindsay-Hogg, who two years later would marry film actress Geraldine Fitzgerald; their son, Michael Lindsay-Hogg (whose real father was thought to be Orson Welles) would later become a film director, and a friend of Dom and Oonagh's son Garech.

Oonagh's photographs from 1934 onwards make it clear that by now while her husband was having an affair with Valerie Brougham, she was likewise involved with Dom Oranmore. In the divorce proceedings brought by his first wife Mildred, it was stated that his relationship with Oonagh began in February 1934. This situation continued for some time, but proved unsatisfactory to all involved, particularly after word of the participants' extra-marital activities started to become common knowledge. Matters were not helped when the press reported in early autumn 1935 that owing to an official technicality, Lord Oranmore and Browne had been detained on a trip to Mexico with an unnamed woman, not his wife, and soon afterwards was seen in New York in the company of Mrs Philip Kindersley.

It was agreed that both Dom and Oonagh should divorce their respective spouses in order to marry each other; this also had the advantage of allowing Philip Kindersley to marry Valerie Brougham. Ludicrous complications ensued when Dom opted not to follow customary procedure and be found by a chambermaid keeping company in a Brighton hotel bedroom with a woman hired for the purpose. Instead, he and Oonagh chose to stay in a hotel in France owned by one of her cousins; unfortunately the manager of this establishment declined to give evidence against his employer's relative. The errant pair was obliged to move on to Austria, where an establishment suited to their purpose was found. Both the Kindersleys and the Oranmores were divorced on the same day and in the same court in November 1935.

Dom and Oonagh were married in Marylebone Register Office on 29th April 1936. Six months later Philip Kindersley married Valerie Brougham, with whom he would have three further children. In June 1938, Dom's ex-wife Mildred married the Hon. Hew Dalrymple.

In June 1937 Oonagh wrote in the visitors' book she had begun after her first wedding, 'Luggala has been given to me by my kind father to share with Dom, Gay and Tessa.' From that date until her death in August 1995, Luggala was the place that meant most to Oonagh and with which she was most intimately associated, even though her involvement in the estate passed to her son Garech in 1970. In the years immediately prior to Luggala being presented to her, Oonagh had spent relatively little time there, presumably because Philip Kindersley had been reluctant to visit Ireland; their social life had been based in England. Of the three Guinness sisters it had been Aileen, together with her husband Brinny and their young children, who most frequently stayed at Luggala in the early 1930s, with Maureen Dufferin scarcely ever doing so. Aileen's albums show that the Plunkets, even though they owned Luttrellstown Castle on the other side of Dublin, often entertained at Luggala, notably bringing the Hollywood actor Douglas Fairbanks – a personal friend who was then staying with them – to Wicklow in November 1933. With Fairbanks came both former model Sylvia Ashley-Cooper, with whom he was then having an affair (and who he would later marry), and her husband Anthony, Lord Ashley. This kind of relaxed attitude to the vows of matrimony was a feature of life at Luggala.

From June 1937 onwards the estate belonged outright to Oonagh, bought by her father Ernest from Viscount Powerscourt for an undisclosed sum. After taking possession

ABOVE AND RIGHT: Until 1937 Luggala was as much used by Aileen as by Oonagh, especially during the summer months when the lake would be used for swimming. Often the two sisters would stay in the house together, along with their husbands and young children and a number of similarly married friends.

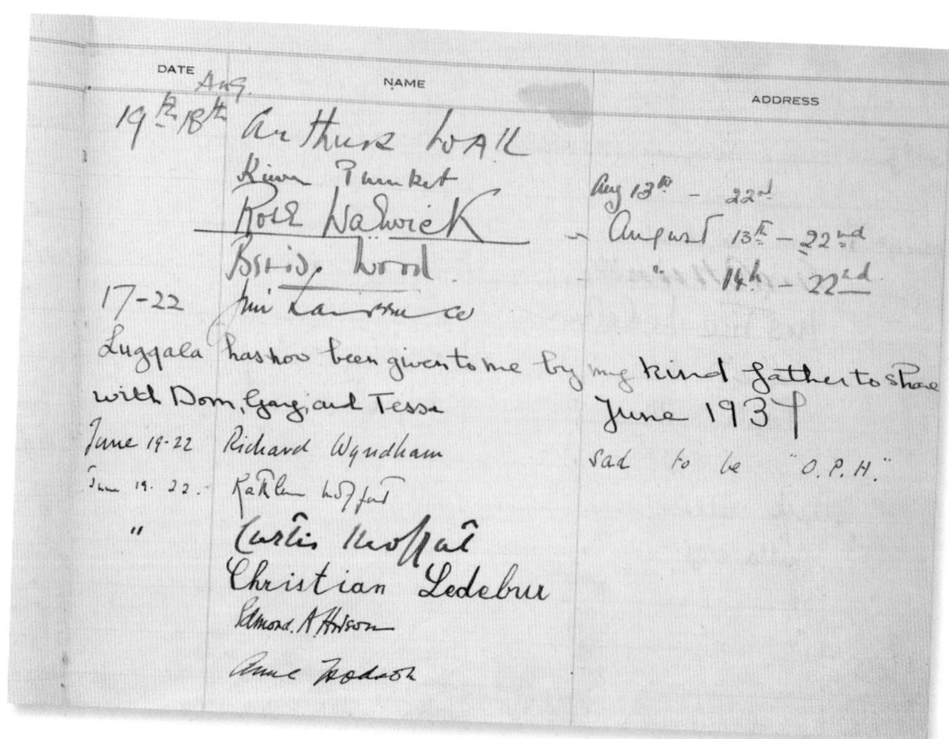

DATE	NAME	ADDRESS
Aug. 19th 18th	Arthur Wall	
	Rowan Plunket	Aug 13th – 22nd
	Rose Warwick	August 13th – 22nd
	Brid Wood	" 14th – 22nd
17–22	Iris Lawrence	
Luggala has now been given to me by my kind father to share with Dom, Gay, and Tessa		June 1937
June 19–22	Richard Wyndham	said to be "O.P.H."
June 19. 22.	Kathleen Moffat	
"	Curtis Moffat	
	Christian Ledebur	
	Edmond A. Hobson	
	Anne	

RIGHT AND BELOW: In June 1937 Ernest Guinness bought the Luggala demesne from Lord Powerscourt and gave it to his youngest daughter Oonagh; in 1970 she would in turn would transfer her shares in the Luggala Estates Company to her son, the Hon. Garech Browne. During the intervening 33 years she entertained regularly at Luggala. An early house party shown here included her close friend Iris Tree and the latter's husband, Baron Friedrich von Ledebur-Wicheln, as well as Tree's previous husband, Curtis Moffat. Also in the group was Richard 'Dirty Dick' Wyndham, whose younger half-brother, the writer and editor Francis Wyndham, would come to stay at Luggala in the 1950s.

OPPOSITE: Oonagh around the time she was given Luggala photographed on the steps of the house with the two children of her first marriage, Gay and Tessa Kindersley, then aged seven and five respectively.

THE GALWAY BLAZERS TAKE THE FLOOR

THE EARL AND COUNTESS OF ROSSE

CAPTAIN M. G. RODDICK, LADY ELVEDEN, MRS. "BROWNIE" HOLLOWAY AND LORD ELVEDEN

LORD AND LADY ORANMORE AND BROWNE

BERGNER'S DOUBLE

Lady Oranmore and Browne has been called Elisabeth Bergner's double. The resemblance is really startling in this photo of Lord and Lady Oranmore and Browne, taken at the successful ball of the Galway Blazers at Castle Hackett, the lovely residence of Colonel Denis Barnard. Poole, Dublin.

The Hunt Ball Season.

Hunt Balls are always full of hilarity, and certainly the Galway Blazers', held after a lapse of several years, was one of the most enjoyable held so far this season; it took place at Castle Hackett, Colonel Bernard's seat near Tuam, and this photograph taken at it shows Lord Oranmore and Browne helping Lady Warrender and the Countess of Rosse to champagne—and what would a Ball be without it.

Lady Warrender, who is the attractive tall, slim wife of Sir Victor Warrender, Bt., M.P., hunted a lot with the Blazers this season, preferring the thrills of hunting over the stone walls of Galway to the fashionable packs in the Shires. Last summer she thought of the brilliant idea of having a cycling tour with her husband and two sons, John and Simon, through England, and thoroughly enjoyed every moment of it, so much so that she is thinking of repeating it this year in Ireland.

Lady Rosse is the Chatelaine of Birr Castle in Birr, where her infant son, Lord Oxmantown, was christened a couple of months ago.

Lord Oranmore and Browne is one of the most popular of the young peers in Ireland, and has a lovely place, Castle MacGarrett near Claremorris, where he and his pretty wife intend to spend most of the year, and entertain in the hospitable manner so characteristic of the Westerner.

THE M.F.H.'S GROUP

(At back, l. to r.) Mr. A. D. Comyn (Hon. Sec.), Mr. Bowes Daly, M.F.H., Miss O'Rourke, Major F. Carr, M.F.H., and Mr. J. S. Young. (Seated) Mrs. Bowes Daly, Lord Sligo, M.F.H., and Lady Warrender

(AT BACK) MR. W. ENDERBY, MR. AND MRS. DOMINIC BROWNE AND CAPTAIN BARON DE ROBECK. (SITTING) MISS DIANA MAITLAND-MAKGILL-CRICHTON, MR. R. MORE O'FERRALL AND LADY MAUREEN BRABAZON

The Blazers Hunt Ball was held with éclat and much bonhomie at Castle Hacket, Tuam, Co. Galway, the owner of which is Major-General Denis Bernard. All the Galway Masters, three of them, were on the premises, and Major Carr, who is one of them, used to be well known in the Albrighton country when Joint-Master of those hounds with the late General Hickman. Some well-known ex-Masters were likewise in evidence: Mr. Enderby, a former Master of the East Galway, and Mr. Dominic Browne, a former Joint-Master of the Blazers. Mrs. Bowes Daly is a sister of the Duchess of Buccleuch, and they are kinswomen of Lord Harewood. Major Watt's amateur band added tremendously to the general hilarity. Major Watt has been either sole Master or Joint-Master of the United Hounds since 1926

(ON RIGHT) MAJOR A. H. WATT'S BAND

(L. to r.) Mr. D. Dineen, Mr. W. Emery, Major A. H. Watt, M.F.H. (United), Mr. F. Floyd, Mr. Ronnie Cameron and Mr. F. W. Harrington

Photos: Poole, Dublin

305

TOP LEFT: During the early years of their marriage, Oonagh and Dominick not only entertained at both Luggala and Castle MacGarrett, but also did much to encourage a lively social scene in the west of Ireland through their attendance at such occasions as the annual Galway Blazers Hunt Ball.

BOTTOM LEFT: On 25th June 1939 Dom and Oonagh's first son, Garech Domnagh Browne, was born in her parents' Dublin house Glenmaroon. On 7th August he was christened at St. Patrick's Cathedral, his seven godparents including his grandmother, his aunts the Marchioness of Dufferin and Ava and the Hon. Mrs Mordaunt Smith, as well as Viscounts Elveden and Ridley, and the Marchese Marconi.

OPPOSITE: An undated cartoon showing Dominick and Oonagh with their extended family. He had five children from his first marriage and she two; together they then had another two sons who survived into adulthood, Garech (born 1939) and Tara (born 1945).

at St Patrick's Cathedral

Christening at St Patricks

mummy Oonagh Garech Dom
at Glenmaroon

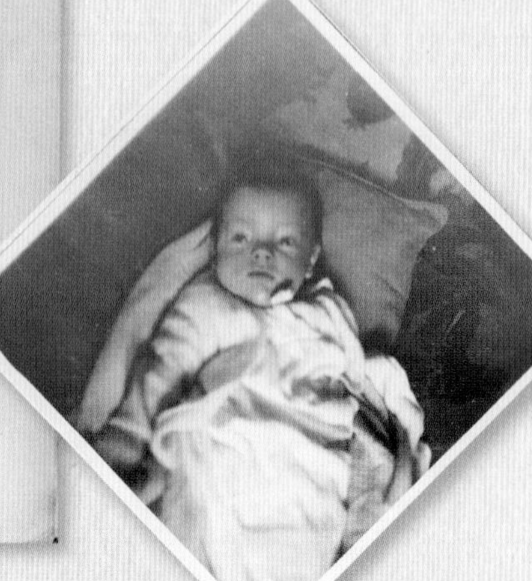

of the house, her first guests there included bohemian actress and poet Iris Tree, daughter of the famous actor-manager Sir Herbert Beerbohm Tree. Iris Tree was then married to the Austrian Baron Friedrich von Ledebur-Wicheln, but from her first marriage to American photographer and society portraitist Curtis Moffat she had a son, Ivan. He would later become a screenwriter in Hollywood (*Giant*, *The Greatest Story Ever Told*) and have an affair with Oonagh's niece, Caroline Blackwood, with whom, it was revealed after both of them had died, he had a daughter, Ivana Lowell. Although Iris Tree and Curtis Moffat had by then divorced (and both of them remarried), he too was staying at Luggala in June 1937. Amidst sundry children, the only other adult guest was the amateur painter Richard 'Dirty Dick' Wyndham, otherwise known as 'Whips' because, Cyril Connolly would later tell his daughter Joan Wyndham, he had been 'one of Europe's great flagellists'. His uncle George, former Chief Secretary for Ireland and the man responsible for introducing legislation (the 'Wyndham Act') that led to the dissolution of the old Irish estates, was said to have been found dead in a Paris brothel in June 1913. Twenty four years later, Oonagh's decidedly louche guest list for her first house party at Luggala set a tone for the very many to follow over the next half century or so.

Between 1937 and 1950, when she and Dom divorced, Oonagh alternated between Luggala and Castle MacGarrett, in the latter hosting shooting weekends as well as the 1938 Galway Blazers' Hunt Ball. On that occasion, Oonagh's evening bag, valued at £250, went missing, having been purloined by a guest at the party. A subsequent press report noted that thanks to diligent police work, 'The entire county was thoroughly combed and the authorities extended their

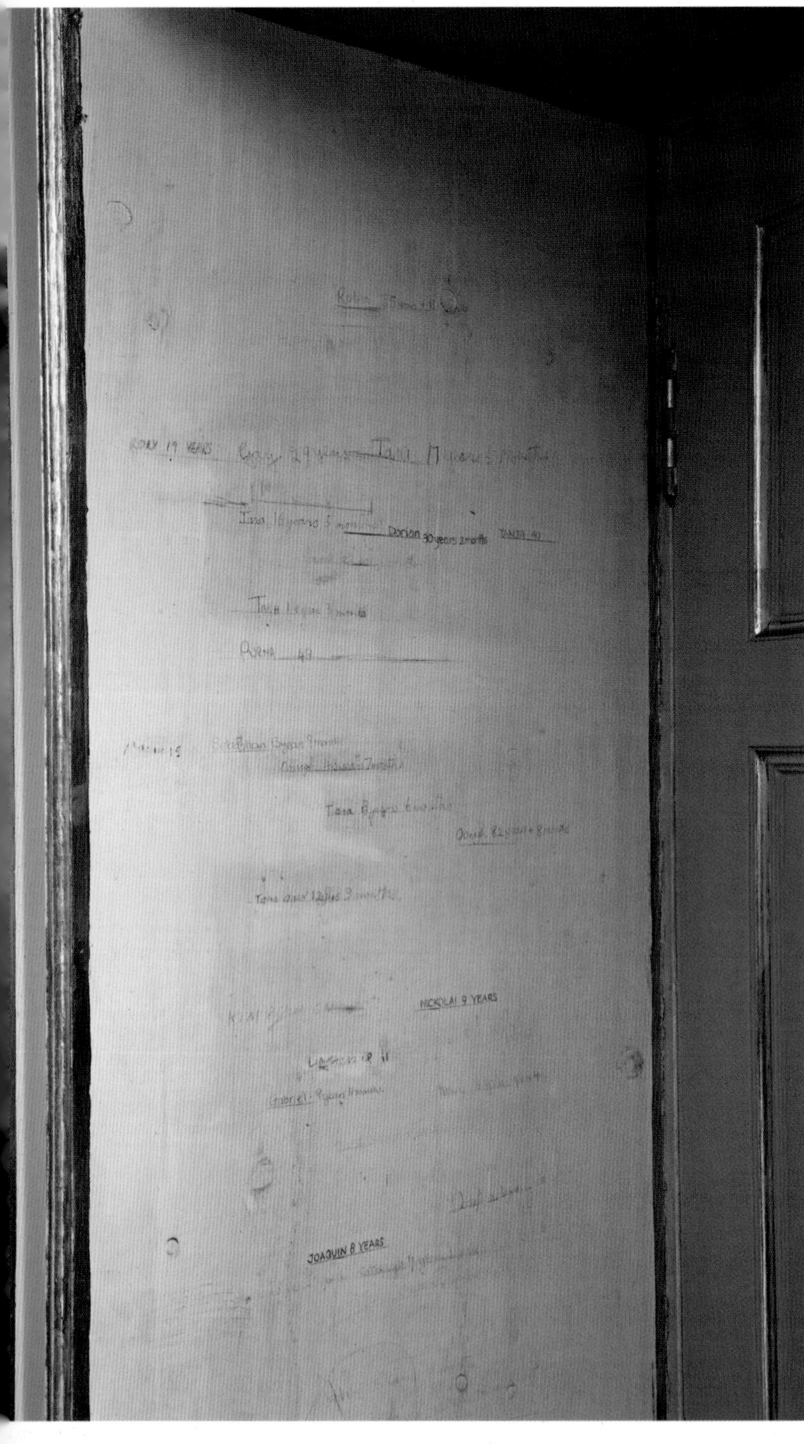

investigations to outside counties.' Eventually the bag was discovered in the possession of a young man who, when taken into custody, explained his behaviour in time-honoured fashion: 'I had taken drink.' Hunting, shooting and other field sports were the dominant activity at Castle MacGarrett, although these did not engage the interest of everyone who came to stay. When Iris Tree visited, she would dread meeting Dom's set of 'hearties' and implore Oonagh 'not to put her between a brace of these at dinner since she was either stricken dumb or would unconsciously begin to imitate them.'

But Oonagh and Dom were just as often at Luggala or in Dublin, where they stayed in Glenmaroon on the city's periphery and became known, in the sycophantic words of an Irish social columnist at the time, as 'the most popular of our young peers and peeresses'. In his 1946 autobiography *All for Hecuba*, the actor and co-founder of Dublin's Gate Theatre, Micheál Mac Liammóir, having committed the rare solecism of calling them the Earl and Countess of Oranmore and Browne, described the couple: Dom 'with his Gainsborough head and his fabulous parties, and Oonagh, his wife, with her bell of pure gold instead of hair, and her vague, laughing Botticelli eyes, her passion for Tschaikowsky, and her minute hats from Marie Laurencin. They come to our first nights with the Malespinas, the Michael Scotts, the Erskine-Childers, and we drive to Glen Maroon to eat oysters...Wherever Dom and Oonagh go there is a feeling of spontaneous festivity; yet their lives have been full of sadness; they are the heirs to the eighteenth century, to stay with them in any of their houses is a continual surprise and delight, an elaborate and haphazard picnic; one wishes they might never grow old.'

On 25th June 1939, just over two months before the Second World War broke out, Dom and Oonagh's first son, Garech Domnagh Browne, was born in Glenmaroon. Following the

ABOVE: Inside the frame of a door leading from drawing room to entrance hall, Oonagh marked the changing heights of her various children as they grew up. Despite redecoration following the fire of 1956 and again more recently, these marks have remained in place and provide a poignant record of Oonagh's life in the house.

OPPOSITE: A 1940 pastel portrait of Oonagh and her son Garech by Gaetano de Gennaro, an artist born in Naples in 1890. He subsequently spent time in France before coming to Ireland in 1940. A decade later he moved to Brazil, where he died in 1959.

LEFT TOP AND BOTTOM: Luggala during the years of the Second World War. Oonagh and Dom remained in Ireland throughout this period and divided their time between Castle MacGarrett and Luggala, with excursions to Dublin, where they were able to stay in her parents' house, Glenmaroon. Since the travel restrictions imposed by war meant visitors from overseas were rare, so too were house parties. Oonagh – always a devoted mother – was thus able to give all her attention to children, both her own and those of her sister Aileen, who remained in the United States until 1946. Note the photograph of Oonagh standing at the door to Luggala dressed in traditional Irish costume, still found at that date in the Connemara region of the country.

declaration of hostilities between Britain and Germany, Dom, then aged 38, was advised that his time would be more usefully spent farming. He therefore remained in Ireland, which adopted a policy of neutrality and used the term The Emergency to describe the next six years. Philip Kindersley, meanwhile, became an officer in the Coldstream Guards, leaving his two children, Gay and Tessa, with their mother; the former, who had been at Cothill, an English prep school, now transferred to Castle Park, a similar establishment in Ireland. Oonagh, who had a powerful maternal streak, also happily assumed responsibility for two further children, her nieces Neelia and Doon. Their mother Aileen, having divorced Brinny Plunket in 1940, removed herself to the United States where she remained until war came to an end. Aileen's grandson, Michael de las Casas, says that when she eventually returned to Europe in 1946, her first remark to Neelia, by then aged 17 and unseen for six years, was 'You've got too much make-up on.'

During the Emergency years, Oonagh and the family spent the greater part of their time at Castle MacGarrett, or during the summer at a house in Ballyconneely on the Atlantic coast. At the outbreak of hostilities in Europe, the Oranmores temporarily moved out of Castle MacGarrett, 'in case the Germans might bomb the house, thinking it was a factory', explains their son, Garech. But before long, realising the unlikelihood of this occurrence everyone moved back again and remained there, undisturbed by bombs and living in considerable comfort, thanks to Oonagh's wealth: there were footmen at meals, by then not a common sight in Irish country houses.

While the west of Ireland was a sanctuary of peace when compared with what was taking place elsewhere in Europe, the war years and those immediately after brought their own troubles to Oonagh, many caused, unintentionally, by members of her family. In June 1943 her elder son, Gay Kindersley, turned 13, left Castle Park and prepared to go to public school. His father had always intended that Gay follow his example and go to Eton. Oonagh, however, was concerned that the school was too close to London, and even closer to Windsor Castle, which she believed put her son's life at serious risk from German bombs. She therefore enrolled him in St. Columba's College, a Protestant public school established one hundred years earlier on the outskirts of Dublin. Philip Kindersley, despite having been a prisoner of war in Italy since the end of the previous year, learnt of this turn of events. Announcing that he had no intention of Gay 'being educated as a Sinn Feiner', through his parents he initiated legal proceedings in the English courts to ensure his son was sent to Eton. When Oonagh ignored an order to hand over her son, an application was made to the High Court in Dublin, which granted a provisional writ of habeas corpus to Gay's grandfather, Lord Kindersley. A succession of court hearings ensued, all of them extensively covered in the British and Irish press, delighted to offer readers a topic other than the ongoing war. For Oonagh, the matter was made worse by the fact that she had to spend most of her time in a Dublin nursing home owing to difficulties with a pregnancy.

In late November, the High Court declared she must give up Gay to his grandfather. Oonagh then appealed to the Irish Supreme Court, but in mid-December its three judges unanimously agreed with the earlier decision, although they stated 'The court was satisfied that the mother's attitude had been actuated by nothing other than genuine love of her son and real regard for his safety and welfare.' On 28th December Oonagh gave birth to a boy; two days later the unnamed infant died. A tombstone at the temple by the lake in Luggala is marked simply 'Baby Browne'. In March 1945 Oonagh would give birth to another son, christened Tara Browne.

Meanwhile, attended by a large contingent of journalists, in mid-January 1944 Gay Kindersley left Ireland with his paternal grandparents and, after a brief stay at Plaw Hatch Hall, was duly enrolled at Eton. For the next five years he would spend school holidays between England and Ireland, where on stepping off the Holyhead–Dún Laoghaire mailboat he would be met by Dom and the chauffeur driven Rolls Royce and taken either to Castle MacGarrett or Luggala.

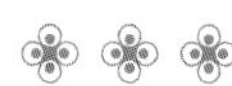

Oonagh's only daughter, Tessa Kindersley, suffered from an asthmatic condition serious enough to prevent her being sent away to school, but not so serious as to impede her great passion for horses. In 1945 on her pony Brown Jack she won her show jumping class at the Dublin Horse Show and performed well in other competitions she entered. A year later, in early August 1946, there was an outbreak of diphtheria in the west of Ireland and so Oonagh, then staying at Castle MacGarrett while Dom was in London, asked a doctor from Castlebar to inoculate Tessa. Fifteen minutes later, the child suffered an adverse reaction to the anti-toxin administered, went into a coma and within two and a half hours had died;

she was aged 14. None of the other children were inoculated, it was a hideous aberration: the inquest recorded a verdict of cardiac arrest due to anaphylactic shock. In the aftermath, her 18-year-old cousin, Olwen Mordaunt-Smith, wrote a few lines of verse commemorating Tessa in which she recalled the girl's 'wondrous beauty with lustrous hair' with a 'body so frail and mind so sweet'. Members of household staff carried her coffin to Crossboyne Parish Church for a service, after which she was taken to Luggala and buried, like her little half-brother, by the lake. Here, in 1950, Oonagh placed a small domed stone temple, originally constructed around 1740 for Sir Compton Domville on his estate at Templeogue, Dublin. Later moved to Santry Court, it was lying in pieces on the ground when discovered by architectural historian Maurice Craig, who encouraged Oonagh to remove the monument and re-erect it at Luggala. In recent years her son Garech has further restored the temple and replaced its lost ball finial.

ABOVE: Oonagh and Dom's older son, Garech, as a three-year-old child at Luggala. At least part of each summer was spent in the house, although time was also found for a cottage at Ballyconneely on the Atlantic coast; Oonagh sold the latter to her sister Aileen after Tessa's death because it had too many sad associations.

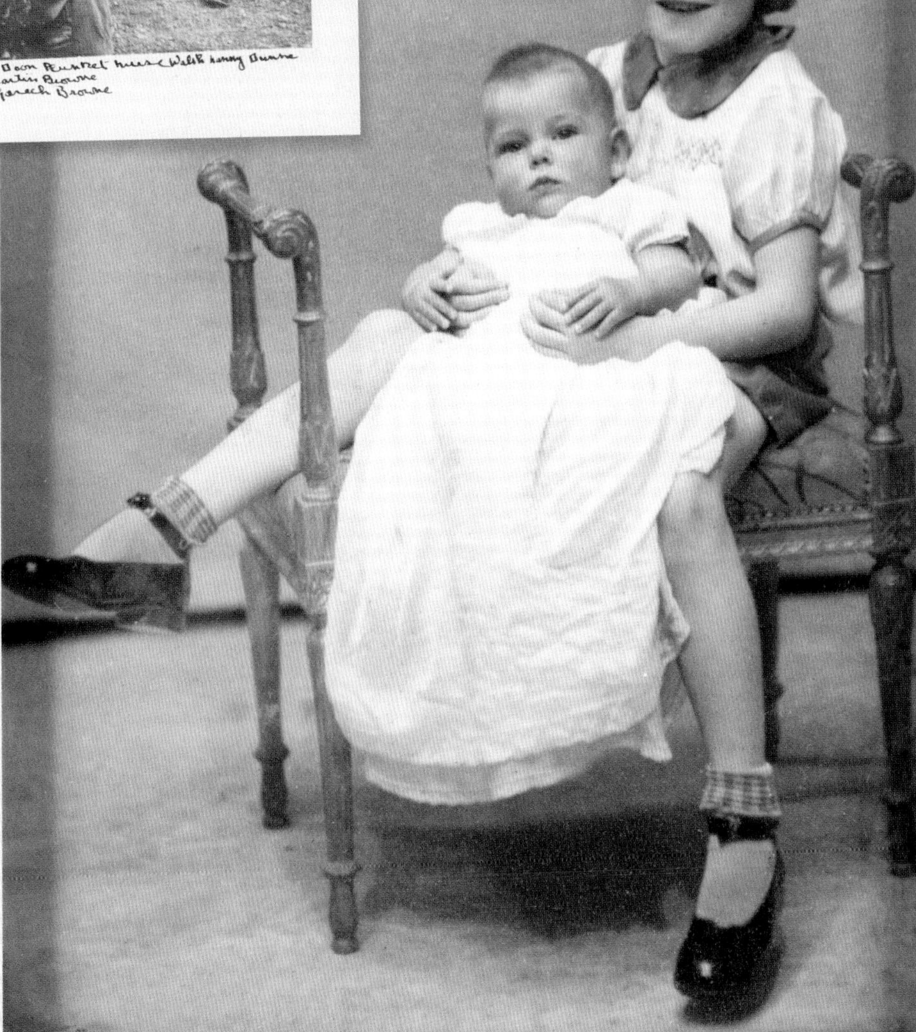

ABOVE AND RIGHT: In late December 1943, Oonagh gave birth to a son who died two days later. The arrival of another boy in March 1945 was, therefore, a source of great pleasure to Oonagh and Dom. Christened Tara, he would be the last child born to Oonagh, although she later adopted two Mexican orphans. Despite an age difference of almost six years, he and his older brother, Garech, were always close.

Tessa wins the Children's Jumping Championship at Ball's Bridge
on Brown Jack, Royal Dublin Spring Show 1946

Gerald Maguire
Gay Kindersley
Dom
out side the four Courts

LEFT: Close to the lake at Luggala is an 18th-century temple rescued by Oonagh in 1950. Here she buried her children and their tombstones, designed by Michael Biggs, can be seen inset into the grass, those of the unnamed baby who died soon after birth in 1943 and Tessa who died three years later.

OPPOSITE TOP AND BOTTOM: In 1943 the education of Gay Kindersley, Oonagh's son from her first marriage, was the subject of an extended court battle between his parents; it was eventually decided that contrary to his mother's wishes he should go to Eton. Meanwhile, Oonagh's daughter from the same marriage, Tessa Kindersley, turned into a gifted rider who won prizes in show jumping. In August 1946, aged fourteen, she suffered an adverse reaction to an anti-diphtheria inoculation and died: the inquest recorded a verdict of cardiac arrest due to anaphylactic shock.

Less than three years after her daughter's death, Oonagh suffered another blow when her father, Ernest, unexpectedly died in March 1949 at the age of 72. There were financial consequences to his untimely demise. In 1946 and 1948 Ernest had settled Guinness shares worth just over £1 million and in which he had a life interest on his three daughters, to whom he had also given gifts in the region of £500,000. Because these transfers of wealth had taken place less than five years before his death, they were liable for substantial duties; taxes due on the gifts, for example, were in the region of £378,000. Ernest's will, which took several years to resolve, was probated at almost £3.2 million in Ireland, of which that country's government took more than £1.3 million.

Stephane Groueff, who was then engaged to Neelia Plunket, would later remember her mother Aileen's despair over 'being ruined'. This, however, did not hinder Aileen in 1950 from engaging London decorator Felix Harbord to embark on a spectacular refurbishment of Luttrellstown Castle. Ernest Guinness's offspring were far from being ruined. Yet while Oonagh and her sisters continued to be beneficiaries of the trust established by their grandfather Lord Iveagh, Ernest's inopportune death left them less personally wealthy than some other members of the ever-expanding Guinness clan. Particularly for Oonagh, the least fiscally sagacious of the sisters, this was going to be a problem in the years ahead.

More immediately, the deaths of her daughter and father put pressure on a marriage already under strain. As with her first husband, Philip, Oonagh had grown to realise she did not share as much in common with Dom as once appeared to be the case. Their circle of friends differed, as did their enthusiasms, he being primarily interested in outdoor pursuits, she in cultural. The breaking point came in 1950 when she learnt he had fallen in love with someone else. Born Constance Vera Stevens, English actress Sally Gray had made her stage debut at the age of 12 in 1928. From the mid-1930s onwards she began appearing in films, the best remembered being *Dangerous Moonlight* (1941). Although offered opportunities to work in the United States, she remained in England, which is how she came to meet Dom Oranmore.

Discovering what had been going on, Oonagh asked her husband to join her on a boat kept at Luggala. When the two of them were alone on Lough Tay, she insisted he finish with Sally Gray. Dom, prevaricating, requested six weeks to do so. Oonagh told him the marriage was over. At the end of July 1950, she was granted a divorce and from then on was officially styled Oonagh Lady Oranmore and Browne. Dom and Sally Gray secretly married in December 1952, the formalisation of their relationship only becoming public knowledge when they attended Elizabeth II's coronation in June 1953.

CHAPTER FOUR

Luggala Lodge: 'The Most Decorative Honey Pot in Ireland'

In February 1950 Oonagh turned 40. The previous year her father had died and six months hence she would divorce her second husband. By the autumn of that year and for the first time she found herself alone and responsible for her own welfare. For a woman who had always led a cosseted life, moving directly from parental home into first one marriage and then another, this was a testing new scenario. Yet it proved a challenge she was well able to meet. Over the next few years Oonagh became known, both in Ireland and overseas, as a woman of consequence in her own right, not as someone's daughter or wife.

Central to Oonagh's newly independent persona was Luggala, which became her base of operation and the place with which she was specifically identified. With Castle MacGarrett no longer available to her, this was the only house where she could entertain on a grand scale and have friends to stay. The role of hostess was one to which she took with aplomb. For the next two decades, whenever Luggala was mentioned, in speech or print, so too was Oonagh: it was impossible to conceive of one without the other. A locale that, at the beginning of the 19th century, had been among the country's most acclaimed places became so once more thanks to its owner.

Oonagh made Luggala internationally renowned, she drew visitors to the house and then, like some Celtic Circe, she held them there. On one occasion she described it as being 'the most decorative honey pot in Ireland'. It was her enchanted kingdom, where she governed alone. In accounts of the house at this time, the most frequently employed term to describe Luggala was 'magical'. The magic was exerted, at least in part, by Oonagh. Writing in 1955, John Godley, 3rd Baron Kilbracken, observed 'Whenever I pass between those gateposts and plunge down into the valley beyond, I feel as though I have left Ireland and entered a strange, unreal, independent principality: Oonaghland. Oonagh holds sway over all the valley, and the mountains and forests which fall down into it from the sky.'

Luggala now became celebrated as somewhere guests were invited for drinks or dinner, only to emerge several days later blinking at the harsh light of the ordinary world, aware that during that lost period of time they had enjoyed themselves immensely without necessarily being clear about the details of how or why, or even with whom. This experience, one that many people have undergone over the past sixty years, has since become known as being 'Luggala'ed'. The house's position at the bottom of a private valley, utterly removed from public gaze, encouraged guests to behave in a more relaxed fashion than they might have done elsewhere, secure in the belief that whatever took place at Luggala would not become known beyond its gates. At a time when morality in Ireland was strictly policed, and standards of behaviour closely monitored, Luggala offered guests liberation from both observation and judgement.

Lord Gowrie first visited the house as a 22 year old in August 1962, having previously been staying in Clandeboye with Oonagh's sister Maureen Dufferin and her son, Sheridan, a contemporary at Eton and Oxford. 'I always found Maureen a trial,' he remembers, 'and she was so conscious of procedure that at every meal I had to sit beside her, although there were lots of other young and interesting people there.' Before the strain of having to pay consistent attention to his hostess became intolerable, her elder daughter, the future novelist Caroline Blackwood, arrived at Clandeboye. 'We got on immediately, perhaps through mutual dislike of her mother. Caroline, with that throaty voice of hers, said, "Let's get out of here and go and stay with my aunt Oonagh. She's absolute heaven and you'll adore her".' Grey Gowrie then accompanied Caroline Blackwood to Luggala where, 'I just went missing. I decided to hide out and spent nearly three weeks with Oonagh and Caroline, and the painter Michael Wishart. I'm not really a drinker, but I think I was tight most of the time. It was very bonding and funny and odd... After what seemed like ages, I suddenly said this won't do. One, I prefer being sober. Two, I must face reality. I was about to take up a job on *The Times*, so I went back to see my girlfriend, plan a wedding and get on with my life. However, the trip did generate a life-long friendship with Oonagh's original and gifted son Garech.'

PREVIOUS PAGE: 'One of the extraordinary things about Luggala,' says the Hon. Garech Browne, 'is that it almost looks like a different place every single day.' According to the time of year, the time of day and the weather, the house and grounds take on a new character.

RIGHT: A typical Christmas houseparty at Luggala during Oonagh's tenure as chatelaine. Among the guests were rumbustious writer Brendan Behan and his wife Beatrice, painter Sean O'Sullivan, Olive, Countess Fitzwilliam and her sister Hester, both daughters of the Hon Benjamin Plunket, Bishop of Meath, and Bridget Richardson, one of Oonagh's oldest friends. Also featured on this page are Oonagh's son Garech Browne, poet John Montague and Lady Frances Eliot, future Marchioness of Lansdowne.

Xmas 1960 Luggala Co Wicklow Ireland

Brendan Behan

Beatrice – Brendan Behan

John Montague Francis Eliot Obbie Fitzwilliam

Beatrice Behan. Francis Eliot. Garech

eatrice Garech Bridget Richardson

Sean O Sullivan Hester Connel

John Montague Obbie Bridget Francis

Grey Gowrie's experience of Luggala was by no means unusual. Author and journalist Claud Cockburn notably described it as 'the only place where I have seen people who – twenty four hours before – had been fussing furiously about urgent engagements to fly to Hollywood, Rome, New Delhi or London, or dash home to look after things on the farm in Tipperary, greet with cheers and big relief the news that the whole place was snowbound and was going to stay that way for days and days'. If inclement weather sometimes forced guests to stay at Luggala, it was never allowed to stop them getting there. Nicholas, Viscount Gormanston recollects a winter morning when Gay Kindersley struggled to dig his way out of the valley, only to meet Randal, 19th Baron Dunsany 'looming out of the snow in his monocle. He wasn't going to be denied his lunch invitation so he'd abandoned the car miles away down by the crossroads and had a very long walk.'

In 1955 John Kilbracken reminisced about a typical evening at Luggala three years earlier: 'one of those nights of which one does not recollect anything too clearly the next day.

We started as a party of about a dozen; sometime during the evening we moved en masse to a housewarming in the next county, where, grotesquely, all the men and all the women seemed to be identical. I remember challenging myself, and accepting the challenge, to dance a very fast old-fashioned waltz with Ricki [Huston] at about three and dancing it very well – just for the minutes it lasted, the whole evening twisted itself back into focus for me. I remember being violently sick in the garden, beside a sun-dial, which was being a moon-dial, at about four...I expect we got back to Luggala at about six.' Not surprisingly on that, as many other days, nobody stirred in the house until around noon. A lot of alcohol was consumed in Luggala, some of it by Oonagh, whose preference was for Haig Dimple whisky. 'When I first knew her,' says actor John Hurt, 'the bottle of Haig's followed her around on a silver salver. The contents went down, but imperceptibly and there always seemed to be just a finger of whisky in her glass...She was one of those people who could take drink. She never was silly, I never remember her being anything other than circumspect and in control of herself.'

THIS PAGE AND OPPOSITE: Luggala's entrance hall, with its original chequerboard stone floor and demi-lune recess above the chimneypiece. Ever since Oonagh's day, the hall has often been used for impromptu music sessions and for informal lunches and dinners. The paper now covering its walls comes from a design at Malahide Castle and was printed in the 1990s by Irish specialist David Skinner. They are lined with portraits of earlier members of the Browne family, but also hold a couple of examples of work by the early 20th-century Irish Cubist Mainie Jellett (1897–1944). On top of an 18th-century mahogany chest sits a marble bust of Lady Elizabeth Monck, one of the great beauties of the late Georgian era; her daughter Catherine married Dominick Browne, 1st Lord Oranmore and Browne. Above is a portrait of another member of the family, George Paul Monck, painted by Robert Hunter (fl.1748–1780). The brass-bound mahogany turf buckets are an essential feature of every Irish country house.

ABOVE: An overview of the drawing room, which has always been the most important room in the house. Above the chimney piece is a splendid gothic mirror that briefly hung in Leixlip Castle, County Kildare, when brought there by the late Mariga Guinness. However her husband, the Hon. Desmond Guinness, did not like the piece and insisted it be returned to the antique dealer from whom the mirror had been purchased, allowing Garech Browne to acquire it instead.

Despite the reputation she acquired as an outstanding hostess, Oonagh was in no respect attention-seeking. 'She was never loud,' says her former daughter-in-law, Margaret Brinckman, 'But she was very observant of people and would always pick up on their idiosyncracies...She didn't say a lot, but there was one little song she would sing, it was always called for at parties and began, "There was an old man called Bill, and he lived on the top of the hill. He hasn't been sober since last October. And I don't think he ever will".'

Nor was Oonagh socially competitive. 'I think she was an innocent,' says author and editor Francis Wyndham, who was a guest at Luggala on several occasions in the 1950s. 'Her sisters Maureen and Aileen were worldly and ambitious and competitive about being smart, but Oonagh wasn't. She was very easy to be with, very undemanding, she liked jokes.' Nicholas Gormanston, who has been visiting Luggala for half a century, remembers that Oonagh 'had a wonderful sense of humour. She loved jokes; if a very pompous person's dignity was punctured, she would laugh out loud.' John Hurt has almost as long an acquaintance with Luggala and recalls that

ABOVE: The drawing room's Pugin-designed wallpaper was introduced by decorator John Hill after the 1956 fire at Luggala. During the house's more recent refurbishment, the same paper, albeit in different colouring, was hand printed by London firm Cole & Son using the original blocks made in the 19th century by J. C. Crace & Son. Above an 18th-century mahogany side table hangs an Irish oval mirror of the same period.

GUINNESS
RAMBLES IN IRELAND
THE Irish COUNTRY HOUSE

LEFT: The drawing room's great bay of three windows looks south-west across the park towards Lough Tay. The room is dominated by a large 18th-century Irish sofa that was originally part of the furnishings of Russborough, seat of the Earls of Milltown. During the house's restoration, it was recovered in burgundy-coloured velvet that was gauffraged, or stamped, by a firm in Lyons using surviving 18th-century wooden cylinders that broke during the process.

RIGHT: A little oval mirror in a gilt frame offers a reflection of the large mirror over the chimneypiece which, in turn, reflects the windows at the other end of the room. The chimneypiece itself was made in the late 1990s by Dick Reid of York, using as inspiration photographs of the drawing room's interior before the 1956 fire.

Oonagh 'never said a thing. Except if there was a very long pause, she might say something really rather banal...but she was nobody's fool, in thrall to nobody.'

In an obituary written for the *Independent* Michael Luke, a regular visitor to Luggala in the 1950s and 60s, wrote that, unlike Aileen Plunket and Maureen Dufferin, 'Oonagh was an intensely private person, a listener rather than a speaker; and all the more observant for that. Because she was so self-effacing, it was easy to cast her in the role of Cinderella. Certainly there were always a number of princes, slipper in hand, eager for that little foot...It was people rather than things which held a finely veiled but intense curiosity for her. Her astute observation of people could express itself in a throwaway comment borne in a small voice of such deceptive innocence that the sharp wit informing it was often felt in delayed reaction.' 'Nothing missed her eye,' remembers artist Anne Madden. 'She saw everything that was going on without apparently looking.'

She was also, during this period, her most physically alluring. Grey Gowrie describes Oonagh as having been 'a very beautiful, fragile and amusing person. She was kind of cat-like and conspiratorial, like someone who hadn't quite grown up.' In his journal, the former English politician Woodrow Wyatt, who spent a week in late December 1957 at Luggala, remembered his hostess as being 'as lovely as the angel on the Christmas tree'.

Because she was so small and slight, Oonagh was often described as child-like. Certainly she always retained a youthful sense of mischief. Poet John Montague, one of her son Garech's oldest friends, remembers 'It struck me, especially at the Christmas season, that she had a very dangerous sense of fun...She specialised in placing husbands and wives in proximity to their previous partners, so that they had to share the same bathroom. There was a certain wickedness which struck me as an Anglo-Irish touch.' John Montague's first wife Madeleine Mottuel describes Oonagh as 'skittish', while Anne Madden remembers her as 'very quick and funny, with a deadpan face'.

As a girl, actress Anjelica Huston often stayed at Luggala with her parents, John and Ricki. She remembers Oonagh as 'childlike and so delicate, like a little bird with the tiniest feet; one of the wonderments for me as a child was being the same size as she was'. Oonagh dressed in a youthful manner, with dresses that had 'a touch of the spring time about them,' low-cut shoes with a strap across the instep 'and a baby blue satin ribbon in her hair'. Anjelica Huston describes Oonagh as being 'like an Alice-in-Wonderland figure. She had a certain kind of jeunesse...she was forever in the guise of a little girl.'

LEFT: A view from the entrance hall into the dining room. On the left of the door is a large mahogany bookcase, its shelves used to hold photograph albums and memorabilia associated with both Garech Browne and his mother. Above the door is a portrait of Charles II, from whom Garech Browne's maternal grandmother Marie Clothilde Russell was descended through the king's mistress, Louise de Kérouaille.

OPPOSITE: Evidence that Luggala continues to be a work in progress is provided by the dining room. This was re-configured by David Mlinaric and Garech Browne during spring 2012 and enhanced by the addition of a large mirror hung above the chimneypiece; the latter, like that in the drawing room, was made in the late 1990s by Dick Reid. In front of the mirror hang a portrait of Garech painted in 1966 by Edward McGuire and below a small oil by Jack B. Yeats, brother of poet W.B. Yeats. The mirror and picture frames were made by Kildare gilder Susan Mulhall in 2012 under David Mlinaric's direction. Much of the room is hung with portraits of Garech and his friends. The chandelier of Bohemian glass was installed by Oonagh during the 1956 restoration of the house.

Yet despite being both smaller and quieter than the majority of her guests, she managed to hold their notice. 'Half witch, half goddess,' observed Michael Luke, 'Oonagh Oranmore was nevertheless "real" in a very unusual, disturbing and exhilarating way. However brief the encounter, her savoury uniqueness made you sit up and look a little more carefully at your own cherished illusions.'

The setting in which she was found helped to ensure every meeting's memorability. 'Tucked into a cleft of the Wicklow mountains under Sally Gap,' wrote Michael Luke, 'purple heather on black rock, a waterfall behind and before a lithe river feeding first one lake and then another and another, the Victorian Gothic folly, as Luggala had become, shone like the discarded crown of a prima ballerina.' For Stephane Grouëff, Luggala was 'located at the bottom of a picturesque geological fault, looking like an illustration from a nursery book of *The Queen of Hearts*.' 'It was like going into a fairy tale,' remembers

LEFT: A corridor along the first floor of the house's west front provides access to a series of additional guest bedrooms and bathrooms tucked under the eaves of the building. At the end is a door leading into the new library's gallery.

OPPOSITE: During Luggala's refurbishment in the second half of the 1990s, a warren of small rooms formerly used by servants was cleared to create a double-height library decorated in the Strawberry Hill gothic style. Work here is not yet complete, as can be seen by the temporary bookshelves holding some of the collection assembled by Garech Browne, an inveterate bibliophile.

Gabriel
BENEDICTIONS
BENEDICTIONS

ABOVE AND OPPOSITE: Along a stone-flagged passage leading from the staircase hall to the kitchen lies Luggala's pantry, its shelves replete with glasses and plates, cups and bowls. Here also are found occasional reminders of the source of the funds that have helped to sustain the house since the 1930s: Guinness.

OVERLEAF: Luggala's kitchen, the ceiling of which rises to a skylight high above all the working units. Although refurbished in the late 1990s, this room retains the same character it had when Oonagh lived in the house.

Anjelica Huston. 'Descending into the dell with the ferns and the overhanging trees, the flocks of deer and the pheasants, and then coming on the magical lake with its sand made up of chips of mica.'

As it had in the time of the La Touches, the flawless beauty of Luggala left an indelible impression on anyone fortunate enough to be invited there. In his 1980 memoir *An Open Book*, Anjelica Huston's father, John, recalled the first time he had visited Luggala 29 years before. Arriving in the dark, he had seen little. 'The next morning at dawn I went to the window and looked out upon a scene I have never forgotten. Through pines and yews in the garden I saw, across a running stream, a field of marigolds and beyond the field – surprisingly – a white sandy beach bordering a black lake...Above the lake was a mountain of black rock rising precipitously, and on its crest – like a shawl over a piano – a profusion of purple heather. I was to go back to Luggala many times, but I'll never forget that first impression. I was Ireland's own from that moment.'

Exactly a year later, the diarist Frances Partridge and her husband Ralph came to stay for the night at Luggala. 'Incredible beauty lay before us as we climbed the last ridge before dipping into the valley,' she afterwards wrote, 'range upon range of mountains spread around us with their tops still golden in the setting sun, and the deep, green, lost valleys below. A big loch of brown peaty water with sheep browsing round a small formal temple, and beneath the domed forehead of a crag the house itself – a fantastically pretty white building in purest Strawberry Hill Gothic style...What a magical atmosphere that house had, charmingly furnished and decorated to match its style, dim lights, soft music playing and Irish voices ministering seductively to our needs.' Sixty years later, Francis Wyndham remembers Luggala as being 'the most romantic place I've ever known,' and recalls 'that sparkling little jewel of a house with the black lake before it'.

The era in which it was offered helped to make Oonagh's hospitality at Luggala even more unforgettable. For most people in Europe, and especially in Ireland, the 1950s was not the last century's finest decade. During that period the Irish economy stagnated, unemployment and emigration were rampant, and an air of hopelessness pervaded much of the country. Scarcely any landowners who had held onto their houses and some portion of the surrounding estates were in

a position to entertain, even if they had wished to do so. After staying for several days in August 1963, Desmond Leslie, whose resolutely eccentric family lived at Castle Leslie in County Monaghan, wrote that Luggala was 'The only 4 star, 4 rosette, 4 "fork" house in the "Irish Michelin".'

Oonagh was one of the very few people both able and willing to maintain a tradition of hospitality that had otherwise largely disappeared in Ireland. So, too, was her sister Aileen Plunket on the other side of Dublin at the newly redecorated Luttrellstown Castle. Across the Wicklow Mountains, from 1952 onwards Sir Alfred Beit and his wife, Clementine, were likewise generous hosts at Russborough. A few years later, the Hon. Desmond Guinness, son of Oonagh's cousin Bryan, 2nd Lord Moyne (and also of Clementine Beit's cousin, Diana Mitford), came to live in Ireland with his first wife, Princess Marie-Gabrielle (Mariga) von Urach. Initially, the young Guinnesses rented Carton House, formerly owned by the Dukes of Leinster, before buying Leixlip Castle, County Kildare. Their presence added a younger generation to the mix, and another hospitable house within easy reach of Dublin, thereby making them accessible not only to the capital's more cosmopolitan denizens but also overseas visitors arriving by boat or plane. In all these places, it was the peculiar mixture of locals and non-residents, of the smart and the straightforward, the urbane and the unsophisticated that gave Irish house parties a distinctive character. This was admirably

MILK
BREAD

ABOVE AND OPPOSITE: Following the end of her marriage to Dominick Oranmore and Browne in 1950, Oonagh spent more time at Luggala, not least because it gave her a house in which to entertain. Before long, she began an affair with writer Robert Kee, who, until the relationship ended around 1957, was a regular presence at Luggala, often accompanied by Georgiana, his daughter from a marriage to Janetta Woolley which had ended around the same time as that of Oonagh and Dom. Oonagh's photograph albums of the period chart the course of her relationship with Kee, as does the frequency of his name in her visitors' book.

summarised by Mark Bence-Jones in the mid-1960s when he wrote, 'The sense of the unexpected has long been one of the charms of Irish fashionable life. One goes to a dinner party in the depths of County Galway and finds M. Jean-Paul Sartre being worsted in a theological discussion by the local parish priest...Irish fashionable life is, in fact, a unique blending of the very smart international world with the traditional "Wild Irish" sporting, tweedy, bog-walking, animal-loving countryfolk. Dior and dogs' dinners go hand in hand.' Nowhere was this more the case than in Luggala from 1950s onwards. 'Nobody could keep away,' declared Michael Luke. 'Dublin intelligentsia, literati, painters, actors, scholars, hangers-on, toffs, punters, poets, social hang-gliders were attracted to Luggala as to nowhere else in Ireland – perhaps even in Europe, from where many would come. And the still centre of this exultant, exuberant chaos was Oonagh.'

Oonagh's coming out as a noteworthy hostess was the twenty-first birthday party she threw at Luggala for her eldest son, Gay Kindersley, in August 1951; although his actual birthday had been two months earlier, the occasion was delayed so as to coincide with the Dublin Horse Show. Over 200 guests attended what the *Daily Express* called 'the most important event of Eire's social year' and, as all the press reported, their arrival and departure were monitored by walkie-talkies to ensure a smooth flow of traffic. Members of the diplomatic corps were asked as well as local landowners, such as the Earl and Countess of Meath, Sir Edmund and Lady Hudson, Brigadier the Hon. James Hennessy, and many Horse Show competitors. A covered walkway from the dining room led them all to a large marquee, where dancing took place to Tommy Kinsman and his Orchestra who had come over from London for the occasion. According to one newspaper account, 'such numbers as the Raspa and the Can-Can were played repeatedly as these were very popular with the young people present,' who continued on the dance floor until 4am when hot soup was served. Long before then, at 10.30pm, there was a pause in the celebrations so that groundsman Alfred Smith, after 35 years the longest-serving member of Luggala's staff, could present a silver salver to Gay on behalf of all the estate workers.

All this was respectfully reported in newspapers over the following days, but some of the night's other episodes did not receive coverage, such as the experience of Oonagh's middle-aged secretary Olga Randel. She was knocked from her seat

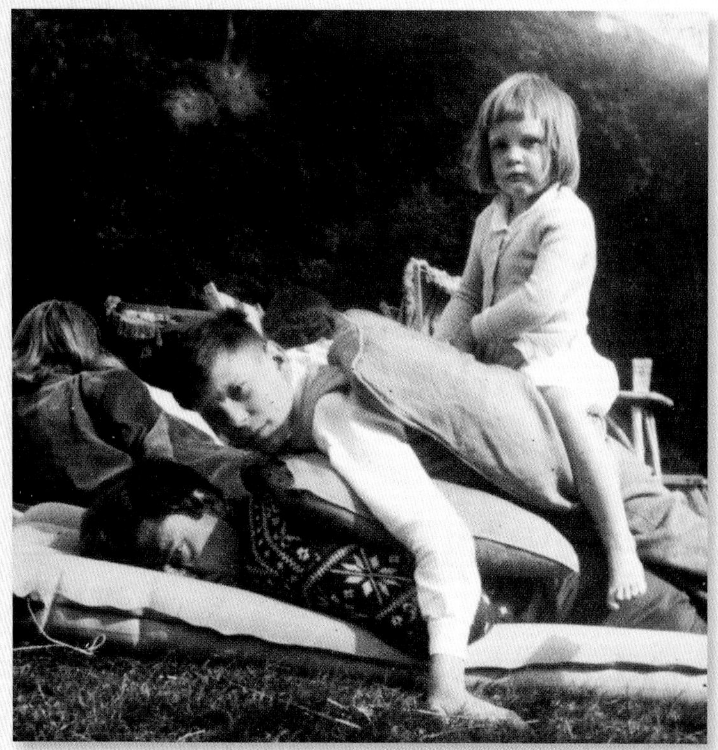

Souvenirs de Ravello
John

after a drunken poet, who had already assaulted another guest for allegedly making a pass at his wife, drove a car at speed into the marquee. Scooped up from the ground by an intoxicated Italian doctor, Miss Randel was laid out on a bed in one of the house's ground-floor rooms. There, in front of a growing crowd of onlookers pressed against the windows, the doctor administered what he insisted was the only correct treatment for her back pain: a suppository.

This party would be the first of many such gatherings during Oonagh's tenure as chatelaine of Luggala. Yet while she alone ruled, she did not reside alone. Newly single, she was as much courted as had been the case before her first wedding. A story is told of how in the days before a telephone was installed in the house, one suitor wooed her by telegram. Each of these required a boy to cycle several miles from Roundwood to Luggala. By the time he got back to the post office, another telegram would be waiting for delivery, the last of them on a particular evening simply bearing the words 'Goodnight darling.'

In 1951, a few months before Gay's twenty-first birthday, Oonagh began an affair with Robert Kee. Almost a decade her junior, the handsome, intelligent and intense Kee had by then written a couple of novels, the first a *roman à clef* of his time as a prisoner of war. However, not yet the celebrated author and broadcaster he would later become, he was then known as co-founder of the publishers MacGibbon & Kee. It seems fair to judge that his interest in Ireland – he subsequently wrote several, much-admired history books on the country and also campaigned against British injustice to Irish prisoners – was sparked by the relationship with Oonagh, which continued for the next five years. During this time, he frequently stayed at Luggala, sometimes bringing his young daughter Georgiana, the offspring of a marriage to Janetta Woolley, which had ended in divorce in 1950.

It was through Woolley that Kee had met Ralph and Frances Partridge, and he remained friends with the couple even after his divorce. In May 1952 he brought

OPPOSITE: In August 1951 American film director John Huston came to stay at Luggala for the first time and was immediately enchanted by both the house and its owner, remaining a close friend thereafter. For some years Huston and his fourth wife, Ricki, rented Courtown House in County Kildare, frequently driving over to Luggala for dinner or, since these occasions frequently ended late, to sleep overnight. Their daughter, actress Anjelica Huston, remembers staying many times in the house when she was a child.

ABOVE: Passionately keen on hunting, in 1954 John Huston bought an 18th-century house in County Galway, St. Cleran's, so that he could ride out with the Galway Blazers. Here Oonagh visited him and Ricki in 1958. St. Cleran's was later bought by American talk show host Merv Griffin and turned into a hotel.

Oonagh to stay with the Partridges at a house they had rented in south-east France. Oonagh, Frances later wrote, 'looked like some veiled Eastern woman in her enormous black glasses. Her small fragile and elegant body, her tiny hands loaded with huge rings hardly promised co-operation to our housewifery, nor was it wanted, but I found her tragic expression and air of being lost rather worrying...after several days in our company, she leaned across the table and asked me, "What is your name?" When I told her, "And what is your husband's?"' This collision of temperaments, and unfamiliarity with their names, was sufficiently overcome for the Partridges to pay a visit to Luggala a few months later.

Parties at Luggala were never composed of a homogeneous group, Oonagh always mixing people of disparate interests and backgrounds – 'the arty, crafty and downright dafty,' as one regular guest summarised them. Oonagh, remembers retired diplomat and poet Richard Ryan, 'simply picked people up and saw them as sport. She mixed everyone up in a great stew and then sat back to see what happened...When you went to Luggala, it was like Camelot. You never knew who you'd meet but you'd certainly never go there without coming out having had a memorable time.'

'To my mind,' wrote Claud Cockburn in August 1959, 'the sort of country house party which best combines the finest flavours of the Edwardian, neo-Georgian and Elizabethan modes is the kind you find at Luggala...The only trouble there is that when you tell about the party afterwards no one can believe you. Well, what can you expect when you start your story by saying: "It was the night the Duc de Brissac and Brendan Behan had that row with the Big Four bank director about the Grand National and this other man soothed them with a poem in Gaelic of his own composition"?' In 1995 Cockburn's son Alexander remembered encountering Seán MacBride, former IRA Chief of Staff and founder of republican/socialist party Clann na Poblachta, as well as future founding member and International Chairman of Amnesty International, in Luggala more than 40 years earlier: 'There was an old Victorian party game in which one contestant would think of a word and then be asked by the others to do certain things "in the manner of the word." Then the group would try to guess what the word was. MacBride was asked to hang his shoes on the chandelier and then take them down in the manner of the word. His word, it turned

Lady Oranmore and Browne, dancing with her son, Mr. Gay Kindersley.

OPPOSITE: Gay Kindersley, Oonagh's son from her first marriage, was a keen amateur jockey who enjoyed considerable success, although at a price: he twice broke his back. In his final season in 1965 he rode in the Grand National but fell at the third fence. Afterwards he established himself as a trainer in Berkshire.

ABOVE: Oonagh's debut as a noteworthy hostess at Luggala was the twenty-first birthday party she threw for Gay Kindersley in August 1951. Over 200 guests attended what the *Daily Express* called 'the most important event of Eire's social year' and although lavishly covered by the press, much of what took place on this occasion thankfully went unreported.

Patrick Cummins

'Patrick Cummins,' declared John Kilbracken in a feature published by *The Tatler & Bystander* in February 1960, 'is the most imperturbable butler in the world. He has to be, at Luggala.' It is an opinion with which everyone who knew the house during Oonagh Oranmore's time as chatelaine would concur. In fact, anybody who stayed in Luggala throughout that period would remember the consistently composed Cummins as vividly as they did his employer.

Born three miles outside the County Cork market town of Mallow in September 1909, Patrick Cummins was one of seven children; his father worked as a labourer on the local estate of Hazelwood owned by the Lysaght family. In his late teens, Patrick went to Jersey, where he found employment as a servant in Villa Millbrook, owned by Josephine, Lady Trent, widow of the founder of Boot's the Chemist. Following occupation of the island by the Nazis in July 1940, he returned to Ireland and was soon working at Castle MacGarrett as valet to Dominick Oranmore and Browne. While he always enjoyed good relations with Dom, he soon found a greater affinity with Oonagh and, as his niece Anna Cotter explains, 'When Lord and Lady Oranmore were splitting up, she asked him to go with her. Uncle Pat almost stole away out of the house, without any clothes or anything and went to Luggala.'

For the next 20 years, Patrick Cummins presided over the staff at Luggala, always composed, always dependable no matter what was taking place among Oonagh's houseguests. 'He was impeccable,' remembers Richard Ryan. 'He glided, he walked from the knees down and everything was done in virtual silence. If you stayed overnight, the following morning there would be a couple of taps on the door and with no acknowledgement of who or what was inside the room a perfect breakfast tray would be brought in with a rose in a vase.'

Cummins had a genius for anticipating the needs of others. 'He always came up to my room in the morning with Alka Seltzer and a glass of orange juice,' says Nicholas Gormanston, who also recalls that on the occasion of his first visit to Luggala in 1962 he had shared the car with Brendan Behan 'so there were many stops in establishments along the way. By the time I got there, I was legless but Cummins simply led the way to the kitchen and forced several cups of coffee down me.' Even when unable to anticipate what was going to happen, he could remain calm. 'If Oonagh tells him, an hour before dinner, that another dozen guests are arriving,' John Kilbracken reported, 'he has a stock reply: "Very, very good m'lady." In fact, that's his reply to everything.' 'The warmth of the reception,' wrote Michael Luke, 'the generosity of the hospitality and depth of cellar, all presided over by a gentle Irish Jeeves, Patrick Cummins, was never allowed to be scuppered by the unforeseen. Such were Cummins's diplomatic skills they always seemed to have been anticipated.'

Despite many years away from County Cork, Cummins never lost his accent. A much-recounted story concerns a December 1959 lunch party given by Oonagh at Luggala and attended by the then American Ambassador to Ireland. On the day in question, Gay Kindersley was riding in a national hunt meeting in England and naturally his mother was anxious to know the outcome but the race coincided with lunch being served, so Cummins was deputed to keep her up to date with any news. As he handed the ambassador a dish of well-browned rissoles, he murmured to Oonagh 'Mr Gay's turd,' a remark that did little to encourage her guest's appetite.

Neither in gesture nor word did Cummins ever indicate disapproval of or distaste for what he might have witnessed. Nor did he overtly favour some guests over others, although it was possible to recognise preferential treatment. 'He was special,' says Grey Gowrie. 'He took to me, so I got a good time.' Madeleine Mottuel, whose grandfather was a French duke and whose family had been ennobled during the Napoleonic era ('I have five marshals among my ancestors') remembers that when she was married to poet John Montague, Garech Browne had asked Cummins for an opinion on his circle of friends, to which came the response, 'Mrs Montague is a gentlewoman.' At the end of a long evening in Luggala, she says, Cummins 'would come and tell me that I was the only one who wasn't drunk, and I would help him put people into their rooms, those that looked like they had arrived together.' Some years later, following the end of her marriage to Montague, she brought her mother to tea with Oonagh at the latter's apartment in Paris: 'Cummins opened the door and threw himself into my arms!'

THIS PAGE: For more than 40 years Patrick Cummins was Oonagh's most devoted servant, acting as butler once she made Luggala her principle base from 1950 onwards. Always smiling, always imperturbable and always discreet, here he can be seen with other members of staff including the equally loyal Gretta Fanning and Patsy Sheridan who later went to work for the Hon. Desmond Guinness at Leixlip Castle.

Cummins' imperturbability was never more needed than at the time of Luggala's fire and its immediate aftermath. Despite the potential for chaos, he remained unflustered. In his 1960 article, John Kilbracken recollected arriving at the house just a few days after the blaze. 'I pulled up at the charred remains of the front door and the desolation was complete...Rubble, torn and scorched wallpaper, broken bricks and mortar, burst-open champagne bottles: they littered the interior in a maze of dereliction.' Suddenly out of this bleak scene emerged Cummins, impeccable in white jacket and perfectly creased dark trousers. 'Her ladyship is taking tea in one of the cow-sheds, m'lord,' he informed John Kilbracken. 'Would you care to join her?'

When Oonagh left Luggala and moved to the south of France in 1970, Cummins, together with Gretta Fanning and Patsy Sheridan, accompanied her. Cummins retired from service in 1983 and returned to Mallow, where he lived in a cottage next to his niece Anna: 'The minute he'd finished breakfast he'd be in to see what needed to be done. He'd be very upset if I had the house tidy because then he'd be left with nothing to do all day.'

Although retired, he would always come back to work for Oonagh whenever her other staff were away. John Montague visited him in Mallow 'and he could only speak of Luggala and all that time.' He was the most loyal man in Oonagh's life, 'her substitute husband and father,' according to Madeleine Mottuel. John Montague says 'He would look after her with all the skills of an undertaker. She used to say, "I don't mind death because I'll be laid to rest by the arms of Patrick Cummins".' It was not to be. Patrick Cummins died in December 1992, almost two and a half years before his mistress.

LEFT: Oonagh's visitors' book gives an idea of the intensity of her entertaining at Luggala during the 1950s, and the diversity of guests invited to enjoy her exceptionally generous hospitality. Among the regular names are those of writers Robert Kee, her lover during this period, and Claud Cockburn together with his wife, Patricia, and children. Cockburn once memorably described Luggala as 'the only place where I have seen people who – twenty four hours before – had been fussing furiously about urgent engagements to fly to Hollywood, Rome, New Delhi or London, or dash home to look after things on the farm in Tipperary, greet with cheers and big relief the news that the whole place was snowbound and was going to stay that way for days and days.' John Huston and his wife, Ricki, were also frequent guests; in his 1980 memoirs he recalled his first visit to Luggala 29 years earlier, observing 'I'll never forget that first impression. I was Ireland's own from that moment.' Over a twenty-year period Oonagh and Luggala were responsible for introducing many people to the charm of Ireland.

RIGHT: Another frequent guest at Luggala during the 1950s was artist Lucian Freud. He had first come to Ireland towards the close of the previous decade to meet the Irish painter Jack B. Yeats and found the country so congenial that he settled in Dublin for a while. At the time he was married to Kitty Garman, daughter of the sculptor Jacob Epstein, and both their names can be found regularly in Oonagh's visitors' book. However, in 1952 he eloped to Paris with Oonagh's niece, Lady Caroline Blackwood, marrying her late the following year. Until the two separated towards the end of the decade, it was with Caroline Blackwood that he came to stay at Luggala. There he found plenty of raffish company, such as Brendan Behan and the art collector Peggy Guggenheim, who spent several days in the house in September 1955. Other habitués included Oonagh's close friends Daphne Fielding (previously Daphne Bath, when married to the Marquess of Bath), Derek Lindsay, otherwise known as Deacon, and impoverished Irish peer John, Lord Kilbracken, together with other members of the country's former ruling class, such as Lord Rossmore and Desmond Leslie.

ABOVE: Another Christmas, another houseful of guests. On this occasion, December 1958, those staying at Luggala included distinguished literary critic Cyril Connolly and his former wife, Barbara Skelton, with whom he was then having an affair even though she had since married publisher George Weidenfeld. Skelton would go on to marry the bisexual Professor Derek Jackson, among whose previous wives was Janetta Woolley, once married to Oonagh's lover Robert Kee.

out, was "lovingly." He took down the shoes, stroking them with profound affection.' Grey Gowrie describes his first visit to Luggala as being 'one of those country house stays with very uncountrified people. You didn't go out and shoot things but crouched inside the house and chatted and drank.'

In a 1970 short story, *How You Love Our Lady,* Caroline Blackwood provides a fictional portrait of Luggala and Oonagh, who is the narrator's mother (just as Oonagh was Caroline's surrogate parent): 'My mother loved poets, painters and talkers. She said she could only bear to be surrounded by "free spirits." She was always speaking about her love for Art and Nature, and sometimes she said that she thought that life should be one long search for the beautiful.' The particular blend of 'free spirits' gathered at Luggala could be found nowhere else. Claud Cockburn wrote of Oonagh's 'extraordinary, and carefully disguised, skill in assembling an ostensibly "random" cocktail of guests, sometimes including people whose feuds have been internationally notorious until they evanesced at Luggala…' 'She did this a lot for her own entertainment,' says Margaret Brinckman, 'because she knew there'd be a reaction. At large dinner parties, there'd be an amazing collection of people, anyone from an ambassador to the bee keeper's son from Castle MacGarrett.' The 'bee keeper's son' was sculptor Edward Delaney, a close friend of Oonagh's son Garech. Once when someone asked who he was, Margaret Brinckman recalls, 'Oonagh just went "buzz, buzz, buzz".'

In a memoir of his father, Edward Delaney's son Eamon tells the story of Oonagh introducing a guest to the Belgian ambassador. Unfortunately, the guest shook the hand of the wrong person, who immediately denied diplomatic status. Not missing a beat, Oonagh made the introduction again. "And this," she said, 'is the other Belgian Ambassador".' Eamon Delaney also recalls the occasion at Luggala when Ireland's finest uilleann piper Leo Rowsome, learning that the French ambassador was present, performed the *Marseillaise*. As a mark of courtesy, everyone stood up – except the ambassador who failed to recognise the tune.

Such episodes of misunderstanding were by no means unusual: in 1957 Cockburn wrote of strolling by the lake at Luggala with a man he had been advised was a famous Italian writer. 'It was thought he would much enjoy a talk about trends in modern English and Italian literature. I speak no Italian, he had no English, and we bumped on and on in French. He had been lively at the outset but seemed to become taciturn. Though I ground out cultural notions like a coffee machine, he failed to respond.' Growing exasperated at the poor response to his efforts, Cockburn muttered 'Oh go jump in the lake,' an imprecation the Italian seemed to understand, since he immediately removed his clothes and entered the water. 'It was while we were sunning ourselves afterwards,' Cockburn continued, 'and he was massaging his enormous thigh muscles, that he made some remark which disclosed to me that he was a famous Italian, all right, a famous Italian rider, not writer.' But as a rule, says film director John Boorman, Oonagh 'liked writers and artists and musicians. I think it was a collector's mentality: an alternative salon.'

The heterogeneous guest list, the late nights, the quantity of drink consumed: all these gave Luggala a reputation for raffishness that spread far beyond its gates. 'I remember a girl friend of mine at Oxford,' says Grey Gowrie, 'who had very liberal parents. But the one place they'd forbidden her to go was Luggala. I later explained to them that she would have been perfectly safe there because everyone was much too drunk to be troublesome.' Likewise Margaret Brinckman, before her marriage to Gay Kindersley, had been invited to a party at Luggala but 'my mother wouldn't allow me to go. It was famous, infamous almost.' When Nicholas Gormanston was first asked to Luggala, his mother advised against accepting the invitation: 'You mustn't go there,' she warned her son, 'you can't afford them.' 'Atmospherically,' Grey Gowrie recalls, 'Luggala was louche in a kindly way. People didn't seem to have much in the way of rules. You could do what you wanted…It was an odd kind of upper-class hippy oasis.'

One reason for Luggala's infamy was the irregular sleeping arrangements found there. It was not unusual for the number of guests to exceed the number of bedrooms. On more than one occasion John Kilbracken wrote that when staying he went to sleep on the drawing-room sofa in front of a fire. The dining room for a period was turned into a dormitory (the entrance hall, then as now, was often used for meals). In *How You Love Our Lady*, Caroline Blackwood writes of 'all the poets and drinkers and talkers' who nightly came to the house of the narrator's mother 'and so often ended up in the "Doss-House" as they called her spare room where rows of mattresses were always laid out on the floor for anyone who felt like staying.'

Luggala, according to Brendan Behan, was a house where you could say anything you liked, 'provided you didn't take too long and were witty'. Fast talk implied fast behaviour, and a glance through the visitors' book during the 1950s helps to explain Luggala's notoriety in more staid circles. There was Brian Howard, back again more than 30 years after he had stayed in the house as a guest of Aileen. Now struggling to break a chronic drug addiction, he wrote to his mother from Luggala in June 1957, 'I am trying to do my cure independently here because the clinic at Lausanne is very expensive. I adore this place and the change of environment may just tip the scales…The fact that meals simply appear, at regular intervals, without my having either to help cook them, or to go out to a restaurant and pay for them, has the result of making me eat enormously.' Nevertheless, the cure was unsuccessful, Howard leaving behind as souvenir of his visit a vast number of broken hypodermic syringes; the following spring he would commit suicide in the south of France.

Then there was Maurice Richardson, succinctly described by English thriller writer Christopher Fowler as 'a manic-depressive, ex-amateur boxer and journalist who hung out with a pretty low-life crowd' and is today remembered, if at all, for his book *The Exploits of Engelbrecht* concerning a dwarf surrealist boxer who, amongst other pursuits, goes ten rounds with a grandfather clock. To this mix can be added the equally louche Michael Wishart, painter, alcoholic and one-time lover of, among others, legendary opium addict Denham Fouts and, a decade later, decorator Nicholas Haslam; between these two men, he was married to Ann Dunn, daughter of Canadian steel magnate Sir James Dunn, with whom he had a son. As a teenager, Wishart shared a hotel room in Paris with Lucian Freud, with whom Wishart's legendarily promiscuous mother Lorna had had an affair. Freud used his youthful Parisian roommate as the subject in several early paintings; Wishart would become a close friend of Freud's second wife (and niece of Oonagh) Caroline Blackwood and of her third husband, American poet Robert Lowell.

Nor should be forgotten the author, film producer and screenwriter Michael Luke, described by Philip Hoare as 'Byronic in his Bohemian good looks, life style and loves.' After his death in April 2005, a *Daily Telegraph* obituary of Luke observed, 'Friends remember a perpetual aura of scandal about him, his stormy love affairs and propensity for fisticuffs, sleeping rough, occasional gigolo practices and other semi-delinquent behaviour which he justified by claiming: "Everyone is honest according to their means".'

In his own obituary of Oonagh, Luke produced perhaps the best and most succinct accounts of her time at Luggala, remarking that one of its singular attributes, 'was the ease with which life could be conducted harmoniously and concurrently on several levels. On the ground there might be the inimitable Claud Cockburn measuring his considerable length on the drawing-room carpet after an exhilarating morning of informed discussion spent not far from the brandy decanter. His supine form lent itself to adaptation by energetic five-year-olds into an impromptu playground. Then, a little higher, seated earnestly on the edge of, or laid back over, sofas and chairs was the *jeunesse dorée*, exploring each other's personalities. Upright, might be found the "grown-ups"; the writer Erskine Childers, the playwright Sean O'Casey, Soho regulars *en permission*, cosmopolitan lovers of the turf, politicians of different persuasions, and threading through all a beady-eyed Lucian Freud, careful to avoid Brendan Behan, in lively exchange with the writer Patrick Leigh Fermor.'

Disparate though their backgrounds might appear, somehow Oonagh managed to find the links between her guests. One example will suffice. Over Christmas 1958 literary critic Cyril Connolly, then chief book reviewer for the Sunday Times, came to stay at Luggala. So too did his former wife, Barbara Skelton, perhaps the most notorious femme fatale of her generation, known as 'Helter Skelter' and enjoying, judged Hugh Montgomery-Massingberd, a 'career of petulant promiscuity'. Among her many lovers was King Farouk of Egypt, who flogged her with the cord of his dressing-gown (she would later write that the king 'resembled a huge sawdust teddy bear badly sewn at the joints') as well as another Luggala habitué, the predominantly homosexual Michael Wishart. While Connolly and Skelton were married in the early 1950s, one of the main sources of discord between them had been his infatuation with Oonagh's niece Caroline Blackwood; she was also staying at Luggala that same Christmas, having separated from Lucian Freud earlier in the year. When Connolly and Skelton eventually divorced in 1956, the publisher George Weidenfeld was cited as co-respondent. When Weidenfeld and Skelton in turn divorced in 1961, it was Connolly's turn to be cited. Skelton went on to marry nuclear physicist Professor Derek Jackson, a bisexual who would have six wives including both Desmond Guinness's aunt Pamela Mitford and Janetta Woolley, the latter formerly married to Oonagh's lover Robert Kee. Given this cast of characters and their myriad peccadilloes, is it any wonder concerned parents would caution their daughters against accepting invitations to Luggala?

By no means all Oonagh's guests were imported, among the best-known of Luggala's indigenous visitors being that corpulent comet of Irish literature, Brendan Behan. Caroline Blackwood's then-husband Lucian Freud had introduced Oonagh to Behan shortly before the opening of the latter's first play, *The Quare Fellow*, which she attended in November 1954. The following year the writer and his wife, Beatrice, spent the first of a succession of Christmases at Luggala, collected by Oonagh's chauffeur and driven to Wicklow in her Rolls Royce. 'The Guinnesses have been good to the people of Dublin,'

RIGHT: From Oonagh's photograph albums, images of houseguests at Luggala during Easter 1957 and Christmas 1959. 'Nobody could keep away,' wrote Michael Luke of the house during this period, going on to note, 'Dublin intelligentsia, literati, painters, actors, scholars, hangers-on, toffs, punters, poets, social hang-gliders were attracted to Luggala as to nowhere else in Ireland – perhaps even in Europe, from where many would come. And the still centre of this exultant, exuberant chaos was Oonagh.'

Easter 1957

Georgie Kee Anne Hill

Robert Kee

Oonagh. Raymond de Trafford. Michael Luke Georgie Kee

Georgie

Raymond de Trafford Oonagh Derek Lindsay
Tara Browne Georgie Kee Charlie Murdoch

Luggala Xmas 1959

Margaret Barry

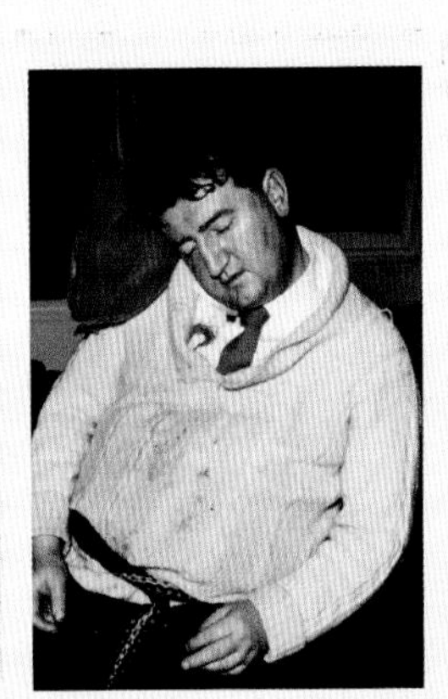

Brendan Behan

Claud Cockburn

John Montague John Killrachan

Patricia Leatham John Killrachan

Behan once declared, slyly adding, 'but then the people of Dublin have been good to the Guinnesses.' Oonagh was certainly good to Behan, prepared to tolerate his boisterous, alcohol-infused behaviour even when this elided into gracelessness. Late one night, Margaret Brinckman struggled to escape from a very drunk Behan in the courtyard at Luggala. 'I remember being very frightened and was only saved from assault by Miguel Ferreras [Oonagh's third husband]. Having been seen off, Behan charged through the arch and into the night shouting "This is what comes of getting mixed up with the fucking Anglo-Irish".'

In 1992, novelist, screenwriter and, from 1960 onwards, husband of Deborah Kerr, Peter Viertel published a memoir, *Dangerous Friends*, impressive for its name-dropping and factual errors alike. Nevertheless, the book contains a vivid account of dinner at Luggala on Christmas Eve 1957. At the time Viertel was renting Mount Armstrong, a house in County Kildare close to that occupied by John Huston, for whom he wrote several screenplays including *The African Queen*. In December 1957, he invited actor Michael Wilding to stay, along with the latter's then-wife Elizabeth Taylor; she failed to appear, being in the midst of an affair with Victor Mature. So on Christmas Eve he took the disconsolate Wilding to dinner at Luggala, where, amongst other guests, they found Brendan Behan, already worse for wear and bellowing toasts of 'Up the Rebels'. At the end of the meal, recorded Viertel, Behan 'rose unsteadily to his feet and, swaying slightly, raised his glass in the direction of our hostess. "To her ladyship!" he roared. "God bless her!" and fell forward onto the table, which gave way under his weight with a tinkling of breaking glass and a jingle of antique sterling silver.' As with the Belgian Ambassador incident, Oonagh remained unfazed. According to Viertel, she 'said, "Oh dear," as if someone had spilled a teaspoonful of salt, rose from the debris in front of her and suggested it was "time for us to move back into the drawing room".' Oonagh, says Madeleine Mottuel, 'would very much float through events and not seem to see or care.'

There was certainly some element of truth to Viertel's account of the evening, since much of it was later confirmed by Beatrice Behan. In a chapter called 'Christmas at Luggala' from her 1973 memoir *My Life with Brendan*, she told what happened after the dinner guests had departed. Behan, it seems, liked to wander the corridors singing 'Adeste Fideles' to the music of an old Irish tune called 'The Coolin'. 'He was in the middle of his song when he tumbled head over heels down a flight of narrow, curving stairs leading to the servants' quarters. He lay at the bottom with his feet wedged against a door.' As a result of his position, the door could not be opened and Behan could not be moved. Eventually one of the maids was despatched to heave him into a sitting position and, a bleeding gash on his head having received attention and his wife having been woken, the Behans were driven back to Dublin in Oonagh's Rolls Royce. Afterwards Behan sent the house a short piece of verse called 'Beannacht an Nua-bhlian' (New Year Greeting):

'Lady Oonagh, Garech, Tara,
Three bright heads be twice as fair,
This time twelvemonths
(And as hard a curse of mine lie on that stair).
The girl that danced the Blackbird lightly,
Michael Wilding, Harold Lloyd,
Tara's bow to shine as brightly,
Bless Caroline and Lucian Freud.'

Incidentally, Peter Viertel wrote that on the journey back from Luggala, Michael Wilding confided 'that he had found Lady Oranmore and Browne to be "a most attractive woman in a sort of beaten-up way." I realised then that his broken heart was on the mend and that the one-time lover of Marlene Dietrich and Elizabeth Taylor was ready for more.'

It has been mentioned that Viertel wrote a number of screenplays for John Huston, being one of the credited writers of *Beat the Devil*, made in 1953 with Humphrey Bogart, Jennifer Jones, Gina Lollobrigida and Peter Lorre. The film's genesis lies in Luggala, specifically during Huston's first visit to the house two years earlier. Also staying on that occasion was Claud Cockburn, perennially impoverished despite being a prolific journalist. In 1949 Cockburn had written his first novel, *Beat the Devil*, published under the pseudonym James Helvick since he had recently left the Communist Party, of which he had hitherto been a high-profile member, and as his son Alexander later observed, 'the name Cockburn did not have benign associations for the publishers and magazine editors crucial to our well-being.'

In 1980 John Huston remembered that when shown to his room on that first occasion in Luggala, 'On the table beside the bed was a copy of a book written by Claude (sic) Cockburn, another houseguest, whom I'd known in my pre-war days. The name of the book was *Beat the Devil* written

RIGHT: In the early hours of 25th January 1956, while Luggala's occupants were asleep, fire broke out in the house. Originating in one of the bedrooms and caused by old faulty wiring, the blaze quickly spread while heavy snow delayed the arrival of the local fire brigades. Even when they reached the house, there was a further delay when the firemen forgot to attach the nozzle to the engine. It was not until 10am that the flames were doused. As a result, the main block was almost entirely gutted, although thanks to the efforts of the family and staff most of the furniture, pictures and other valuable items were saved. So, too, were Oonagh's three West Highland terriers, Googi, Puff and Winkie, with whom the firemen afterwards posed for photographs.

of chartered quantity surveyors estimated the cost of reinstatement to be £25,358, leaving a difference of £6,417. Surviving correspondence makes it clear that Oonagh would have gone ahead with the project regardless of expense. She wanted her house back, and as quickly as possible. 'My general instructions,' wrote Hope to the main contractor in April, 'are that the house should be reinstated exactly as it was formerly and as soon as possible.'

Speed being a priority, Hope and his team had the job completed within a year, so that by March 1957 Oonagh was back in the house. On her visits to Luggala during the months when this was not possible, she stayed, and entertained, in what was called the Cowshed, a range of outbuildings on raised ground behind the main site. Plans were drawn up for this structure to be extended so that Oonagh could offer more accommodation and spare the likes of John Kilbracken from spending the night on a sofa. Designs from Hope's office show a curved block holding six guest bedrooms on the north end of the Cowshed, but this work was never executed.

While Alan Hope was responsible for the structural restoration of the old house, John Hill assumed responsibility for its decoration. Older brother of the painter Derek Hill and brother-in-law of London bookseller Heywood Hill – both of whom stayed at Luggala – John Hill ran the long-established Mayfair firm of Green & Abbott. Previous clients included both the aesthete Stephen Tennant and his own equally demanding brother Derek who, in 1954, had bought St. Columb's, a former rectory, in County Donegal. In addition, Hill had already carried out decorative work for Oonagh at Luggala in 1947 so he was returning to familiar territory. This time he followed his own instinctive love of the Victorian period and focused on emphasising the house's inherently romantic character, particularly through the use of specially printed wallpapers. In the drawing room, for example, Hill arranged for the English firm of Cole & Son to produce a paper called Gothic Lily originally designed by Pugin for the House of Lords at the Palace of Westminster. Some areas were papered in 19th-century chintz while others, such as

OPPOSITE: From the design of its Crace wallpaper, this bedroom is known as the Single Shamrock Room. On the walls hang, from left to right, a portrait of Garech's uncle, the Hon. Geoffrey Browne (1912-1986), his paternal grandmother, Lady Olwen Ponsonby (1876-1927) and an earlier member of the family, the Hon. Henry Browne (1824-1843) who, according to a label on the picture, was 'killed accidentally by the explosion of his own gun'. The oval mirror is Irish and was Oonagh's favourite; it formerly hung in the drawing room.

ABOVE: The main guest bedroom on the first floor. On one wall hangs a tapestry designed by Ireland's most distinguished artist, Louis le Brocquy, for many years a visitor to Luggala, who died at the age of 95 in May 2012. The 19th-century Irish four-poster bed made by Strahan of Dublin was bought in the contents sale conducted by Christie's at Malahide Castle, County Dublin in May 1976, whilst the walnut drop-leaf table at the foot of the bed was used as a writing desk by Oonagh throughout her life.

OPPOSITE: Above the chimneypiece decorated with a typical Irish shell motif is the 1940 pastel portrait of Oonagh and Garech as a baby by Gaetano de Gennaro, while to the left hangs a portrait of writer Gerald Hanley by Anthony Palliser.

ABOVE: One of the pair of lamps that sit on Oonagh's former writing table, an 18th-century Irish mahogany chair and a self-portrait by Anthony Palliser all help add to the ambience of this bedroom.

the entrance hall and Oonagh's bedroom, had papers designed by 20th-century painter and graphic artist Edward Bawden. 'Today,' wrote the Knight of Glin in 1965, 'the interior, with its elaborate wallpapers, chandeliers and plushy comfort is more early Victorian in feeling than late Georgian.' However, he added, 'the hospitality and gaiety of the house is very much more evocative of the eighteenth than of the nineteenth century.' Decorator David Mlinaric, who began staying at Luggala in the 1960s and would work there in the 1990s, says 'It was one of the first houses I visited that was "decorated" as they all are now. Nobody then had imaginative wallpapers or colour schemes; people had very plain houses...Here there was always an element of a refreshing colour palette that wasn't necessarily historically accurate.' A distinctively 1950s touch was the use of fitted carpet throughout the house, that in the dining room being yellow with a winding border of floral garlands.

As if to mark the rebirth of Luggala, a year after completion of work on the house Oonagh's own life underwent a significant change. Her relationship with Robert Kee had come to an end not long after the fire but she did not remain single for long: in February 1958, within days of her 48th birthday, she began a new relationship. Unlike her previous husbands, the new man did not come from the ranks of the aristocracy but was a fashion designer apparently from Cuba and called Miguel Ferreras. Within her own family there was previous form for this startling behaviour: in December 1956 Aileen Plunket had married Valerian Stux-Rybar, a Yugoslav

ABOVE AND OPPOSITE: Garech Browne's dressing room and bedroom are located on the ground floor, in rooms formerly occupied by his mother and situated behind the drawing room. The walls are covered in another Crace paper, this one previously used in the staircase hall until Luggala's most recent restoration. The dressing room pictures include a watercolour of Garech by Anthony Palliser, while on one of the bedroom walls is hung a series of studies by artist Barrie Cooke of Janet 'Tiger' Cowley; the finished picture hangs in the dining room.

interior decorator. Like the latter, Oonagh's new husband had no money of his own, came from a background regularly subjected to reinvention, was widely rumoured to be homosexual, and was certainly much younger than his spouse – probably by some 15 years, although it is impossible to be absolutely certain about this since Ferreras was inclined to be coy about his exact age. Furthermore, his courtship could best be described as whirlwind and the resultant marriage as causing considerable surprise, if not dismay, among the bride's family and friends. Oddly enough, both his and Stux-Rybar's marriages would end within months of each other.

Despite his claims to the contrary, it cannot be said that before meeting Oonagh Miguel Ferreras was widely known as a fashion designer; tellingly, in its report of the wedding, the *New York Times*, a stickler for accuracy, misspelled his name as Ferraras, while Britain's *Daily Express* called him Miguel Sereres. The *New York Times* also described the groom's deceased father as being 'of Madrid', but thereafter Miguel Ferreras, who took American citizenship only in 1960, claimed to have been born and raised in Havana; members of Oonagh's family would later draw attention to this vagueness over his origins. According to Ferreras, he had initially studied architecture in Paris before the Second World War, but if this were the case he had to be older than 31, his admitted age in 1958. He came to the United States, he said, in 1947 or 1948 (the date varied from one press interview to the next) on a student

visa to study fashion design, spending several years in the New York atelier of Charles James, the most brilliant but most temperamental American couturier of his generation. Ferreras must have possessed a certain talent to have survived time with James, a man not known to have suffered fools, or pretty much anyone else, lightly. In July 1961 the couturier told a *New York Times* reporter that his former pupil, 'has great mechanical competence, great bluster, which, as Barnum & Bailey showed us, is so necessary, and what would pass for taste in the provinces.'

In the early 1950s Ferreras, by now married to Margaret Clarke, a Canadian with whom he had two daughters, opened his own New York salon on East 56th Street. Here he failed to attract many customers and, as was described by the *New York Herald Tribune*'s Mary Blume in July 1961, he 'lost masses of money'. Neither his clientele nor his output was ever substantial: a piece in *Life* magazine in May 1958 informed readers 'He does some 60 designs a year, sells his small output from $325 to $1,200.' For much of the 1950s Ferreras' name cropped up in the press intermittently but not always favourably. In September 1957 it was widely reported that the clothes he had designed for singer Lena Horne's new show *Jamaica* left her unable to move, let alone dance, and had to be remade entirely. It must have been a struggle to keep going, and he seems to have taken whatever work was available, such as designing the maternity dresses that appeared in advertisements for Mennen skincare for babies.

Meeting Oonagh in the winter of 1957 was opportune for Ferreras. 'I first met my husband several months ago,' she informed journalists after the wedding. 'We were introduced by mutual friends in New York and have seen one another constantly since.' Conducted by a Presbyterian minister, the marriage ceremony was held in Oonagh's suite at New York's Drake Hotel on Park Avenue and 56th Street, where she always stayed during her time in the city. Her niece Caroline Blackwood acted as bridesmaid, while a man the groom claimed was his brother Joaquin (but, the Brownes later thought, was in fact a former lover) performed the part of best man. Two months later, the men reversed roles when Joaquin Ferreras married Elena Santeiro Garcia, widow of José Manuel Alemán, former Minister of Education in Cuba, who had left his native country for Florida in 1948 taking with him, it was alleged, some $174 million from the country's Treasury. As the Suzy Knickerbocker column noted at the time, 'If there's one thing the Ferreras boys do, it's marry well.'

After honeymooning in New York and Cuba, in May 1958 Oonagh and Miguel returned to Luggala where her son Garech had organised a welcome party for his new stepfather: a traditional Irish hooley in the converted cottage on the east side of the house's courtyard. Guinness and whiskey were served, along with baked potatoes, pigs' trotters, grilled kippers and apple pie, all the food laid out on the floor and eaten without the aid of knives or forks. The 70-odd guests sang and danced jigs until the early hours of the morning. Photographs of the event show Oonagh wearing a black hooded Connemara cape while her new husband, in Aran sweater and Tam o' Shanter, unsuccessfully struggles not to look like an extra from Disney's *Darby O'Gill and the Little People* (released the following year).

Ferreras' costume for the party is an apt metaphor of the incongruity of his marriage to Oonagh, a union that seems to have been in difficulty almost from its start. One problem was that, like her first husband Philip Kindersley, he did not like Ireland and failed to share her affinity for Luggala. She tried to overcome this by proposing a studio be built for him in the grounds of the estate: Alan Hope came up with numerous designs for an elegant pavilion but none of these was used.

Ferreras' aversion to her native country meant that in the late 1950s and early 1960s Oonagh spent more time than hitherto away from Luggala, much of it passed in Paris, where she had an apartment on rue de l'Université, or in Venice where each summer she habitually took a floor in either the Palazzo Polignac or the Palazzo Papadopoli. Finally, in 1961 she paid for her husband to open his own couture salon in splendid premises on rue du Faubourg St-Honoré in Paris. Ferreras, as he repeatedly pointed out, was the first American couturier in the French capital since Mainbocher more than 30 years before. Mainbocher's corset, immortalized in 1939 by one of Horst's most famous photographs, seems to have been something of an inspiration for Ferreras: his first Paris presentation in late July 1961 opened with an elasticised nylon girdle, intended to be worn under all the clothes that followed.

As a couturier, Ferreras attracted plenty of publicity but was not so successful at winning clients. High-profile names – the Duchess of Windsor, Elizabeth Taylor, members of the DuPont family, Ann Woodward (who had famously shot her husband William Woodward Jr in 1955), even Brigitte Bardot – bought his clothes but not in sufficient quantity to make the establishment profitable. Naturally he claimed otherwise, but it is telling that once divorced from Oonagh, he was never

RIGHT: Oonagh and Miguel Ferreras soon after their unexpected 'wedding' in February 1958. Conducted by a Presbyterian minister, the ceremony was held in the bride's suite at New York's Drake Hotel on Park Avenue, where she always stayed during visits to the city. Her niece Caroline Blackwood acted as bridesmaid, while the groom's alleged brother was best man.

able to have his own label again. He also argued that French couturiers were jealous of him; if so, this emotion was probably inspired less by his talent and more by his access to generous funds courtesy of his wife. Strikingly, almost every review he received included mention of Oonagh and her wealth. Although evidently he possessed personal charm, he lacked tact: in July 1961 he told the *New York Herald Tribune*'s Mary Blume that women who spent $700 on a ready-to-wear dress 'have no imagination...American society women all look alike.'

The new couture house was launched with a splash in Paris, literally since the party to mark its opening was held on a bateau mouche on the Seine, a firework display featuring his initials MF. From the start, however, press reviews were less than enthusiastic, with the *Daily Telegraph* reporting from the first show, 'We virtually hung on our eyelashes in Ferreras's crowded salon to see his debut, but the story is, alas, of clothes, not a collection.' Similarly the *Associated Press* coverage syndicated around the world informed readers, 'The crush in his handsome white and gold salons, with potted palms behind a plate glass wall, was terrible. But in spite of a friendly reception, his unwaisted sheaths offered no serious threat to the Mainbocher legend.' The following January, at the time of his second couture collection, Nancy Mitford

The Mystery of Miguel Ferreras

In September 1997 *Harper's & Queen* published an article called 'Dance with a Stranger' by journalist Nicholas Farrell. The piece dealt with the strange, opaque history of Oonagh's putative third husband Miguel Ferreras, then living with his last wife in a small New York apartment on East 78th Street and claiming to be aged sixty nine. In the course of his life, Ferreras made a great many claims, some of them conflicting and some incapable of validation even after Farrell's forensic investigation.

It is hard to find anyone who met Ferreras while he was with Oonagh who has a kind word to say about the man. 'I thought him an unbelievable nightmare,' says Grey Gowrie while conceding that, 'my attitude was probably coloured by Caroline [Blackwood] who thought he was awful. But he wasn't charming and seemed entirely alien to Luggala. One likes one's Latin lover to be a bit of a smoothie, and Miguel charged around growling and had no conversation; he was like a small, dark, bad-tempered bulldog.'

Ferreras certainly felt out of place in Luggala, where nobody displayed any curiosity in his fashion, the only field in which he was of some consequence. 'It rain too much in Ireland,' he told Farrell in 1997, 'and the Guinnesses are very provincial. Besides, I do not like the Guinness stout.' More importantly, he did not like Oonagh's friends and the sentiment was reciprocated in abundance. 'He couldn't talk to us,' explains John Montague, 'he didn't have the same interests. Once, when he got bored by the company, he was seen going outside and heading down to the lake. Then he came back, opened the window into the drawing room and stepped inside with a deer kid in his arms.'

In photographs of Luggala during those years, Ferreras's short, stocky frame can frequently be spotted sunken into a chair, a morose expression on his face while everyone around him is clearly having enormous fun. In a house habitually filled with fast talkers, it didn't help that his English was both heavily accented and inelegant. Ill-tempered by disposition and no doubt disgruntled, while simultaneously elated, by his dependence on Oonagh's money, occasionally he would be unable to conceal his anger. Over Christmas 1961 Ferreras physically assaulted the drunken Brendan Behan in the snow, incorrectly claiming the writer had sexually interfered with Tara Browne, then aged 16; Oonagh immediately placed a blanket over Behan to keep him warm. Behan, who knew how much Garech and Tara hated Ferreras, informed him that if he wasn't out of Ireland in three days, he wouldn't be leaving at all.

John Montague's former wife Madeleine Mottuel considers him to have been 'good looking in a South American way, a bit spiffish, the sort that pleased women although he wasn't necessarily that way himself. I think his main interest was to be recognised. I was often sitting by his side at meals so I'd had his conversation more often than most, especially as a lot of their friends were very hard, snobbish and snubbing him.' 'Everyone was rather nasty to him,' Grey Gowrie confirms. 'He wasn't thought to be up to snuff.' Employees felt the same way. Gretta Fanning, who worked for Oonagh from 1961 onwards, says of Ferreras, 'He'd give you the impression he was a kind of bully. I wouldn't like to have any dealings with him, I kept out of his way. He was a horrible man.'

In 1960 Godfrey Carey, now a Q.C. but then an 18 year old fresh from school, was hired as tutor to Tara Browne, principally on the basis that Carey's father was Oonagh's doctor. Ferreras conducted the job interview, which took place over dinner in a restaurant, after which he took Carey to what the latter subsequently described as 'a poof's parlour. Not a woman in sight.' It was, he says, 'not a suitable place for a young man, so I made my excuses and left.' This was in Paris where Oonagh had an apartment on the rue de l'Université and where Ferreras preferred to spend as much time as possible, especially after opening his own couture house in 1961. What did Carey make of his charge's step-father? 'Not a lot, in fact I thought him a rather sinister man. I didn't get the impression he was hugely kind to Oonagh and he certainly made a complete misjudgement of me.' Less than six months after taking up the position of Tara's tutor, Carey had left, pursued by accusations from Ferreras that he had been having an affair with Oonagh. 'I think that was rather stretching things: I don't believe I had a reputation as a philanderer at that stage.'

Like many other people, Carey found it difficult to discern a connection between Oonagh and her husband ('She marry me for sex,' an unchivalrous Ferreras later informed Farrell). 'Oonagh was an ungrown-up, rather fairytale person,' says Grey Gowrie., 'When I knew her, her line towards Ferreras was "Help! How on earth am I going to get out of this"?'

Eventually she did so, albeit at a price. It seems, however, that off-loading Ferreras would have been costlier had lawyers employed by Oonagh not gone to the trouble of investigating his background, which was murkier than he liked to admit.

The precise details of Ferreras's life prior to his arrival in the United States in the late 1940s are hard to verify. Although American social security records state he was born on 28th January 1927, Garech Browne says he has a copy of Ferreras's real birth certificate supplied by his mother's lawyers. It appears that Ferreras had been born José Maria Ozores Laredo in Madrid in 1922 (not 1928 as he would later claim). Ozores Laredo joined the Spanish Army in August 1941 and, having volunteered for Franco's Blue Division, fought with the Nazis on the Russian Front. Following brief imprisonment for desertion, he then re-volunteered with the Blue Division, remaining with it until wounded in 1943 when he was sent home to Madrid – and there arrested twice for theft. He next volunteered for the Third Reich's Waffen-SS and, having been made an under-lieutenant, saw combat in Rumania, Russia, Hungary, Yugoslavia and Germany, before being taken prisoner in Italy in 1945 and repatriated to Spain a year later. A Cuban called Joaquin Ferreras claimed he had fought alongside Ozores Laredo in the Blue Brigade and that, after hostilities ended, the two men had been deported to Cuba from Portugal. Ozores Laredo took the name of Joaquin Ferreras's brother Miguel, who had died of consumption in 1949 and subsequently moved from Cuba to the United States.

Whatever parts of this story are true – and it was all denied by Ferreras in 1997 – no wonder he preferred to present himself as having come directly to the United States from Cuba, and as being too young to have fought in the Second World War. Garech Browne proposes that since he had taken the name of a dead man, 'my mother was never even legally married to Miguel under English or Irish law.'

The information gathered about his background by her lawyers meant Ferreras was more willing to clear out of Oonagh's life 'and he didn't get any money at all.' All the details of his murky history will probably never be known, especially since Miguel Ferreras died in April 1999, a couple of years after being quizzed about his past by Nicholas Farrell.

The Daily Mail
[illegible]lite House, Carmelite Street,
DAILY MAIL, Saturday, April 26, 1958

PAUL TANFIELD

They danced till dawn in bawneens and clogs

BROADWAY'S Spanish-American dress-designer, 32-year-old **Miguel Ferreras,** husband of the former **Lady Oranmore and Browne,** was quite bewildered by the abandoned gaiety of his riotous "belated" honeymoon party.

No one has seen anything like it for years. And no wonder . . . it was planned by his wealthy wife, nee **Oonagh Guinness** (who knew what was good for him) . . . organised by his 18-year-old stepson, **Garrett Browne,** who was wearing a white homespun suit and heavy clogs.

DONKEY-CARTS

It took place in a cottage that was converted from a barn in an isolated valley in the Wicklow Mountains . . . All the 76 guests were wearing Irish dress by request.

They came from isolated cottages for miles around in their donkey-carts, dressed in their bawneens, knee breeches, and Tam o'Shanters. Women favoured big red petticoats and pantaloons.

They found Mr. Ferreras carrying his wife about in his arms. She was wearing a black hooded cloak that is peculiar to elderly and middle-aged women in Western Ireland. His garb came strictly from Hollywood.

ON THE FLOOR

There were no cocktails, champagne or 'fancy drinks'—It was draught from the barrels and Irish whiskey, lashings of it. The drink set the company jigging, swigging, and singing until daybreak.

There were no knives or forks. And those who had plates helped themselves directly from dishes on the floor—where there was.

Roast turkey, roast goose, boiled pigs trotters, pigs head, boiled nettles, apple tart, ham griddle, currant bread, a massive basketful of potatoes in their jackets, and even kippers grilled on a griddle over an open fire.

Lad who appeared to eat most . . . to dance most . . . was 13-year-old Tara Browne, wearing a heavy white homespun suit with a red jumper, clay pipe and clogs. He's another son of Mrs. Ferreras, and he's soon off to Eton.

They came from miles around to the cottage in the Wicklow Mountains, and helped themselves to the tasty dishes laid out on the floor. Knives and forks were definitely out.

Mr. Ferreras and wife. She wore the black-hooded cloak of Western Ireland.

AWAY DULL CARE LET THE DANCING BEGIN

★ *In white homespun suit and heavy clogs, Garrett Browne raises his glass in a signal for the dancers to take the floor.* ★

The Star

Nice work . . .

MR and Mrs Gay Kindersley flew to Madrid today, 24 hours after their racehorse, Gama II. Mr Kindersley is to take part in two international amateur horse races there.

An expensive trip for an amateur rider? Mr Kindersley smiled. "Although they are amateur races there is a £400 prize for each of them," he said.

They will be away until Monday—all expenses paid by the racing authorities in Spain.

Not so bad for an amateur.

Evening Standard

DAY AT THE RACES IN MADRID

Off to Spain today fly Mr. and Mrs. Gay Kindersley. In Madrid tomorrow he is taking part in two international amateur horse races. One is on the flat the other is a hurdle race. He said: "I shall ride Gama, my wife's horse, in the flat race. Over the sticks I shall be riding a friend's horse."

wrote to her sister Deborah, Duchess of Devonshire, that the *Figaro* had commented of Ferreras, 'he would do better to open a flower shop.'

And so it went on for the next few seasons, with the designer – and his loyal wife – insisting that the business was a success, but sales and press notices indicating otherwise. Although he regularly talked of adopting a bold and radical approach to fashion, in an era of Courrèges and Cardin, his clothes, while never less than competent, were actually rather staid and conformist. As expenditure habitually exceeded income, Oonagh's enthusiasm for the project began to wane, and so too did her desire to remain married to Ferreras. 'They sort of slid apart,' said her son, Garech, in 1997. 'She began to notice he was disappearing off and spending her money.' It didn't help that neither Garech nor his brother Tara cared for their step-father.

Even so, in 1964 Oonagh and her husband announced their intention to become parents through adoption; by this

ABOVE: After several months' honeymooning, in May 1958 Oonagh and Miguel Ferreras arrived at Luggala where her son Garech Browne had organised a traditional Irish hooley in the converted cottage on the east side of the house's courtyard. Oonagh wore a black hooded Connemara cape while her husband, in an attempt to adapt to his new circumstances, donned an Aran sweater and Tam o' Shanter. Already the differences between the couple were apparent.

OPPOSITE: Despite Miguel Ferreras' aversion to Luggala, Oonagh continued to entertain regularly in the house, with large house parties such as this one at Christmas 1960 when the guests included Lady Frances Eliot, Derek Lindsay, Simon Lennox-Boyd (later Viscount Boyd) whose mother was a Guinness and Desmond Mackey who owned an antique shop in Dún Laoghaire, County Dublin called Curiouser and Curiouser which, it was said, summarised how customers felt after buying something from him.

Luggala Xmas 1960

Simon Lennox Boyd, Francis

Hester Connell Donagh Beatrice Behan
Miguel

Derek Lindsay

Desmond MacRoy

Francis Eliot

Charmian Scott

The Shorter Oxford English
The Shorter Oxford
OXFORD

time she was in her mid-fifties and too old to have any children. That spring, Hearst columnist Aileen Mehle, otherwise known as Suzy Knickerbocker, announced the Ferrerases were planning to become members of the Greek Orthodox Church so that they could adopt two babies from Athens; this report was immediately denied. However, within months, Oonagh, who always adored children, had adopted twins, a boy and a girl whom she had found in Mexico the previous year when visiting John Huston; the director was then making *The Night of the Iguana* with Richard Burton, Ava Gardner and Deborah Kerr, the last of these married to screenwriter Peter Viertel. In July 1964 the babies were brought to Paris and given the names Desmond and Manuela.

The adoption wasn't sufficient to save her marriage and within two months of the twins' arrival in Europe, Oonagh informed Ferreras of her intention to seek a divorce, which she obtained before the end of the year, again in Mexico. To this plan her estranged husband acquiesced, perhaps fearing a drawn-out battle with Oonagh could lead to the more dubious

OPPOSITE: Miguel Ferreras's career as a couturier was underwritten by Oonagh and assisted by members of her extended family, such as the Hon. Desmond Guinness, who in 1964 held a fashion show of Ferreras's latest collection in his home, Leixlip Castle. Here the models included Tara Browne's wife Nicki.

ABOVE: In 1961 Oonagh (seen here with her son Tara Browne) paid for Miguel Ferreras to open his own salon in splendid premises on Paris's rue du Faubourg St Honoré. As Ferreras repeatedly pointed out, he thus became the first American couturier in the French capital since Mainbocher more than thirty years before. However, the enterprise was not a success, and with the end of the marriage came the salon's closing.

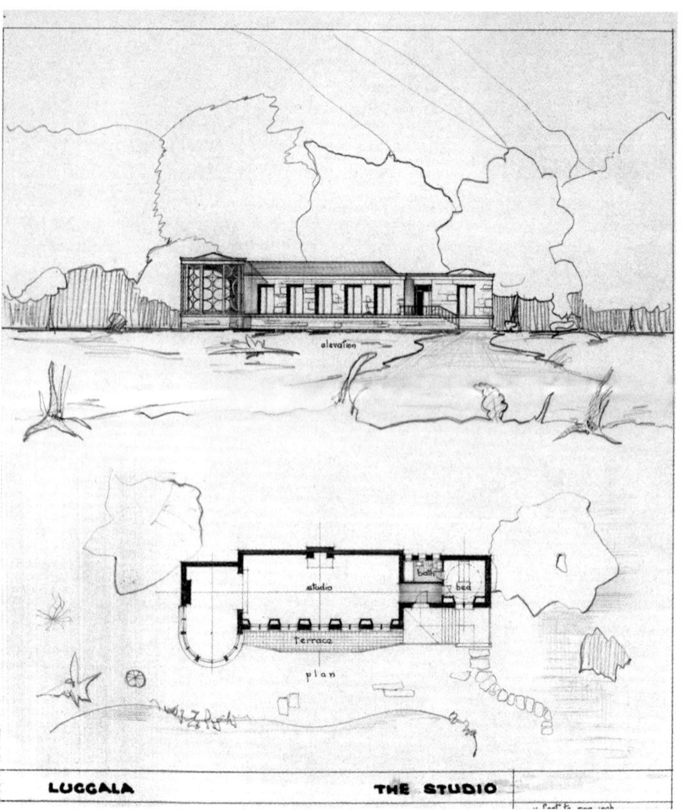

aspects of his past becoming public or because he had already begun a relationship with the woman who in 1965 would become his latest wife, and he her eighth husband: Flor de Oro Trujillo. Eldest surviving child of brutal Dominican Republic dictator Rafael Trujillo, who was assassinated in 1961, she had first married, at the age of 17, her fellow-countryman and legendary playboy Porfirio Rubirosa (who went on to marry, among others, Doris Duke and Barbara Hutton, before dying in a car crash in Paris just a few months after his former wife wed Oonagh's ex-husband). Curiously, not long before, the marriage of his putative brother Joaquin to Cuban widow Elena Santeiro Garcia had also come to end and his divorce was likewise quickly followed by union to another wealthy woman. Miguel Ferreras' marriage to Flor Trujillo lasted seven years. During this time, he regularly declared his intention to open another couture house, courtesy of his latest wife's money, but it never happened. When journalist Nicholas Farrell came across him in 1997, he was living with his fourth spouse on New York's Upper East Side and claimed to be working as a fashion consultant.

As for the Maison Ferreras in Paris, it was briefly maintained by Oonagh; in January 1965 she informed the *International Herald Tribune*'s Hebe Dorsey of her intention to become directrice of the salon. At the start of the following

ABOVE: Soon after returning to Ireland with Miguel Ferreras, Oonagh commissioned architect Alan Hope to come up with designs for a studio to be built at Luggala in which her husband could work. In the end, no studio was constructed, Ferreras preferring to spend as little time in Ireland as possible.

OPPOSITE TOP: One of Tara Browne's closest friends in the late 1950s/early 1960s was Lady Lucinda Lambton, daughter of future Conservative minister Lord Lambton. Godfrey Carey Q.C., hired as Tara's tutor in 1960, remembers that several months later when he and his charge were in New York Tara announced he had to return to London for Lucinda Lambton's coming out party: Carey never saw him again.

OPPOSITE BOTTOM: During her years with Ferreras, Oonagh divided her time between Luggala, where her husband did not enjoy himself, and Paris's Left Bank, where she had an apartment on rue de l'Université. Here the social life was equally frenetic: Godfrey Carey recalls large groups of people dropping by every evening for drinks before the whole group would go out for dinner.

Lucy Lambton
and
Tara Browne
135 Rue de l'université
Paris VII

Miguel Ferreras

Beatrice Behan

Xmas Eve 1962 Luggala

Brendan Behan

Brendan Behan

Lucy

Oonagh Miguel

135 Rue de l'université
Paris VII
February 1961

Lucy

Miguel

Lucy Lambton

Tara Veronique

Veronique

month, a collection was shown created by a 34-year-old designer called Jacques Fougeirol who, it transpired, had been responsible for most of Ferreras' work in the immediately preceding seasons. By the time of the July couture shows, however, the business had closed down and Oonagh's involvement with the fashion world had come to an end. In the same year she legally changed her name so that she could once more be known as Oonagh Oranmore and Browne. Within months her sister Aileen had also divorced her husband, Valerian Stux-Rybar, and in similar fashion reverted back to the name of her previous spouse.

Without a husband and with two small babies, Oonagh began spending more time at Luggala, although the responsibilities of motherhood meant it hosted fewer parties than had once been the case. But there were still occasional high-profile occasions, such as the open-air lunch Oonagh gave for several hundred guests in early July 1965; this was on the day after a ball at Powerscourt held on behalf of the French hospital charity les Petits Lits Blancs and attended by Prince Rainier and Princess Grace of Monaco. Both of them came to Luggala for Oonagh's lunch. 'It was just a big picnic,' Paddy Moloney of The Chieftains later described the occasion. 'The Chieftains played, and Dolly McMahon sang, followed by Leo Rowsome on pipes.'

By now, another generation of musicians was coming to stay at Luggala, brought there by Oonagh's sons from her second marriage, Garech and Tara Browne. Both men had distinctive characters and tastes. But whereas Garech from an early age displayed an interest in Irish traditional music, Tara's taste was more in line with emerging trends in 1960s London, where he lived in a mews house in Eaton Row. Always precocious, from his early teens he was highly sociable and more absorbed with parties than studies; parental efforts to persuade him to attend Eton were unsuccessful, for example, as were attempts at private tutoring.

On 12th November 1963 the *Daily Express*'s William Hickey column carried a story headlined, 'Guinness heir Tara weds in secret – to an Irish farmer's daughter.' The bride was Noreen Ann MacSherry, originally from County Down (where her father Sean farmed) but living for some time in London where at one point she worked as a clerk in a bank. Three years older than her husband (who had turned 18 the previous March), at the time of their wedding, which took place in France, Noreen – always known as Nicki – was six months pregnant; the couple's son, Dorian, was born within days of the *Daily Express* story appearing. A second son, Julian, was born in February 1965.

Even before he married, Tara's social life revolved around London, but in March 1966 it came to Luggala, the venue for a party celebrating his twenty-first birthday. In some respects, the occasion was not unlike a similar event held fifteen years earlier for Oonagh's eldest child, Gay Kindersley. Once more a large marquee was attached to the house and filled with cloth-covered tables and chairs. A long-serving member of staff, Sam Hamilton, the estate manager who had worked for Oonagh since 1938, said a few words of congratulation and, as before, Irish friends and neighbours like Molly Cusack-Smith and the Beits were present.

But so too were guests quite unlike those seen in the house at Gay's party in 1951: the Rolling Stones' Mick Jagger and Brian Jones, the latter's girlfriend, Italian model and actress Anita Pallenberg, John Paul Getty Jr and his future wife Talitha Pol, and other members of the period's fashionable London scene, like Sir Mark Palmer, the Hon. Victoria Ormsby-Gore, designer Bill Willis, antiques dealer Christopher Gibbs, photographer Michael Cooper – whose camera captured much of the weekend – and decorator David Mlinaric, the last of these responsible for embellishing the marquee. Instead of Tommy Kinsman and his Orchestra, the night's main musical entertainment was provided by American rock band The Lovin' Spoonful, which had top 10 UK hits that year with 'Daydream' and 'Summer in the City'. Stir in local names such as sculptor Eddie Delaney and actress Siobhán McKenna and it made for a heady mix. 'As the Liverpool chatter got mixed up with the Irish racing vernacular,' excitedly wrote a reporter for the *Irish Sunday Independent*, 'and as the A.A. man got all the cars safely down the Monte Carlo rally-driveway, I found a taxi driver who was still waiting to be paid three hours after delivering a well-known musician who had been up to Dublin to look at Nelson.' (Nelson's Column, a well-known landmark in the capital, that was shortly afterwards destroyed by an IRA bomb.)

Despite the advent of more relaxed manners in the 1960s, in many ways life at Luggala continued to reflect that of an earlier age. Richard Ryan recalls the first time he and some friends were invited to dinner at the house. 'It could have been an evening in Trollope. Everyone there was in black tie and we didn't know about such things. We were referred to as the Communists from UCD [University College, Dublin] because we were "normal" people, we weren't Anglo-Irish lords...I remember saying sometime around 11 or 11.30, "I don't know what this is all about," strolling down to the lake and plunging in.'

Oonagh continued to employ a full complement of staff, from a chauffeur who drove the bespoke Rolls Royce Silver Wraith ordered by her in 1952 (and still in Luggala), to a chef and assistant in the kitchen, with a number of maids helping in the house. Overseeing them all was butler Patrick Cummins, seconded by Patsy Sheridan, who would later work for Desmond Guinness at Leixlip Castle. Sean Byrne, whose family lived not far away by Lough Dan, was employed at Luggala in 1966 as assistant to then-chef Eddie McNamara, his day beginning at 6.30am when he would have to clean out and light the kitchen range before helping with preparation of breakfast. At 2pm he had an hour's break, during which he would go for a walk in the grounds, after consulting Patrick Cummins to make sure his path did not cross with that of Oonagh. One afternoon, however, he was beside the lake when stopped by a woman in coat and headscarf who engaged him in conversation. Only too late did he realise it was his mistress, who invited Sean to call her Oonagh, 'but Jaysus, I wasn't even supposed to meet her, let alone call her by name.' Worse followed when she insisted he come with her to the house and then join her in the drawing room for a glass of orange juice, especially since the front door was opened for them by Patrick Cummins. Afterwards, 'I wasn't in the door of my room, when Cummins was on top of me like a dog, furious angry and shouting, "What do you think you were doing"?'

Oonagh's circumstances changed once more in the months after Tara's party, as his marriage came to an end. The differences between him and Nicki, not least in their backgrounds and interests, caused a breakdown between the couple. A legal battle then began over custody of their children, Dorian and Julian. This became more acute in October 1966 when the two boys were brought by Tara from London to Luggala for what was supposed to be a ten-day holiday with their grandmother. At the end of this period they 'disappeared'. Nicki Browne travelled to Ireland to find her sons but was unable to locate them, and on her return had the

ABOVE: In August 1963 Oonagh's youngest son Tara Browne married Noreen Ann MacSherry, always known as Nicki. Three years his senior, she came from County Down, where her father Sean farmed. This photograph shows the couple in November 1966 when, contrary to appearances, they had separated and were engaged in an acrimonious dispute over custody of their two sons.

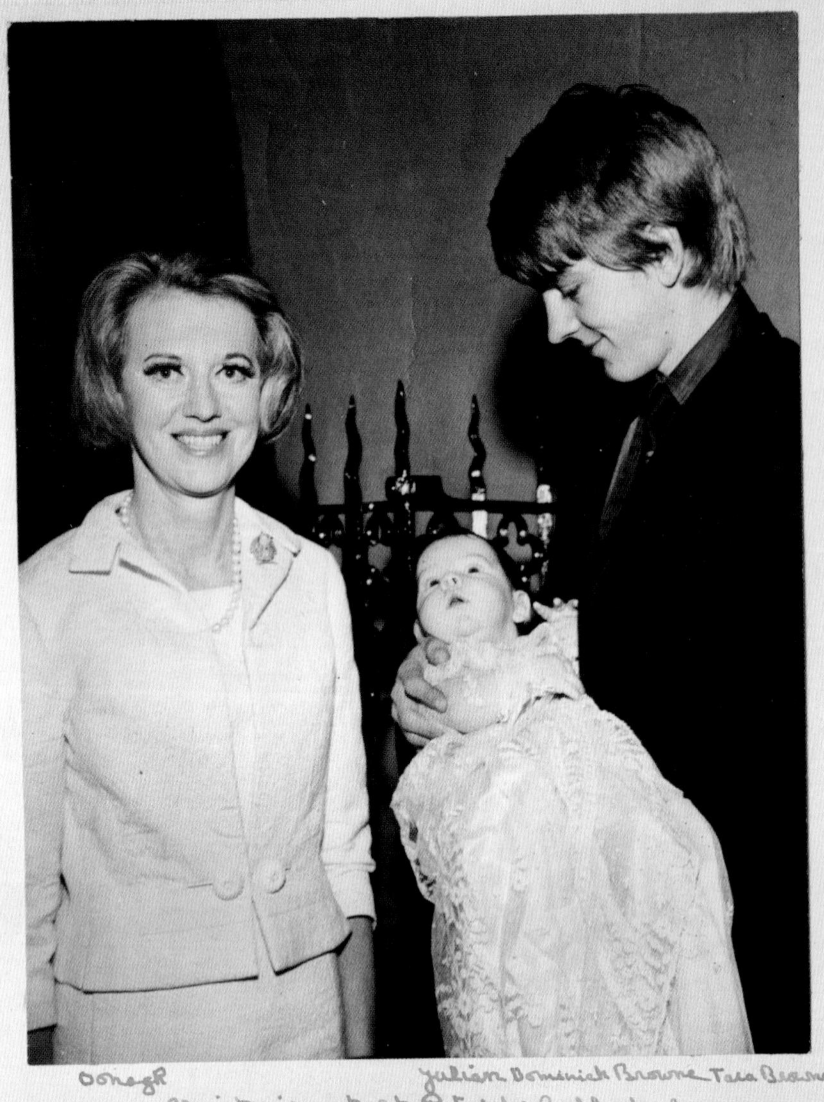

LEFT AND BELOW: At the time of Tara and Nicki's wedding, she was six months pregnant with the couple's first child, Dorian, who was born in November 1963. His brother, Julian, was born in February 1965 and christened in St. Patrick's Cathedral, Dublin. During these years, despite living in London Tara and Nicki often came to stay at Luggala, bringing with them such friends as the Rolling Stones' Brian Jones, his actress girlfriend Anita Pallenberg and poet Roger McGough.

OPPOSITE: The party at Luggala to mark Dorian Browne's christening in December 1963 drew a customarily diverse group to the house. Among those seen in the photographs taken on the day are Lord Dunsany and his daughter the Hon. Beatrice Plunkett, film director Michael Lindsay-Hogg, the 29th (and last) Knight of Glin, Viscount Gormanston and broadcaster and music collector Ciarán Mac Mathúna, whose radio programmes did so much to encourage Garech Browne's interest in traditional Irish music.

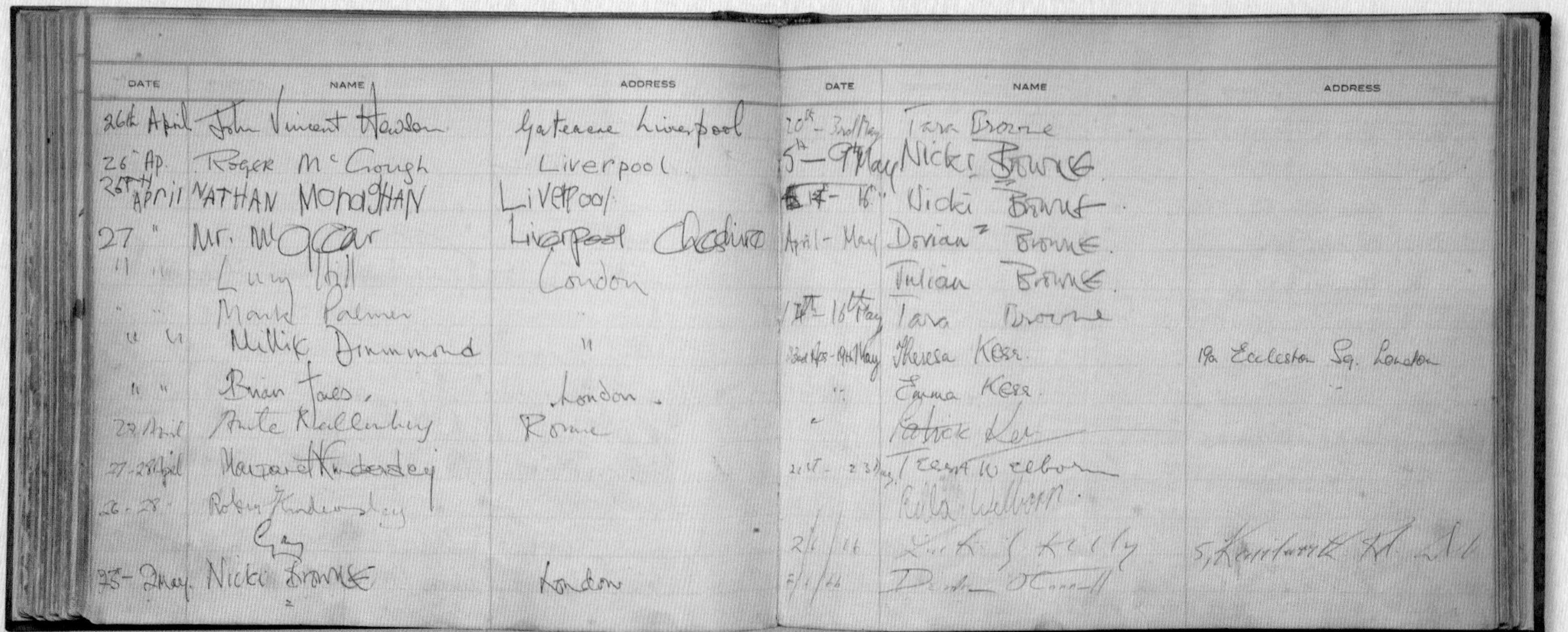

Mr Marcco The Knight of Glin

Randal Dunsany Garech Browne

Mrs Marcco

Nicholas Gormanston Tara Browne

Dorian Brownes Christening party Dec 27th 1963 at Luggala

Seamus O'Kelly

Ciaran MacMathuna Miss Murphy

Beatrice Plunket Caroline Wignell

Niki Browne James Mickey

Deacon Lindsay Mrs Marcco

Dorian Brownes Christening Party Dec 27th 1963

Tara Browne

Oonagh James Mickey

Nicholas Gormanston Randal Dunsany

Michael Lindsay Hogg

Mr Marcco The Knight of Glin Randal Dunsany

Davies

pair made wards of court. However, a petition to the High Court for the return of Dorian and Julian to England was unsuccessful, the judge ruling that Tara, who was neither represented nor present at the hearing, had a right as the boys' father to express his point of view. The case had more than a few echoes of that fought 23 years earlier between Oonagh and Philip Kindersley over their son Gay's future. But this time, before matters could be resolved in court, one of the protagonists was killed.

Earlier in the year, the *Daily Express* carried a brief report that Tara had 'run into a slight snag with his sports car hand-painted in red, green, blue, purple op-art at a cost of £1,000. He has lost his licence for speeding.' He cannot have had the licence back long when, soon after midnight on Sunday, 18th December, Tara, who was known to be a fast driver, crashed his Lotus Elan into the back of a parked van in South Kensington, London; two hours later he was pronounced dead in St. Stephen's Hospital on the Fulham Road. 'He was coming to Ireland that day,' his brother Garech remembered forty years later. 'He was coming for lunch. His children were here at Luggala with my mother. I was in Dublin and I was going to drive down to meet him. Instead, I had to phone my father at seven o'clock in the morning to tell him his son was dead.' Tara's body was brought to Ireland. A funeral service was held at Christ Church, Dún Laoghaire followed by his burial at Luggala, where he lies beside the bodies of his two siblings. The following month a memorial service for Tara took place at St. Paul's, Knightsbridge.

Around the same time, High Court proceedings over the future welfare of Tara's two children were concluded. An agreed statement issued by his wife and mother explained that the judge had ruled that Dorian and Julian should 'remain wards of court until further order, under the care and control of their grandmother, Oonagh, Lady Oranmore and Browne, and said that every effort should be made to enable their mother to play an increasing part in the children's lives.'

At the age of 56, Oonagh was now responsible for four young children, the two she had adopted in 1964 and Tara's sons. Inevitably this had consequences for Luggala, which over the next few years became much more centred on nursery than social life. As Oonagh's photograph albums from this time indicate, the most important gatherings tended to be for a child's birthday party, and the average age of guests dropped accordingly.

At the top of a page in the Luggala visitors' book is a note in Garech Browne's handwriting and dated 1st June 1970. This declares, 'Through the Luggala Estate Company my mother gave me Luggala.' In *Flings over Fences*, an account of Gay Kindersley's colourful life published with his collaboration in 1994, author Robin Rhoderick-Jones states that 24 years earlier the trustees responsible for administering Oonagh's family money 'decided that her financial position, so seriously affected by the disastrous investment in Maison Ferreras, had now deteriorated to such an extent that it would be necessary for her to become a tax exile in France. Worse, she would have to give up Luggala.' Another book published during Oonagh's lifetime, Frederic Mullaly's *The Silver Salver*, observed that 'Thrift – as virtue or vice – was foreign to Oonagh's make-up and her son Tara would later confide to a friend that his mother's overdraft had peaked at somewhere around £650,000 during the 14 years of her second marriage,' that is, whilst she was married to Dom Oranmore.

Whatever the precise truth, it cannot be denied that Oonagh lacked prudence where money was concerned and in her later years was no longer a wealthy woman. In 1970 she retired as director of the Luggala Estates Company, which had been set up in the 1950s to administer the estate: Garech now took her place. Although for the next quarter century she was a regular visitor, she could not call the place her home. She first went to France and bought a house in Antibes called La Tourelle, originally single-storey but greatly extended to

OPPOSITE: In March 1966 Oonagh threw a memorable party at Luggala to mark Tara's twenty-first birthday. The occasion was a curious mixture of the old world and the new: Sam Hamilton, who had worked on the estate since 1938, said a few words on behalf of the staff, and Irish guests included Molly Cusack-Smith and Sir Alfred Beit and his wife Clementine, but also sculptor Edward Delaney and actress Siobhan McKenna. At the same time, the house welcomed a group of Tara's friends from London, such as the Rolling Stones' Mick Jagger and Brian Jones, the latter's girlfriend, Italian model and actress Anita Pallenberg, John Paul Getty Jr and his future wife Talitha Pol. They joined with other members of this group like Sir Mark Palmer, the Hon. Victoria Ormsby-Gore, designer Bill Willis, antiques dealer Christopher Gibbs and decorator David Mlinaric. Music was provided by American band The Lovin' Spoonful, which had top 10 UK hits that year with *Daydream* and *Summer in the City*.

Luggala 1966
Dorian Browne
Tara Browne
Brian Jones

Candida Betjeman

Lady Queensberry

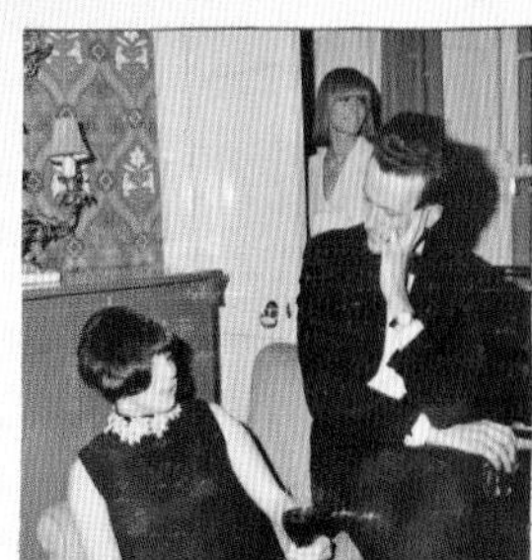

Greg Phillips

WESTERN DAILY PRESS & BRISTOL MIRROR
Bristol.
Cutting from issue dated......19 DEC 1966

GUINNESS HEIR DIES SEEING GIRL HOME

Western Daily Press Reporter

Tara Browne, 21-year-old Guinness heir, died yesterday after his sports car hit a parked van in London.

Nineteen-year-old Suki Potier, of Victoria Grove, Kensington, was in his light blue Lotus Elan.

They had watched television and had dinner together.

Miss Potier's mother said, "Suki is very shocked, but she has no broken bones."

£1 MILLION

Mr. Browne, son of Lord Oranmore and Browne, was to inherit nearly £1,000,000 as his share of a trust fund in 1970.

His mother, Oonagh, Lady Oranmore and Browne, was thought to be in Ireland at the weekend and police were trying to contact.

For the last three weeks he had been staying at the Ritz Hotel, Piccadilly.

His wife, 24-year-old Mrs. Noreen "Nicky" Browne, whom he married secretly in France in 1963, lives in a £20,000 mews house in Eaton Row, Belgravia.

Mrs. Noreen Browne, daughter of a County Down farmer, two months ago started a High Court action for the return of their two sons by her husband.

The children, Dorian, aged three, and Julian, aged one, were made wards of court on October 13.

VANISHED

Next day Mrs. Browne made an emergency application in the High Court. She wanted to know where the children were.

Her husband was said to have vanished with the children in Eire after taking them, with her permission, for a 10-day holiday.

They were said to be ...

... a chance of answering his wife's evidence.

When it was resumed, all the parties were represented by counsel, but neither Mr. Browne nor his mother was present. No statement was issued after the hearing, which was in camera.

The Boston Globe

Guinness Heir Killed; Mod Leader

United Press International

LONDON — Tara Browne, 21-year-old heir to the Guinness Brewery fortune and a leader of London's "Mod" social set, was killed early Sunday when his sportscar smashed into a parked truck in London's South Kensington district.

A 19-year-old girl, Suki Potier, escaped death in the crash and was hospitalized with severe shock.

Browne was the son of Irish Lord Oranmore And Browne and his former wife Oonagh, niece of the 92-year-old Earl of Iveagh. Lord Iveagh is chairman of the brewery firm which produces Guinness Stout.

Tara, who made headlines in 1963 when he secretly wed an Irish farmer's daughter in France, was due to inherit nearly $2.8 million as his share of a trust fund in about four years.

He died in West London's St. Stephen's Hospital two hours after the expensive Lotus Elan sports car he was ...

Dublin. 19 DEC 1966
Cutting from issue dated......

Guinness heir dies after crash

THE HON. TARA BROWNE, a Guinness heir, died in hospital early yesterday after a midnight crash in his sports car in South Kensington, London. His girl passenger, Miss Suki Potier (19), escaped with shock. She was treated at hospital.

The accident happened at the junction of Redcliffe square and Redcliffe gardens. The light blue Lotus Elan car was in collision with a parked van. Mr. Browne (21), was taken to St. Stephen's Hospital, Fulham road, where he died two hours later.

Miss Suki Potier is the younger daughter of Mr. and Mrs. Gilbert George Potier, of Victoria grove, Kensington. Mrs. Potier said yesterday: "My daughter is very shocked, but she has no broken bones." Her daughter was being brought home by Mr. Browne after watching television and having dinner.

A spokesman for the Ritz Hotel, London, said that Mr. Browne had been staying there for the past three weeks.

DUE TO SHARE FORTUNE

Mr. Browne, whose father was Lord Oranmore and Browne, was due to inherit almost £1 million as his share of a trust fund in four years' time. His mother, Oonagh, Lady Oranmore and Browne, was thought to be in Ireland this week-end.

Lord Oranmore and Browne's marriage to Oonagh, Lady Oranmore and Browne was dissolved in 1950. He is 64.

Mr. Browne's wife, Mrs. Noreen Browne (24), daughter of an Irish farmer, started a High Court action in October for the return of her two young sons by her husband. The children, Dorian (3) and Julian (1), were made wards of court on October 13th. The next day Mrs. Browne made an emergency application in the High Court through her counsel. She wanted to know where the children were.

Her husband was said to have vanished in Ireland with the children after taking them with their mother's permission for a ten-day holiday. She had searched for them without success, Mr. Justice Pennycuick was told.

Mr. Browne married his wife in France in 1963. She is the daughter of Mr. Sean MacSherry, a Co. Down farmer. She once worked as a clerk in the Bank of England. They lived in a mews house in Eaton row, Belgravia. Mrs. Browne, known as "Nicky", still lives there.

Mr. Browne, a car enthusiast, had run sports models since he was in his teens.

The Hon. Garech Browne said in Dublin last night that as a result of his brother's death a reception by Claddagh Records to launch two new records, which was to have been held in Dublin this evening, ... postponed.

Glasgow. ... 1966

GUINNESS HEIR DIES IN CRASH

TARA BROWNE, 21-year-old heir to a Guinness fortune, is dead. He was killed, probably, in an attempt to save his girl passenger.

His 110-mile-an-hour Lotus Elan sports car crashed into the back of a parked van early yesterday.

Tara is believed to have swung the car in the last seconds before the impact to protect 19-year-old model Suki Potier. She escaped uninjured

Two hours later, in St. Stephen's Hospital, London, the battle to save the life of Tara was finally lost.

Too shocked

He died with everything to live for . . . days after talking of his hopes of a reconciliation with his wife, 24-year-old Nicky

Suki, too shocked to talk of the crash, was given sedatives yesterday at her home in Knightsbridge. Her father Mr. Gilbert Potier, said: "He saved my daughter's life, I am convinced of that.

"It appears that he swung the car in an attempt to save Suki from the full force off the crash.

"It was a very gallant act. It's tragic it should have cost him his life."

TARA BROWNE . . . he would have inherited £1,000,000.

Tara, mop-haired, controversial, a friend of top pop singers, was due to inherit £1,000,000 when he was 25. He crashed in South Kensington while driving Suki home from a dinner party.

Tara, whose marriage to 24-year-old Nicky Macsberry broke up earlier this year, met Suki about three weeks ago.

His children, three-year-old Dorian and Julian, 18 months, have not been told that their father is dead.

Changed plans

On Saturday he was due to fly to the home of his mother, Oonagh Lady Oranmore and Browne, in Ireland's Wicklow Hills, to visit them.

At the last moment he changed his plans.

A maid at his mother's home said: "He has been coming to visit the children nearly every week-end since they arrived here."

Rolling Stone guitarist Brian Jones, a friend of Tara, wept as he said: "I am numbed. It's ghastly. He was so full of life."

● *BOY WHO HAD EVERYTHING —Centre Pages.*

● *"SUKI" POITER . . . suffering from shock.*

LA TRIBUNE
10, place Jean-Jaurès

L'héritier des Brasseries Guinness se tue en voiture

Tara Brown, 21 ans, héritier de la fortune des brasseries Guinness (il devait recevoir dans quatre ans sa part de la succession, soit près de un million de livres sterling), s'est tué dimanche, à l'aube, dans un accident de la circulation, sa voiture de sport ayant percuté un camion à l'arrêt dans le quartier de Chelsea, près de Londres.

La jeune fille qui l'accompagnait a été blessée et transportée à l'hôpital.

On December 22nd the people who have signed their names on this page had lunch here at Woodtown before going to Tara's funeral. Garech Browne.

Oranmore and Browne
Sally Oranmore & Browne
Geoffrey Browne
Dominick Browne
Sara Browne
Gerard Campbell
Suki Potier
Serena Gillilan
Glen Kidston
Victoria Ormsby Gore
David Mlinaric
Martin Wilkinson

ABOVE: Always an impetuous driver, in the early hours of Sunday 18th December 1966, Tara crashed his Lotus Elan into the back of a parked van in South Kensington. Amazingly his passenger, model Suki Potier, escaped with bruises and shock, but Tara was not so lucky: two hours after the accident he was pronounced dead in St. Stephen's Hospital on the Fulham Road. His body was brought back to Ireland and a funeral service held at Christ Church, Dún Laoghaire. The following month a memorial service took place at St Paul's, Knightsbridge, attended by the members of his London circle of friends.

OPPOSITE: Following his funeral, Tara's remains were brought to Luggala and laid to rest beside the temple on the shores of Lough Tay. Here he joined his unnamed baby brother and his half-sister Tessa Kindersley.

accommodate its new owner, the four children in her care, her staff and, as ever, her many guests. Here she lived until the late 1970s, after which the household had a peripatetic few years, including some time in Bermuda before settling for a while in Switzerland. Oonagh then moved again, to Guernsey but it was not a success. In November 1988 she wrote plaintively to Madeleine Mottuel, 'I never loved England and Guernsey I hate. I have of course lead [sic] a very spoilt life of luxury and do not like the change.' In 1993 she decided to return to Ireland, buying a house close to Enniskerry, County Wicklow. The homecoming was not what she had hoped. So much had changed, she had long ceased to be chatelaine of Luggala and her financial resources were limited. Within two years she made the decision to go back to Guernsey but this last move never happened. On the evening of 2nd August 1995, Oonagh died. She had picked up the telephone intending to call her sister Aileen but not yet dialled the number when her heart failed. She was found, mouthpiece still in her hand, by Gretta Fanning, who had loyally worked for Oonagh since 1961. 'She was a wonderful person,' says Gretta, 'Very kind and very thoughtful. We had wonderful times over the years.'

On 5th June 1997 Oonagh's ashes were scattered on the lake at Luggala. She has no tombstone: Luggala itself is her most fitting memorial.

ABOVE: In June 1970 Oonagh retired as a director of the Luggala Estates Company, which she had established in the 1950s; her place was taken by Garech Browne. Although regularly returning to Luggala for the next quarter century, she could no longer call it her home. Instead she moved to the south of France and bought a house in Antibes called La Tourelle. Originally single-storey, the building was greatly extended to accommodate its new owner, the four young children in her care and her staff as well as her very many guests. Here she remained until the late 1970s.

RIGHT: Oonagh (on the extreme right) in old age with some of her family. Included in this picture are her two adopted children Desmond and Manuela, as well as her son Tara's two children, Dorian and Julian, who she raised after their father's death, Robin Kindersley, Gay and Philippa Kindersley. Garech Browne stands immediately behind his mother and to his right is Gretta Fanning, who worked for Oonagh until the latter's death.

LEFT: The three Golden Guinness Girls in old age, at a party to celebrate Aileen's ninetieth birthday in May 1994. She sits on the left, Oonagh in the middle and Maureen to the right. This was the last occasion on which they were photographed together, Oonagh dying the following year, Maureen in 1998 and Aileen in 1999.

BELOW: After living overseas for the previous 23 years, Oonagh revisited to Ireland in 1993, living in a house outside Enniskerry, County Wicklow. This had the advantage of being close to Luggala which she continued to visit until the end of her life. Here she is seen with her son Garech two months before she died. In a small notebook Garech recorded his mother's death on the evening of 2nd August 1995. She was found, telephone mouthpiece in her hand, by Gretta Fanning, who had loyally worked for Oonagh since 1961.

2nd August 1995
My Mother Oonagh
Lady Oranmore
and Browne
died today. She
had been here
at Luggala last
Sunday. She died
swiftly after a glass
of Horlicks having picked
up the telephone to ring her
sister Aileen the telephone was
still in her hand but she
had not got through. G. de B. PTO

The Legend of Tara Browne

Whenever Tara Browne's name is mentioned – in print, in conversation, on the internet – so is that of John Lennon. The reason: Lennon's song, 'A Day in the Life', the final track on the Beatles' 1967 album, *Sgt. Pepper's Lonely Hearts Club Band*, was inspired by the death of Tara after his Lotus Elan crashed on the corner of London's Redcliffe Square and Redcliffe Gardens in the early hours of 18th December 1966. The following month, having read a report of the coroner's verdict on the accident in the *Daily Mail* of 17th January 1967, Lennon was inspired while sitting at his piano to write the song's opening verse:

'I read the news today, oh, boy/About a lucky man who made the grade...I saw the photograph/He blew his mind out in a car/He didn't notice that the lights had changed/A crowd of people stood and stared/They'd seen his face before/Nobody was really sure if he was from the House of Lords.'

The lyrics are certainly not a straightforward account of the December car crash; in 1968 Lennon told Hunter Davies 'I didn't copy the accident. Tara didn't blow his mind out. But it was in my mind when I was writing that verse.' Nevertheless here is evidence of the impact Tara made during his short life, and the interest he continues to rouse more than 45 years after his death.

In October 1966, two months before the crash, Tara was the subject of a seven-minute documentary made for the French television programme Melody Variétés. Literally following a day in his life, the film begins with two acknowledgements on the part of Tara, tall and slim, with a mop of blond hair and speaking in French throughout. He states that his father is a peer 'et c'est une aide pour moi,' and that he gets up in the morning very late. Interestingly, the living room walls of his London mews house, on Eaton Row, are shown covered with the same Pugin paper used for the drawing room at Luggala. Then follows a review of Tara's various interests: the garage where he sold Lotus cars, driving his customised AC Cobra – its body psychedelically painted for him by Pop Art collective Binder, Edwards & Vaughan (BEV)– his association with the Robert Fraser Gallery on Duke Street (a section of the film in which Marianne Faithfull appears), and also his involvement in men's fashion, not least the shop Dandie Fashions at 161 King's Road which he co-owned. Clothes, like cars, were amongst Tara's greatest passions. In March 1966 the French men's magazine *Adam* had carried a photograph by Willy Rizzo of Tara and four of his friends, Christopher Gibbs, Sir Mark Palmer, the Hon. Julian Ormsby-Gore and Viscount Gormanston, all extravagantly dressed in the period's high fashion, with the caption 'Ces yéyés siégeront à la Chambre des Lords' (best translated as 'These hip young men are going to sit in the House of Lords').

The image conveyed by the French film is of a shy yet confident young man, slightly disconcerted by the attention but not averse to it. That impression is confirmed by surviving friends. Writing in *The Spectator* in August 2011, Hugo Williams remembered Tara at the age of fifteen as being 'two years younger than me but years ahead in sophistication and fun, dealing jokes, insults and ridiculous boasts from an inexhaustible deck like a child delightedly playing snap. In his green suits, mauve shirts with amethyst cuff-links, his waves of blonde hair, brocade ties and buckled shoes, smoking menthol cigarettes (always Salem) and drinking Bloody Marys, he was Little Lord Fauntleroy, Beau Brummell, Peter Pan, Terence Stamp in *Billy Budd*, David Hemming in *Blow-Up*.' Williams described Tara as 'barely literate, having walked out of dozens of schools. He smoked and drank but he hadn't got on to joined-up handwriting yet.' Formal education held no interest for him, as Godfrey Carey can confirm. Hired as Tara's tutor in Paris in February 1960, Carey would wait for his pupil every morning at 9am, but rarely saw him for at least another two hours. Soon it would be time for lunch, followed by a siesta, after which plans would get underway for the evening's social activity. Towards the end of Carey's four-month stint, the entire household flew to New York to stay at the Drake Hotel; after just a few days, Tara announced he had to return to London for Lucinda Lambton's coming out party. Carey never saw him again.

As Irish writer Paul Howard noted on the fortieth anniversary of Tara's death, 'He was part of a different aristocracy . . . the counter-culture that built up around the art and music scene in a city in the throes of massive social and cultural change.' The soundtrack to the Melody Variétés documentary is provided by George Harrison's Indian-inspired song 'Love You To', released on the Beatles' *Revolver* album in August 1966. Tara described the Beatles as being 'les rois' of the English music scene, but he also knew the members of several other bands, including the Rolling Stones and The Lovin' Spoonful, the latter playing at his 21st birthday party. When Tara crashed his car on 18th December 1966, his passenger was a model called Suki

ABOVE: Tara Browne's 21st birthday party at Luggala in March 1966 attracted a large number of guests from his social circle in London. Their stay was recorded by photographer Michael Cooper, remembered today for his many images of the Rolling Stones and for the cover image of the Beatles' 1967 album *Sgt Pepper's Lonely Hearts Club Band*. Here he caught some of the party's visitors to County Wicklow, including the Stones' Brian Jones and his then girlfriend Anita Pallenberg, John Paul Getty II and his future wife Talitha, designer Bill Willis and Tara's wife, Nicki.

Potier, who suffered only minor injuries. Not long afterwards, she became involved with the Rolling Stones' Brian Jones, with whom Tara had been having a drink before he left to collect Suki for dinner. 'I'm numbed,' Jones announced after being told of the accident. 'It's ghastly...he was so full of life.'

One of the more bizarre internet rumours concerning him first emerged in the United States in the late 1960s. This proposes that Tara did not die when his Lotus crashed; instead it was Paul McCartney who was killed that year and then secretly buried, his features transposed onto those of Tara, who has forever after been playing the part of McCartney. The two men certainly knew each other: in his 1997 authorised biography, *Many Years from Now*, McCartney recalled that he first took LSD in Tara's mews house. And Tara stayed in the Liverpool home of McCartney's father in December 1965 when he and McCartney went out riding mopeds and the latter crashed, cutting his lip and chipping a tooth. This incident may be the origin of the Tara/McCartney swap story.

'A Day in the Life' was not the only commemoration of Tara: Irish composer Seán Ó Riada, a friend of Garech Browne, wrote a piece to the words of Hans Arp called *In Memoriam Tara Browne*, while The Pretty Things' 1967 album *Emotions* included a song called 'Death of a Socialite' featuring the lines 'People, they see you and love you without knowing what your name is/It might be one day or two days but never for always.' When John Paul Getty Jr and his wife Talitha had a son in June 1968, they named the baby Tara, as did Keith Richards and Anita Pallenberg their own short-lived second boy, who was born and died in 1976. But the Beatles' song remains the best-known association with Tara Browne. On 18th June 2010 John Lennon's hand-written lyrics to 'A Day in the Life' were sold by Sotheby's in New York to a private collector for $1.2 million.

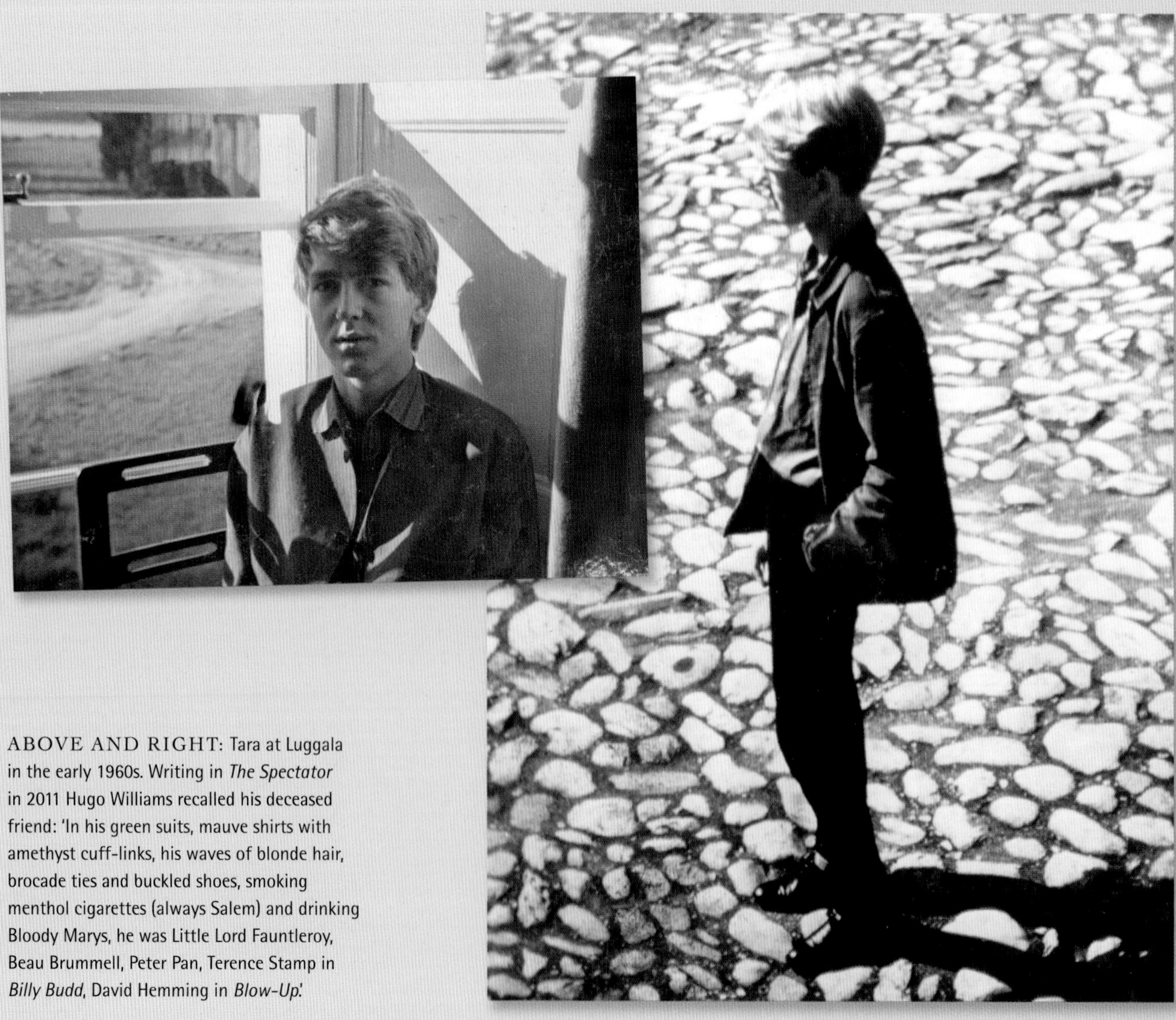

ABOVE AND RIGHT: Tara at Luggala in the early 1960s. Writing in *The Spectator* in 2011 Hugo Williams recalled his deceased friend: 'In his green suits, mauve shirts with amethyst cuff-links, his waves of blonde hair, brocade ties and buckled shoes, smoking menthol cigarettes (always Salem) and drinking Bloody Marys, he was Little Lord Fauntleroy, Beau Brummell, Peter Pan, Terence Stamp in *Billy Budd*, David Hemming in *Blow-Up*.'

ABOVE AND RIGHT: Tara's bedroom, the Double Shamrock Room, at Luggala, left as it was during his lifetime. The only addition is the collection of uillcann pipes belonging to his brother Garech, stored on the bed. On the walls are hung a series of photographs and paintings of Tara made during his short life. Among these is picture of Tara painted by Gilberte Brassaï, wife of Hungarian-born photographer George Brassaï. The couple lived in Paris and were friends of Oonagh and her children.

CHAPTER FIVE

Garech Browne: 'Custodian of this valley of Luggala'

John Montague tells a story of being in north Belfast with Garech Browne. It was several decades ago during the time of the Troubles and the two men unexpectedly found themselves caught up in the midst of an Orange Order parade. Garech observed the event with interest and with a running commentary that included such remarks as, 'They look a bit like an army of Laurel and Hardys, yes? But I do think that some of the music is rather interesting. Didn't James Galway play the flute in one of these bands?'

It will be appreciated that the pronouncements were not well received by those closest to the speaker, especially given his appearance: 'With his classic Aran gansey roped by a lovely Aran crios, or embroidered sash, and his long Cavalier hair bound by a velvet ribbon, Garech would have stood out in any company.' Inevitably a member of the jostling crowd decided to confront him, querying his patriotic credentials and pointing out that the Orangemen marching past were 'the Queen's men'.

'The Queen?' responded Garech. 'Do you know her? I've met the Queen,' he then continued. 'I must say, I found our conversation a bit boring. John here says that she actually reads T.S. Eliot, but I did not find that we had much in common. What did you think of her?' To which his interrogator had no response, and the group that had gathered in happy expectation of trouble melted away, leaving the two friends 'in a kind of charmed circle'.

The anecdote tells a great deal about Garech Browne, the distinctiveness of his character and appearance, the indifference to public opinion, and the assumption, which has sometimes been interpreted as arrogance or naïveté, that everyone else's outlook and background are the same as his own. This is far from being the case.

The Hon. Garech Domnagh Browne was born on 25th June 1939 in Glenmaroon, the Dublin residence of his maternal grandparents. The first child of Dom and Oonagh Oranmore and Browne, he was christened in St. Patrick's Cathedral (restored by an earlier Guinness) and given seven godparents including his grandmother, his aunts the Marchioness of Dufferin and Ava and the Hon. Mrs Mordaunt Smith, as well as Viscounts Elveden and Ridley, and the Marchese Marconi.

As a result of war breaking out within two months of his birth, Garech's early years were spent between Castle MacGarrett and Luggala. His first visit to the latter, he says, occurred when he was about a week old: 'My father brought me here and showed me to Sam Hamilton in the gate lodge, but of course I don't remember that.' The greater part of his time, however, was passed at Castle MacGarrett, with excursions during the early part of each summer to Ballyconneally where his mother had a cottage, later sold to her sister Aileen Plunket.

Garech's formal education was, by his own choice, limited. Around the age of ten he went to Castle Park, a preparatory school in the Dublin suburb of Dalkey. Not long afterwards, his parents formally separated and then divorced. 'My father sent for me and asked who I wanted to live with, him or my mother. I said my mother.' As a result, he began to spend more time at Luggala, since the estate belonged outright to Oonagh.

Aged 13, Garech passed the Common Entrance examination on his second attempt. However, by that time he had lost his place at Eton so he was sent to Institut Le Rosey, the international boarding school in Switzerland where his contemporaries included the present Aga Khan as well as another Irish boy, Thady Wyndham-Quin, future 7th (and last) Earl of Dunraven. It did not take Garech long to realise he disliked his new surroundings. 'I think I began to realise schools were run like prisons,' he says, 'and I didn't want to spend my life in one. Also the only things I wanted to learn – music, literature, real history – they didn't teach.' In his second term at Le Rosey, he sent himself a telegram which read, 'Unforeseen circumstances. Come home immediately. Your loving mother.' This was presented to the school authorities and a flight to London duly organised.

OPPOSITE: A watercolour study of Garech Browne by his friend, the Anglo-Belgian artist Anthony Palliser. This bears the inscription 'For Garech on his birthday, a first sketch for the portrait...25.6.89'. The finished painting can be seen on page 7.

for Gareth
on his birthday
a first sketch
for the portrait…
26.6.89.

LEFT: Garech Browne as a child at Glenmaroon by Muriel Brandt (1909–1981). Born in Belfast, Brandt later moved to Dublin and became a member of the Royal Hibernian Academy. She painted portraits of many notable figures in Ireland during the 1940s and '50s.

Garech was next sent to Bryanston in Dorset, on his cousin Caroline's husband Lucian Freud's advice. His time at this establishment was equally brief, since once again he organised an unscheduled departure, leaving in a taxi, the driver of which put him up for the night. 'From his house I frantically tried to ring my mother but I couldn't get hold of her; she was staying with Mr Robert Kee in a hotel in Brighton.' After spending a further week with friends, at the insistence of his father Garech returned to Bryanston to apologise to the headmaster, Thorold Coade, for his unannounced exit: 'His first words to me were, "Didn't you know it was against the school's rules to take a taxi?"'

Efforts to educate Garech now came to an end. Indeed, the only official qualifications he has ever obtained is a licence to drive horse cabs and motor cars. When younger, one of his enthusiasms was the acquisition of old carriages, of which he built up an impressive collection – stagecoach, brougham, sidecar, wagonette, Victoria, gig and so forth. 'I drive them for pleasure,' he told Gloria MacGowran in 1977, 'but also hire them out to private individuals or for films.' John Montague recalled that in the 1960s Garech could be seen 'cantering through Dublin, perched high upon the coachman's box with his long whip'. During that time, Terence Connealy described Garech as 'elegantly archaic' yet completely serious when speaking of his carriage collection, and recalled an incident when he was rebuked by a hotel doorman for tethering his horse and brougham to an adjacent lamppost. 'Well,' enquired Garech, 'who is going to hold the reins while I have a drink?'

Garech, says artist Anne Madden, 'is totally uninstitutionalised, completely and wholly due to the fact that he never really

went to school.' Aged fifteen, he moved to Paris where his mother had an apartment. There he took a course in French civilisation at the Sorbonne while studying the French language at the Alliance Française, 'where I met a very nice Irishman who was a friend of Samuel Beckett'. The teenage Garech soon began to attract attention, not least because of his unusual appearance, which included hair longer than the era's customary length. 'I've hated barbers since I was at Castle Park,' he says, shuddering at the memory of 'clippies and hair down the back of one's neck'. Was he aware that he stood out? 'Probably, but it never bothered me.' Accompanied by Garech, John Montague once went to visit an elderly aunt in hospital. 'Looking with exhausted, rheumy eyes at my long-haired friend, she clasped my hand and murmured: "Who is that lady with you"?' Similarly Paddy Moloney remembers his initial encounter with Garech, at a music session in Tulla, County Clare in 1956. 'I thought he was a girl at first', Moloney told author John Glatt more than 40 years later. 'He had long hair, which was very unusual in the 1950s, and a babyface. But then of course I heard him speak and he had a very low voice. It was very strange.'

ABOVE: The teenage Garech, already firmly establishing his distinctive appearance. At a time when conformity in dress was the norm, he opted to wear items of Irish clothing like the Aran jumper seen in these photographs. Although not yet in a ponytail, his hair was also much longer than was customarily the case for men in the 1950s.

ABOVE: Garech dressed to drive one of his American carriages. The only official qualification he has ever obtained is a cabbie's licence to allowed him to drive for hire. It was number 99. John Montague recalls that in the 1960s Garech could regularly be seen 'cantering through Dublin, perched high upon the coachman's box with his long whip.'

OPPOSITE: 'Portrait of a Boy' – the teenage Garech painted by Lucian Freud in 1956. Three years earlier Freud had married Garech's cousin Lady Caroline Blackwood and the couple were regular visitors to Luggala. However, the marriage ended in 1957 when Blackwood moved to the United States; she and Freud divorced the following year.

From 1956 onwards Garech began to spend more time in Dublin, where he rented a mews house in Quinn's Lane, behind St. Stephen's Green. 'I lived on £10 a week,' he recalls. 'The rent was £5 a week and I lived on the rest.' In Ireland his idiosyncratic mien and preference for wearing traditional Irish clothing like Aran sweaters and crios – a hand-woven belt originally worn by Aran islanders – attracted even more notice than had been the case in Paris: on at least one occasion he was physically assaulted in a bar. 'Some felt,' explained Terence Connealy in March 1970, 'that the dreamy-eyed pint-sipping Garech whose wardrobe ranges from dun gansey with fawn slacks crossed by a crios to Edwardian topcoats and ruffled Regency blouses, was having them on.' Garech's response was to remark, 'No hard feelings to those pugilists who seemed to think I was slumming, but really it was a bit rough to have one's good intentions doubted so violently.'

On initial acquaintance, his dress and manner have sometimes proven rebarbative. Director John Boorman recalls that when he first met Garech in 1970, 'I thought him repulsive, he seemed so stand-offish and snooty, that was my first impression.' But on the second occasion the two men saw each other, 'I was very intrigued by him and we became friends.' Similarly, in his 2001 memoir *Company*, John Montague remembered the first time he encountered Garech, walking down the street with Brendan Behan: 'Before glimpsing him, I heard his haughty, port wine voice – a voice that resonated with Ascendancy privilege – which instantly got my Gaelic hackles up. But I was gradually forced to realise that underneath that straw-coloured thatch, and behind that Lord Snooty baby face, lay a real if untrained intellect, and considerable staying power.' Garech has often been bemused to discover his outward form misinterpreted as an attempt to shuck off or conceal his origins. As Eamon Delaney, son of Garech's old friend Edward Delaney, has explained, 'He hadn't rejected his background outright – far from it – but combined the aristocratic and the native, so that these Yeatsian polarities could truly integrate and flower.'

'I'm a shy man who likes attention,' says Garech, But he is also a man undeterred by the possibility that the attention his appearance or his activities receive might be hostile. His interest in Irish music has often inspired bafflement, even antagonism. In the mid-1960s the politician Erskine Childers, who had grown up not far from Luggala at Glendalough

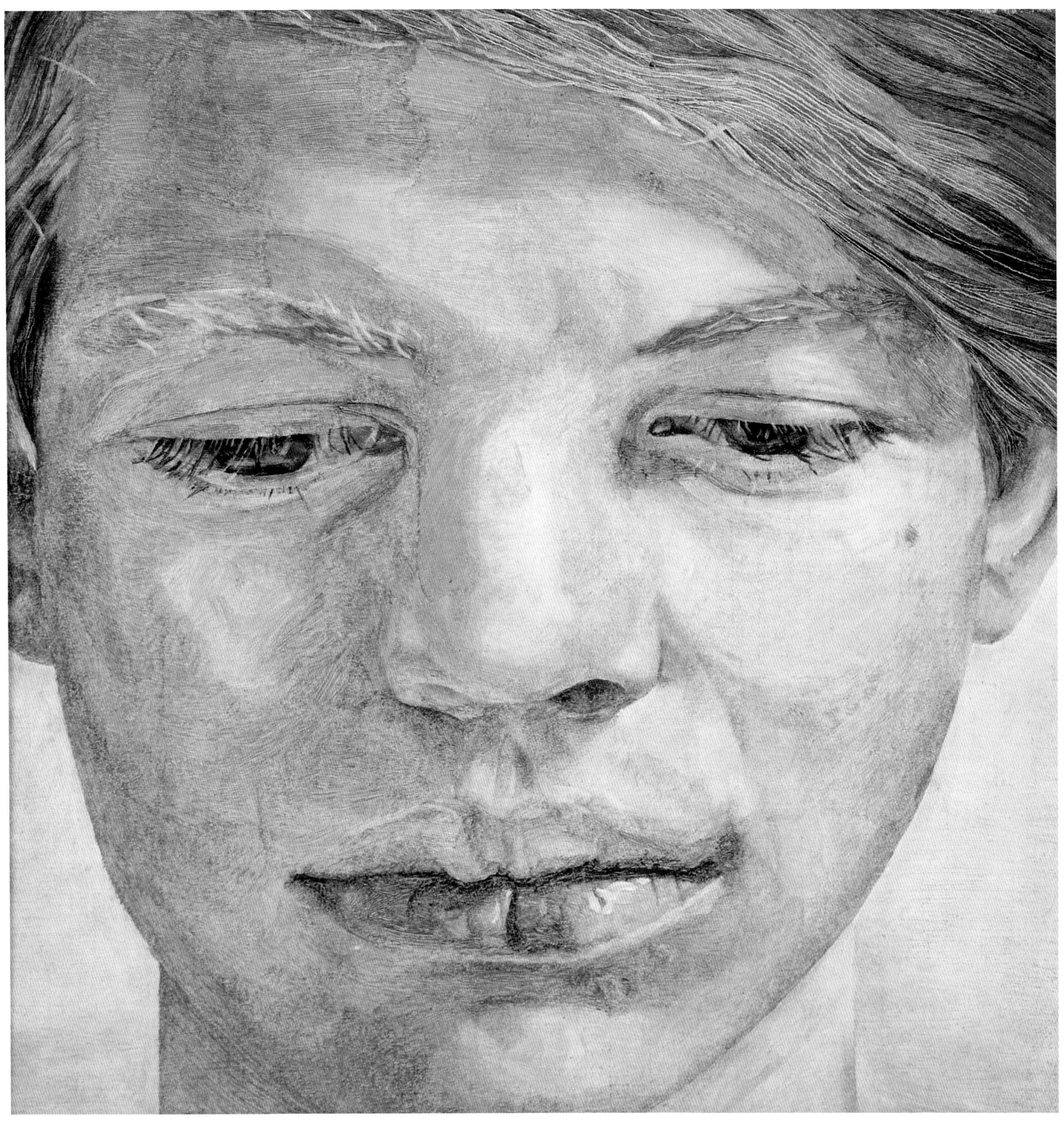

ABOVE: The young Garech at Luggala with an Irish harp. From childhood onwards he has loved the country's traditional music and played a key role in its revival. 'When I was seven,' he remembers, 'I was given a radio at Castle MacGarrett and whenever music came on I'd be found leaping around my bedroom when I was supposed to be asleep hours earlier.'

House and would be elected President of Ireland in 1973, spoke for many of his fellow citizens when he asked why Garech wanted to issue recordings of 'squealing pipes and old women wailing songs by the hearth-side when it's an image of a modern Ireland we wish to present to the world'. It was thought in some quarters that Garech's involvement in the revival of Irish traditional music was retrograde and self-indulgent, the hobby of a rich man likely to be dropped as soon as it no longer held his attention. Few people appreciated that, on the contrary, his engagement with this music was lifelong and had originated in his Mayo childhood. The first song he ever performed, aged about four, was the traditional air *Three Lovely Lassies from Bannion*. This was originally sung by Delia Murphy whose father owned Mount Jennings, an estate next to Castle MacGarrett. Her grandson is uilleann piper Ronan Browne whose father, Dr Ivor Browne, was one of the founders of Claddagh Records. Ronan Browne remembers first meeting Garech in July 1987 at an annual traditional music festival, the Willie Clancy Summer School, held in Miltown Malbay, County Clare. 'At the end of the night we were all in Ambrose Kelly's pub in Mullagh. It went on very late and about two o'clock in the morning the guards [police] came into the pub. Knowing the lie of the land, I dragged Garech out through a window and we hid in the nettles till the guards had gone. Then we went back inside and carried on till daylight.'

Contrary to what might be thought, given his background, Garech's interest in Irish traditional music was never that of a dilettante or dabbler. 'I learnt huge amounts from him – and still do,' says Ronan Browne. 'His knowledge is deep and firmly held; he has a grasp of the minutiae of Irish music.' Garech's accumulation of knowledge on the subject began early. 'When I was seven,' says Garech, 'I was given a radio at Castle MacGarrett and whenever music came on I'd be found leaping around my bedroom when I was supposed to be asleep hours earlier. You have to remember that around 150 people worked on the estate and many of them played music...Tom Kirrane was the Irish teacher at Ballindine [a village immediately south of Castle MacGarrett] and he'd take me all over the place and we'd look for things and people who played music.'

In 1955 broadcaster Ciarán Mac Mathúna began presenting his weekly Irish music programme *A Job of Journeywork* on Raidió Éireann, and Garech was at once an avid listener. He took to visiting local towns in the vicinity of Castle MacGarrett such as Craughwell, County Galway

ABOVE: Garech photographed in the Drake Hotel, New York in May 1964 with his long-standing friend Viscount Gormanston. Bearer of the oldest vicomital title in Britain or Ireland, Nicholas Gormanston became the 17th Viscount before his first birthday when his father died in action at Dunkirk during the Battle of France, 1940.

Garech Browne: Ireland's Last Dandy

Is there a better – or more gorgeously – dressed man in Ireland than Garech Browne? It seems unlikely since no one else takes as much care over his appearance or over co-ordinating the colour, texture and fabric of his clothes. For all that, Browne is neither vain nor exhibitionistic.

He does not particularly care to have attention drawn to what he is wearing and can seem almost abashed when this occurs. He is far from being a poseur, dislikes the company of those who are merely so and is probably most at ease when least noticed. He can, however, talk eloquently on the history and development of costume and loves to describe each element of his extensive wardrobe.

Garech Browne is a true dandy, not in the rather frivolous sense by which this term is customarily dismissed here, but in the more serious fashion that dandyism has always been understood among the French. Because, curiously enough, although dandies originated in England, they were always better understood in France. Browne would certainly appreciate Balzac's remark in the latter's *Traité de la vie élégante* of 1830 that 'dress consists not so much in the garment as in the way it is worn'. He would also no doubt concur with Baudelaire's argument more than 30 years later that dandies 'all partake of the same character of opposition and revolt... Dandyism is the last splendour of heroism.'

Of all texts published on this subject, the finest is Jules Barbey d'Aurevilly's *Dandyisme*, dating from 1845. While admitting that dandyism 'is almost as difficult a thing to describe as it is to define,' the author noted one primary characteristic 'is always to produce the unexpected, that which could not logically be anticipated by those accustomed to the yoke of rules.' Dandyism, therefore, 'while still respecting the conventionalities, plays with them'.

This perfectly describes Garech Browne's own approach to clothing, which is simultaneously individual and yet conformist. Individual in his fondness for mixing unusual tones and materials, he still complies strictly with what could be construed as old-fashioned rules of correct dressing. He insists, for example, on wearing braces – 'they make your trousers stay up and I find them comfortable, as a matter of fact' – and also always closes his shirt sleeves with cufflinks.

If the colouring of his clothes is original, the cut is not: tradition rules when it comes to tailoring, and he is a stickler for good form in matters of style. But he has no desire to look the same as every other well-dressed man. 'I don't want to be a sheep,' he remarked about his personal mode of dress 20 years ago. 'Very boring to be a sheep.' Having found a style he felt suited him, he has remained loyal to it ever since; he has worn the same beard, albeit grown steadily greyer, for more than two decades and his hair is forever worn tied back by a piece of ribbon.

Having recently celebrated his 60th birthday, Garech Browne says he has always loved good clothing. He remembers being aged 11 when his first suit – a two-tone corduroy number – was made by a tailor called Scott with premises in Dublin's Lincoln Place. In adulthood he chose to follow the example of his father (now aged 97) and late grandfather, and has had his coats and suits made by London tailors Lesley Roberts. His shirts are made by Turnbull & Asser, his shoes by Lobb's. Ties and braces come from a wide variety of sources including Hermes, Charvet and Lanvin.

Whenever his clothing is specifically made for him, he provides the raw materials. These come from various sources, including silk poplin from Egypt, Thai shot silk and heavy raw silk from India. Then there are the traditional Harris tweeds he has bought from the recently deceased Scotswoman Marian Campbell, as well as Irish tweed from Clifden's Ronnie Millar and the Foxford Mills, and báinín from Ó Máille's in Galway. His shoes are made not just from leather but also the skin of sika deer and ostrich and even elephant ears. Buttons, most often of mother-of-pearl, come from The Button Queen in London.

His wardrobe is extensive but consistent; suits tend to be ordered in groups of four or five, and all of them carry the date

THIS PAGE AND OVERLEAF: Garech photographed at Luggala in August 1999. In the picture above he wears an Egyptian silk poplin striped jacket and waistcoat made for him by Lesley & Roberts six years earlier. Overleaf, in the photograph to the left he is wearing a Thai silk jacket and waistcoat with plain Thai silk trousers, all made by Lesley & Roberts in 1986, while to the right, standing inside Luggala's front door, he is dressed in a striped green tweed jacket, the fabric coming from Miller's of Galway, combined with cavalry twill trousers, again all coming from Lesley & Roberts in 1986.

of manufacture inside a breast pocket. In addition, they are without exception immaculately finished and in many cases interchangeable: a waistcoat from one ensemble, for example, is worn with the jacket and trousers from another.

The most striking aspect of Garech Browne's appearance is his fondness for colour. 'I love different shades and not having everything strictly the same,' he remarks by way of explanation for a blue check jacket being thrown over a brilliant yellow waistcoat ('I like waistcoats and always have').

Taking pleasure in colour is a trait of the dandy. It is believed that Beau Brummel retired from the army in 1797 after his appearance at parade in a pale blue tunic with silver epaulettes caused consternation among his superiors. In 1845 Jane Carlyle described the most famous dandy of the day, the Comte d'Orsay, as wearing 'black satin cravat, a brown velvet waistcoat, a brown coat lined in velvet...black trousers.'

This complex intermingling of texture and tone also epitomises Garech Browne's approach to dress. He will wear the finest silk beneath the coarsest tweed, he will allow one pattern to jostle with another for predominance, and is not afraid of striking sartorial notes which on another man might be perceived as discordant. In addition, there is an attention to detail which must usually escape everyone but Browne himself. A late 19th-century French dandy, the Prince de Sagan, used to have his black silk top hat lined in green leather, a small luxury likely to be appreciated only by himself. Similarly, Browne will use the most brilliantly-hued silks inside his suits where they will be seen by his eyes alone. This is the mark of the true dandy. He himself explains, 'You know, in Edo Japan one was not allowed to dress fabulously. Men were completely limited in the colour of their kimonos, so they had brighter shades hidden underneath.'

When Balzac wrote, 'one may become rich, but one is born elegant,' he might have had Garech Browne in mind. He has enjoyed the income to dress well but this does not explain his interest in clothes. After all, there are plenty of even wealthier people in this country who look neither so polished nor stylish as he. Conformity in dress has been a regrettable characteristic of the 20th century male, who rarely ventures outside the strictest palette of sombre shades and those few items of clothing regarded as acceptable. To be original is to invite disapproval. This is why Baudelaire's vision of the dandy as revolutionary is so perceptive. Dandyism is a form of contained rebellion in which certain rules are broken but others strictly obeyed. It is also often a form of aesthetic self-expression, an opportunity to give public voice to private interests.

In Browne's case there is an obvious correlation between his advocacy of Irish traditional dress and Irish traditional music: he not only wears the clothes and cloths of Connemara but also, more than 30 years ago, founded Claddagh Records which has done so much to revive the fortunes of this country's original performance arts. The problem dandyism has faced this century may be summarised by Bertrand Russell's decidedly facile judgement of the politician Anthony Eden: 'Not a gentleman: dresses too well.' What nonsense comments such as this must seem. Garech Browne, on the contrary, shows that it is possible to be a perfect gentleman and a perfect dandy.

This is the text of an article written by the author and originally published in the Irish Times *on 22nd August 1999.*

ABOVE: On the edge of woodland in front of the house stands 'The Good Shepherd', a twelve-feet tall bronze sculpture by Edward Delaney. Born in Claremorris, County Mayo, in 1930, Delaney came from a family which had long worked on the Castle MacGarrett estate. Therefore, although he and Garech only met and became friends in adulthood, they soon discovered many connections and remained close until Delaney's death in 2009.

where Raftery, 19th-century Ireland's famous blind bard, is buried and where 'I found a lot of old men who sang his songs in Irish.' His fascination with the country's ancient cultural traditions, he says, in no way perturbed his parents. 'It didn't bother them in the least. I can't see why it would have done. After all, it wouldn't have been so long since the Brownes of Galway spoke Irish. I bet the first Lord Oranmore spoke it... My father was a close friend of Liam O'Flaherty, my mother subsequently of Brendan Behan and Paddy Kavanagh, and she wore her Galway shawl and petticoat quite frequently.'

The first Lord Oranmore may have spoken Irish, but Garech has struggled to do likewise. There were many native speakers in his family's area of County Mayo, and he heard the language used by the people who worked at Castle MacGarrett. His first attempt to learn, he says, was from his governess Miss O'Callaghan. 'She was from the local area but she didn't teach terribly well. "The fox is on the wall": I couldn't get excited about that even then.' Later, 'I thought I'd pick up Irish in Connemara or on the Aran Islands, but by and large they all spoke English.' In 1970 he made his most serious effort to grasp the language by participating in a five-week course run by Gael Linn, an organisation dedicated to fostering interest in Irish.

'I realised that it wasn't enough to be a patron of folk music and traditional dancing if I didn't know the native tongue.' Ultimately, despite his best efforts, the attempt to master the Irish language was unsuccessful, a consequence perhaps of his earlier abandonment of formal education.

Whatever about language, in relation to Irish music his ear proved intuitive and sound. Around the time he was taking classes in the Sorbonne, Garech paid a visit to Inishmore, one of the Aran Islands off the west coast of Ireland and birthplace of his father's friend Liam O'Flaherty. 'On the boat over, I heard a woman humming and I could tell the tunes were extraordinary. I went over to her, and it was Máire Áine Ní Dhonnchadha, and she was shocked, she'd no idea she was singing. She let me come to hear her where she was staying.' In 1970 his company Claddagh Records would issue *Deora Aille*, an album of Máire Áine Ní Dhonnchadha singing the music of Connemara. 'The great gift of Máire Áine,' wrote John Montague in 2001, 'was as profound as Portuguese fado or Spanish flamenco. She was the custodian of the ancient sean-nós tradition [unaccompanied sung stories], and no one who had heard

ABOVE: Two pages from Garech's visitors' book, featuring a portrait of him by Edward Delaney who can be seen photographed in front of one of his own sculptures. Delaney was responsible for the design of a number of Claddagh Record album sleeves, not least those for the first recordings of The Chieftains: he once boasted that many people bought the LPs for the sleeves and threw away the albums.

ABOVE: Writing in *The Guardian* in November 1966, Benedict Nightingale described Garech Browne as 'a reformed playboy' and ascribed this reform to the establishment of Claddagh Records, after which 'he took to coming into an office of an afternoon' and, according to Nightingale 'became a symbol of resurgent Celtic culture.' Here Garech is seen at one of the Claddagh Records parties of the period.

OPPOSITE: Garech speaking at the launch of a Claddagh Records disc of poems read by Thomas Kinsella, *Fair Eleanor, O Christ Thee Save*, which was released in 1971. On the platform with him are Ruth Ó Riada (widow of the composer Seán Ó Riada) and Cearbhall Ó Dálaigh, who three years later became President of Ireland. Through his advocacy of traditional music, he has done much to encourage links with other countries and is the recipient of the Order of the Cross of Terra Mariana in recognition of his work on behalf of Estonian-Irish cultural relations.

her harsh, powerful voice could forget it. But she had never recorded that voice, nor even sung on the radio: only Garech was able to lure her onto record, clasping her hand in grave sympathy while she sang one of the most esoteric of Ireland's secret songs, "Úna Bhán".'

Over the years ahead Garech would regularly spend time in the west of Ireland listening to musicians and learning from them. The paternal grandmother of Ronan Browne's wife Máire Ní Chonláin was a well-known story-teller, singer and keener at wakes called Cáit Bean Uí Chonláin. Garech visited her in Spiddle, County Galway, in the early 1960s, when he sat on the floor listening to her talking and singing. 'She teased him in Irish because he couldn't understand what she was saying, but she hugely respected him.' On another occasion, the two met at a fleadh ceoil – a traditional music festival – where she bought him a pint. Afterwards, says Ronan, she 'appears to have made much not only of herself, a woman, buying a pint for a man but that she was buying a pint of Guinness for the "heir" to the Guinness fortune!' Garech also took lessons from the country's finest uilleann piper, Leo Rowsome, the first performer to be recorded by Claddagh Records. With regard to his own

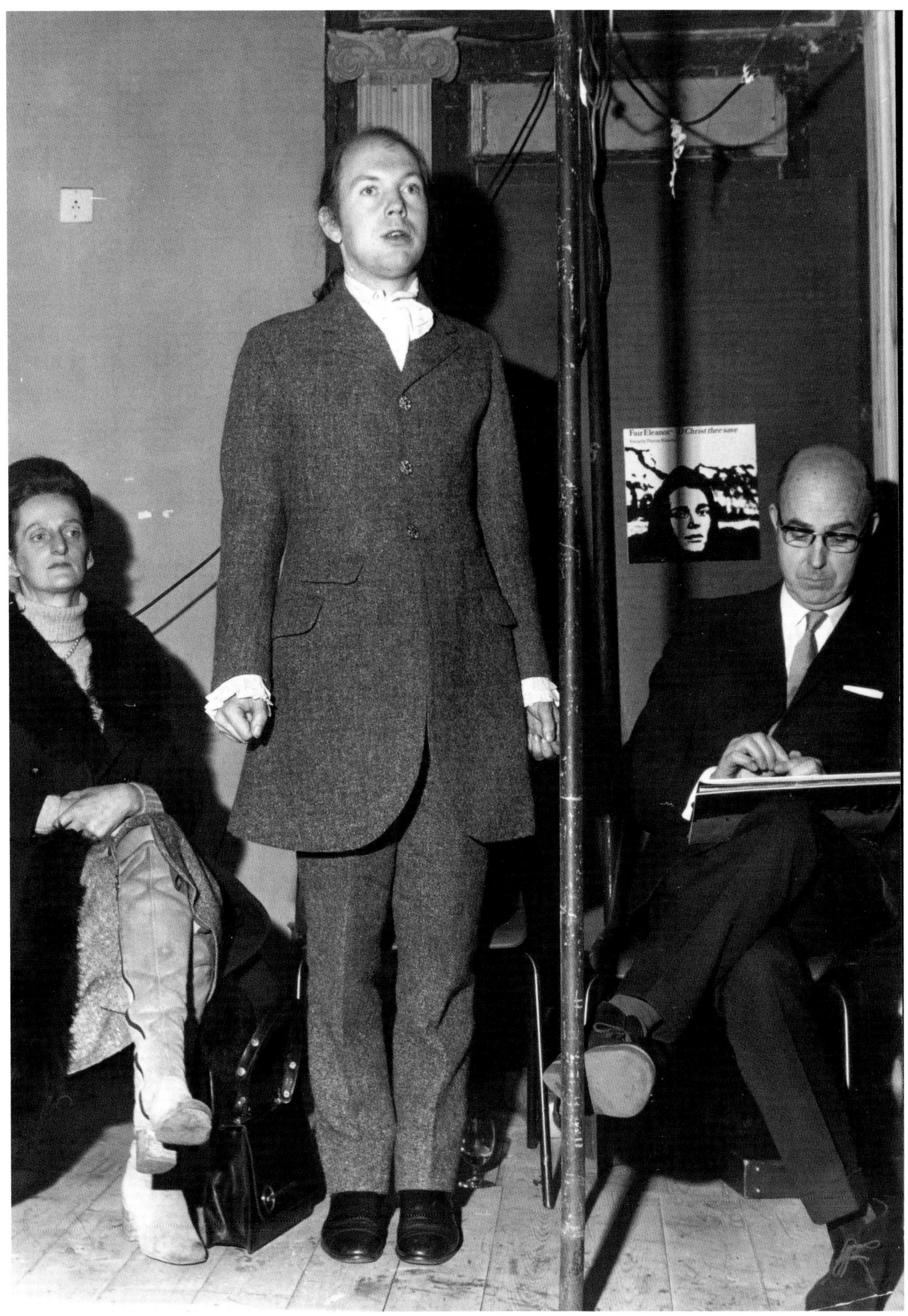
Christ thee save

ABOVE AND RIGHT: Music has always been a central part of Garech's life, and like a chieftain in ancient Gaelic Ireland he relishes live performance by musicians in his house. This, in turn, has attracted many visitors to Luggala over the years, among them actor Dennis Hopper and his then-wife Victoria, long-standing friend Marianne Faithfull, the Rolling Stones's Ronnie Wood who, like Faithfull, lived in Ireland for many years, and actress Charlotte Rampling, seen here dancing with The Chieftains' Paddy Moloney. In 1973 Rampling spent time at Luggala when the estate was used by director John Boorman for the filming of *Zardoz* in which she appeared with Sean Connery.

performance on the pipes, in 1968 Garech said, 'since it became speedily obvious that I wasn't going to become even reasonably competent I quit playing for listening'.

Garech's contribution to the revival of interest in Irish music, at home and overseas, is appreciated and honoured among fellow aficionados. His commitment to supporting Irish music and traditional culture made him that once-common but now rare phenomenon: a patron of art. 'What Alan Lomax did for American folk music,' says U2's Bono, 'Garech Browne did for Ireland's musical library. He knew our folklore, our story and song were more than clues to who we were. It was who we were and maybe are. He understood that in so many ways the Irish had sung themselves into being: these rhythms and melodies were in a very real way our actual ancestors and our archaeology, the body, the place we used to live in, as vital a record as any holy mound or Neolithic tomb. Some of the melodies he has recorded in the sean-nós tradition can be traced back to North Africa...they feel older than the world, they are clues to our difference.'

By the time he came to settle in Dublin in 1956, Garech was already well versed in Irish music. Soon he began frequenting the handful of places where it could then be heard in live performance, such as the Brazen Head pub on Lower Bridge Street and the Pipers' Club, Thomas Street. He also took to attending fleadhs throughout the country, so much so that he acquired the punning nickname Lord of the Fleadhs. It was during this time that he and musician Paddy Moloney came to know one another. A year older than Garech, Moloney's background was very different, having been born and raised in the north Dublin suburb of Donnycarney, the son of an army sergeant. After leaving school at 16, Moloney went to work for a builders' providers called Baxendales but played music at night and weekends, being proficient on a number of instruments including the tin whistle, button accordion and uilleann pipes. The two men, then both still in their teens, met at a fleadh in County Clare in 1956 and found they had much in common, not least a passion for Irish music. Back in Dublin, Moloney took to dropping into Garech's mews on Quinn's Lane and the pair became known among mutual friends as Ballcock and Browne, an allusion both to the first aviators to cross the Atlantic, and to Moloney's day

ABOVE: On the shore of Lough Tay, Seán Potts and Paddy Moloney play tin whistles. The two men were founding members of The Chieftains in 1962.

ABOVE: A set of uilleann pipes, an instrument which evolved from ancient Irish warpipes and is played by means of a small set of bellows strapped around the performer's instrument and right arm. In the 1950s Garech tried to learn how to play the uilleann pipes but later admitted, 'since it became speedily obvious that I wasn't going to become even reasonably competent I quit playing for listening.'

job. Moloney also started to spend time at Luggala where the interior of an outbuilding in the courtyard had been transformed to resemble a traditional Irish cottage to be used for parties, musicians and the people of Roundwood, all of whom wore traditional dress. Regular music sessions were held in this building, including a large gathering organised by Garech annually around Michaelmas (29th September). 'The staff would come marching out from the house,' says Paddy Moloney, 'with bowls of potatoes in their jackets, and big lumps of crubeens and cabbage. There'd be a barrel of plain Guinness and pints were poured out of that.' Moloney remembers one occasion when John Kilbracken brought a girlfriend who had long black hair and as the two of them swirled around in dance, locks of her hair dipped into glasses of stout, splashing everyone as she swung by. 'There were pipers playing like Seamus Ennis and his father Jimmy. I remember us all telling stories and spitting out the fire at seven in the morning, and then going up to Roundwood for mass the following day with the staff.'

In 1962 Garech's record company, Claddagh, decided to issue its third album and he asked Paddy Moloney to assemble the musicians for the disc. 'This was a fantastic chance Garech had given me,' Moloney recalled 25 years later. 'And I knew exactly what I wanted to achieve...I wanted to create a different flavour of music with songs and airs.' Moloney carefully selected a group whose members who would understand and share his vision, and together they became the original line-up of what was called The Chieftains. Originally Moloney proposed they be given the name The Quare Fellows, after Brendan Behan's 1954 play, but John Montague suggested The Chieftains, taken from the title story of a collection of poems he was then writing called *Death of a Chieftain*.

The first Chieftains album was released in 1963 with striking sleeve artwork by Edward Delaney; later he would boast that many people bought the record for its cover and then threw away the disc. The group recorded a further three albums with Claddagh before The Chieftains moved to another label, Island Records, in 1975. For the previous seven years Paddy Moloney, who had given up his job with Baxendales in 1968, worked full-time at Claddagh as managing director. Garech had put his own money into the venture, Moloney explained in 1997, and now 'I had to make it a viable commercial concern.' During that period, the company was at its busiest, producing several records annually, each one launched with a memorable party.

ABOVE AND RIGHT: The courtyard at Luggala. The upper storey over the archway contains a series of guest bedrooms and bathrooms and further to the right is a double-height library created by Garech during the house's refurbishment. Still ongoing, this began in 1996 as somewhere to store his substantial collection of books.

ÓRiada's Farewell
Seán ÓRiada plays traditional Irish music on the Harpsichord.

Many of those early parties took place in the Quinn's Lane mews, but in 1964 Garech moved to considerably larger premises after he bought Woodtown Manor in Rathfarnham, County Dublin. The year before a newspaper report had noted he was house hunting: 'At present he lives in a converted Dublin mews but gives his big parties at Luggala... Garech is a collector of musical pipes, a student of Irish folk music and a popular host. His friends are mainly Ireland's leading traditional players. And that is why Garech wants a bigger home. His musical friends and his collection of pipes – gathered by himself from all over the world – have grown too big for the mews.'

Woodtown was the solution to his predicament. Of seven bays and two storeys, and dating from around 1750, the house had been occupied in the 19th century by Samuel White, whose family then owned Luttrellstown Castle, later home to Garech's aunt, Aileen Plunket. Garech acquired Woodtown, he explains 'because it was a rather beautiful house and the right size and the right distance from Dublin, and half-way to Luggala where my mother lived.' Sited on the lower slopes of the Dublin Mountains and with superlative views of the city below, Woodtown contained a series of large, plain but wonderfully proportioned rooms, perfect for entertaining.

The house's previous owner had been American Expressionist painter Morris Graves, 'an appallingly handsome man,' remembers John Montague, 'tall and bearded and guru-like'. Since 1954 Morris and his partner, singer and actor Richard Svare, had been living in Ireland in a series of rented properties. In 1958 they came across Woodtown, then in poor condition and being used to shelter livestock. 'The floors were all gone,' Svare would later remember. 'We put in central heating, windows, all that." The two men spent years restoring the house, working on the project with Dublin architect Michael Scott, a friend of Garech's father. However, in 1963 Svare left Ireland and moved to Stockholm to found the Scandinavian Theatre Company. The following year Graves returned to the United States after selling Woodtown. 'Ricki Huston wrote me a letter,' remembers Garech, 'saying congratulations on buying one of the most beautiful houses in Ireland.'

Over the next few years Woodtown acted almost as a surrogate Luggala, a place to which – like his mother – Garech could invite a wide and eclectic circle of friends and encourage them to interact with each other. Many of those

RIGHT AND OPPOSITE: A rare upright harpsichord stands in the dining room at Luggala. Dated 1764, the instrument was made in Dublin by Saxon-born Ferdinand Weber (1715-1784) who moved to Ireland in 1739 and remained in the country for the rest of his life. It was on this harpsichord that Seán Ó Riada, like Garech Browne a key figure in the revival Irish traditional music, recorded his last album not long before he died at the age of 40 in October 1971. Featuring a picture of the instrument on its cover, that disc, *Ó Riada's Farewell*, was released posthumously to acclaim. 'Seán was the most delightful, charming, knowledgeable man that I've ever met,' Garech recalled 40 years later.

Claddagh Records

In October 1958 Garech Browne, then aged 19, discussed with his friend Dr Ivor Browne, later well known as a psychiatrist, the problems Irish traditional music faced in securing a wider audience than was then the case. At the time both men were students of Dubliner Leo Rowsome who played the uilleann pipes – the bellows-blown bagpipe that evolved from ancient Irish warpipes. Chairman of the Pipers' Club (from which emerged the traditional music organisation Comhaltas Ceoltóirí Éireann) and one of the the finest performers of his generation, Rowsome could find no record company prepared to issue a long-playing album of his music. It was believed a market did not exist for such material. 'Ivor said he'd been around every company trying to get Leo recorded, but none of them would do it,' remembers Garech. 'They all said it was fine to make a 78 record but no one would dream of listening to an entire album of pipering.'

Garech had already been thinking about establishing his own music label. In Luggala, two adjoining bathrooms separated by a partition wall allow conversation between users, and one evening he and his cousin Caroline Blackwood were taking baths at the same time: 'I said to Caroline that what I wanted to do was start a record company and a publishing company, but Liam Miller had already set up Dolmen Press so there was no need for me to do that.' On the other hand, there clearly was a need for a record company prepared to capture and distribute the music of traditional performers. In an Ireland anxious to embrace modernisation, musicians like Rowsome were regarded as an anachronism, a roadblock on the way to progress. 'What I thought,' says Garech, 'was that all around Ireland at that moment were showbands which by and large made a pretty frightful noise, and I thought if we did what we can do, which is traditional music, then it would be better for us.'

Following that discussion between Garech and Ivor Browne in the former's mews on Quinn's Lane, other people were drawn into the project, including poet John Montague and genealogist Liam Mac Alasdair. It was discovered that the cost of producing a single LP was in the region of £500, then the average annual salary of a school teacher in Ireland. However, the small group of friends pluckily pooled their resources and pressed ahead. In the autumn of 1959 they issued an LP containing forty minutes of Leo Rowsome's playing called *Rí na bPíobairí – The King of Pipers.*

The company responsible for this and later recordings was given the name Claddagh Records. Today known for the rings symbolising love and friendships but originally a fishing village, Claddagh is a district close to the centre of Galway city where the river Corrib meets Galway Bay. Garech chose the name because 'it had the symbol and the name, and because we are the Brownes of Galway.'

'Claddagh Records was launched at Garech's mews flat in Quinn's Lane,' John Montague later recalled, 'with a firkin of Guinness porter (of course) in the corner, and a party which roared on until dawn, the first of many such sprawling, splendid parties.' However, since he was still not twenty-one and therefore deemed a minor, it was not legally possible for Garech to become director of a company. Only in 1960 were Claddagh incorporated and Garech able to assume the position of company chairman. Thereafter the business, while always remaining small, began to flourish as it released progressively more recordings. While Garech was in Japan (his mother's twenty-first birthday present) the Leo Rowsome disc sold out, thereby validating its instigators' intuition. The record received excellent reviews, the *Irish Times*' distinguished music critic Charles Acton calling it 'a splendid sample for everyone with any interest in our true national pipes.'

It was several years before Claddagh issued a second LP – '£500 was a lot of money then' Garech points out – but gradually as the 1960s progressed and moved into the following decade, more and more albums were produced. It is indicative of Garech's interests that the company's second recording should have been not of another musician but of a poet. Suggested by John Montague, Patrick Kavanagh, like Rowsome the finest exemplar of his craft, was persuaded into a studio to read.

The distinctive richness of the Claddagh catalogue is due to its mixture of music and spoken word. Pre-eminent in the former category are the early recordings of The Chieftains, but a wealth of other names deserves to be noted, among them Tommy Potts, Liam O'Flynn, Matt Molloy, Christy Moore and Ronan Browne. Composer

Seán Ó Riada was one of the most influential figures in the revival of interest in Irish traditional music, and shortly before his early death in October 1971 Garech, who had become a good friend, persuaded Ó Riada to come to Luggala and record a programme of Irish dance music and song airs on an upright harpsichord made in Dublin in 1764 and still in the house today. The resultant album, *Ó Riada's Farewell*, was released posthumously to acclaim. Claddagh also recorded classical music, not least Frederick May's 1936 String Quartet in C Minor, thirty eight years after its composition, as well as Veronica McSwiney's interpretation of the nocturnes of John Field (the early 19th-century Irish composer credited with creating this piano form) and mezzo-soprano Bernadette Greevy's recordings of Brahms and Bach. But the company's particular strength is its catalogue of traditional Irish music. 'Our crusade for the preservation of Irish music,' observed John Montague, 'could be compared with the influential early recordings of American jazz and blues. The rich, bittersweet voices of Robert Johnson, Big Bill Bronzy, John Lee Hooker and others would have died with them if they had not been recorded, but because they were preserved, they became the foundation on which modern jazz has grown and flourished, as modern Irish music has also, because of those early recordings.'

John Montague's involvement with Claddagh Records helped to ensure the company's Spoken Word series features an unprecedented number of outstanding writers, by no means all of them Irish, reading their own work. The list ranges from Seamus Heaney, Derek Mahon, Austin Clarke and Ted Hughes to Robert Graves, Hugh MacDiarmid, Liam O'Flaherty and, of course, John Montague. In 1966 Samuel Beckett oversaw the recording of extracts from his theatre work being read by the actor Jack MacGowran. In the studio, Garech remembers, 'Jackie sounded so like Sam, I had to look up to see which one of them was speaking.' The issued album's musical accompaniment was provided by two of Beckett's relations and the author striking a gong.

One of the other distinctive features of Claddagh Records releases from the start has been the exceptionally high calibre of the sleeve artwork and notes. 'We always believed that you should get an author who could write to produce the sleeve notes,' says Garech, 'and we used artists like Patrick Swift and Louis Le Brocquy

the Chieftains
ceirníní claddagh

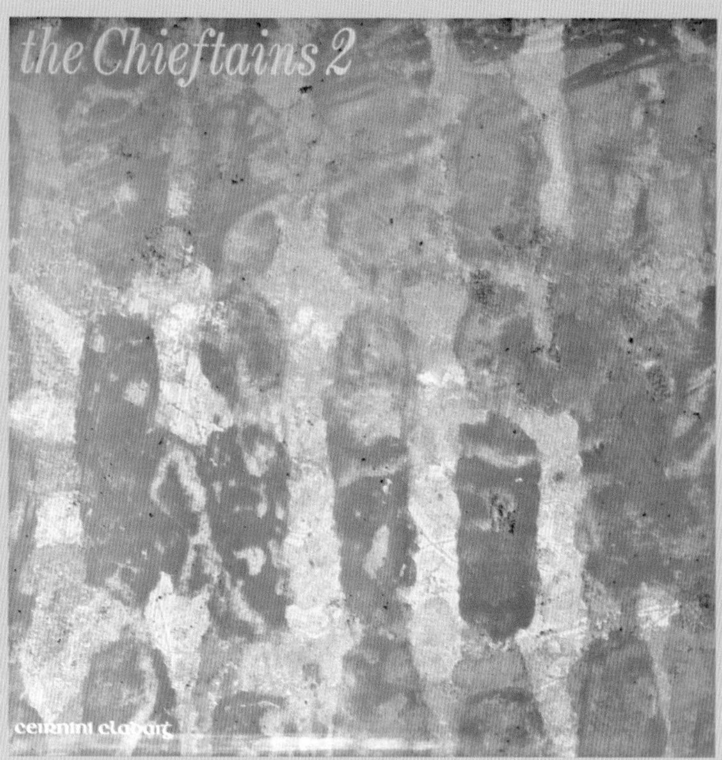
the Chieftains 2
ceirníní claddagh

the Chieftains 3
ceirníní claddagh

The Chieftains 4
ceirníní claddagh

and Eddie Delaney...We were very fussy about typefaces and overall design. What we tried to do was get the arts to speak together'.

Claddagh's back catalogue is unrivalled, but its archive also includes irreplaceable recordings that have never been issued: American poet John Berryman reading his own work, and Jack MacGowran reading Beckett's poems. More than half a century after its establishment, the company continues to operate, albeit in a less hectic fashion than was the case in the 1960s and '70s. But after playing an invaluable role in Irish culture during the second half of the last century, Claddagh Records is now entitled to rest on its laurels. 'In troubled times it got us through, and with much style,' says Ivor Browne's son Ronan, a noted uilleann piper. 'Claddagh set the bar very high for everyone who followed.' Anjelica Huston, who has known its founder all her life, agrees: 'I think Garech in a way was uniquely responsible for world acceptance of Irish music, Irish culture.' In December 2000 Garech was awarded an honorary degree by Trinity College Dublin as recognition of his work in preserving, promoting and encouraging interest in Irish traditional culture.

OPPOSITE: The first Chieftains album was released by Claddagh Records in 1963. Garech recalls 'I wanted to form a group of traditional musicians, smaller and therefore more mobile than Ceoltóirí Chualann, and without accordions. I chose Paddy Moloney as the piper. I discussed the idea with Seán Ó Riada and he gave me his blessing. I found a bodhrán player, then quite rare, in Castletown Geoghegan. I wanted a harper; years later, Paddy found Derek Bell. No musician could be changed in the group without Claddagh's permission.' The Chieftains recorded four albums with Claddagh before moving to another label in 1975.

ABOVE: Claddagh is best-known for its recordings of traditional musicians, beginning with uilleann piper Leo Rowsome in 1959 and continuing with such iconic albums as *Ó Riada's Farewell*, the last record made by Seán Ó Riada before his death in 1971. But it also issued many fine classical music recordings, not least that of Frederick May's String Quartet in C Minor. And Claddagh was responsible for recording many leading Irish and Scottish poets reading their own work, as well as actor Jack MacGowan reading Samuel Beckett. The 1966 album's musical accompaniment was provided by two of Beckett's relations, as well as the author striking a gong.

ABOVE: In 1963 an Irish newspaper reported that Garech, who had hitherto been living in a rented mews in central Dublin, was house hunting: 'Garech is a collector of musical pipes, a student of Irish folk music and a popular host...His musical friends and his collection of pipes – gathered by himself from all over the world – have grown too big for the mews.' The following year he bought Woodtown Manor in Rathfarnham, County Dublin.

friends find it hard to remember whether the parties they attended during this period took place in one house or the other they were so close in spirit. And from 1970 onwards, Garech also moved between the two places until maintaining them both became too much. In 1997 Woodtown was sold to Dublin property developer Sean Dunne. 'I loved it dearly,' says Garech, 'and so did Purna [his wife]. She cried when I sold the house.' Sean Dunne subsequently received permission to convert the house into suites for an adjoining hotel, and to build a retirement village in the grounds. To date, neither of these projects has come to fruition. In May 2006 a sale at Luggala of almost 400 lots of furniture and fine art, most of which had come from Woodtown and was therefore superfluous to his requirements. The occasion, like so many with which he has been associated, attracted international attention and started rumours that he was selling Luggala. In fact, as Garech told the *Daily Telegraph* at the time, 'The sale is just the next stage in the life of Luggala. I was living among clutter with things under the bed.'

Garech became a custodian of Luggala in 1970. Nothing offers a better insight into the singular character of the house during the past forty-plus years than its visitor's book, an item certain in time to be more valuable than any of the signed first editions of poetry and prose found on the shelves of Luggala's library. This vast leather-bound volume sits in the drawing room, an object of wonder to anyone who casts an eye over its contents. Here is the most eloquent testimony to the breadth of Garech's interests and the width of his circle of friends. There are, of course, signatures of musicians in abundance, many of them outstanding representatives of Ireland's traditional culture. Even more than had been the case during Oonagh's time at Luggala, music has been heard in the house under Garech's tenure, not least thanks to the near-constant presence of performers during this period. For a number of years fiddler Martin Byrnes lived at Luggala, ostensibly employed as gardener but just as often found playing his instrument. In the early 1990s Ronan Browne, then young and single, likewise regularly stayed in the house as a kind of unofficial resident musician: 'Garech would always hope I'd play for his visitors, but he never insisted. I'd do so but often I would drag everyone down to the kitchen, explaining the sound was better there. Garech loved that.' The Luggala visitors' book indicates the

June,
9:30 P.M.

Dear Garech —

I'm so sorry I wasn't [illegible] out when you arrived about an hour ago — please forgive it, I couldn't make it sooner.

I'll phone or write soon.

This is a day which I hope begins a long happy period of your life.

With every best wish.

Morris

ABOVE AND LEFT: Built around 1750, Woodtown had been bought in 1958 by American Expressionist painter Morris Graves with his partner, the actor Richard Svare. Assisted by architect Michael Scott, they spent the next two years restoring the dilapidated house. However, in 1963 Svare moved to Sweden and Graves decided to return to the United States. He sold Woodtown to Garech, who remembers that John Huston's wife Ricki 'wrote me a letter saying congratulations on buying one of the most beautiful houses in Ireland.' For the rest of the decade Woodtown acted almost as a surrogate Luggala and many of Garech's friends have trouble remembering whether parties they attended during this period took place in one house or the other. After being given responsibility for Luggala by his mother in 1970, Garech moved between the two places until finally selling Woodtown in 1997.

In June 1970 my mother Oonagh gave Luggala to me. Until September 1973 I lived both in Woodtown Manor and Luggala. Now I live in Luggala.

29-30 Sept. '73. Richard Ryan.

Joan Sweeney

28 September. Tiger Costley Luggala.

20th 21st oct. 73. John Hurt

Oct 6 – 22. Zara Jellicoe

11.11.73 Hugh O Byrne T.D., Dail Eireann 1973

ABOVE: In his visitors' book Garech noted his assumption of responsibility for Luggala in June 1970, even while he was still living in Woodtown Manor.

BELOW AND OPPOSITE: During the refurbishment of the house in the late 1990s, Garech created a new library in the west wing of Luggala opening up a space which had previously been divided into a series of small rooms spread over two floors. His enormous collection of books contains many first-editions inscribed to him by authors such as Brendan Behan, Liam O'Flaherty and Seamus Heaney.

diversity of musicians who have spent time at the house since 1970, from piper Paddy Moloney and singer Dolores Keane to composer Frederick May, singer Marianne Faithfull – who has known Luggala for more than forty years – and Sting, who in September 1980 signed himself 'itinerant'.

Actor John Hurt first came to Ireland for the 1964 Dublin Theatre Festival when he was appearing in *Little Malcolm and his Struggle Against the Eunuchs* at the Gaiety Theatre. 'There I met Garech Browne who introduced me to all things Irish,' he says. 'Garech was always around, he was an extraordinary force really in that particular period of Irish history.' Three years later, Hurt was back to play the lead in John Huston's *Sinful Davey*. Much of this was filmed at Luggala, which he describes as having been 'a complete revelation of another whole society and culture that I was very keen to understand.' Hurt acknowledges a lot of alcohol was consumed at Luggala, 'but what I want to make very clear is that it wasn't a piss-up. It was alcohol-driven in many ways, but all of us were filled with ideas...some people, some of us, went way over the top, but out of all this came an incredibly creative period. And when I went back, it didn't dissipate; it was what you thought it was, time and time again. All the musicians that were around, the poets, the writers, all of them were being allowed their full volume of influence.' It is safe to say that Hurt speaks for many people, present and past, when he remarks 'I'm not important to Luggala, but Luggala's important to me.'

Garech, says long-standing friend Sarah Owens, 'has taught me more about my culture than any educational system.

To Garech with undiminished affection Brendan Behan Beatrice Behan.

For Garech Browne
After hours in the Shelbourne Hotel
"Look on a hero"
Seamus Heaney.

To Garech
with love
from
Liam O'Flaherty

16 X – 1958

BRENDAN
BEHAN

LEFT AND ABOVE: Among Garech's closest friends is actor John Hurt. The two men first met when Hurt came to act in a play in Dublin in 1964 but only properly got to know one another when he returned to Ireland three years later to perform the title role in John Huston's *Sinful Davey*. Much of this was filmed at Luggala, which he describes as having been 'a complete revelation of another whole society and culture that I was very keen to understand.' Hurt speaks for many other people who know the place when he says 'I'm not important to Luggala, but Luggala's important to me.'

One only has to look at his myriad loyal and diverse friends to begin to understand the diversity of his curiosity. He continually astounds me in the range of his interests that are so eclectically reflected in his library.' Like all autodidacts, Garech is an ardent reader and just as he has always collected books, so too has he gathered around him their authors. In this, as in so much else, his mother provided a precedent and an early introduction. While still a teenager, Garech socialised with the likes of Brendan Behan and Patrick Kavanagh, with Robert Kee, Cyril Connolly, Patrick Leigh-Fermor and Claud Cockburn. The written word, and its makers, he regards with respect but never awe: he became aware of the latter's foibles too early for this ever to be the case. Like Oonagh, he has the ability to unite inside the walls of Luggala individuals who might not otherwise socialise together. Writer and hibernophile Pierre Joannon, Honorary Irish Consul in south-east France, speaks of a night in the house when he met Liam O'Flaherty, a socialist, and Francis Stuart who had broadcast propaganda from Nazi Germany during the Second World War. 'It was a fantastic evening,' says Joannon. 'You could feel the complicity between the two men as they were jokingly insulting one another. I remember thinking my god such a scene is unthinkable in France. Yet here we were with these two giants of literature at ease with each other.'

Garech seems to have a particular affinity with poets, not least John Montague who is one of his oldest friends with an association stretching back more than 55 years. The house offers a particular welcome to poets, many of whom have since been drawn or painted by another long-standing friend, Anglo-Belgian artist Anthony Palliser who in 1980 would serve as best man at Garech's wedding. The two first met when they were guests at the Paris wedding of Louise de la Falaise and Thadée Klossowski in June 1977. The subsequent party took place on an island in the Bois de Boulogne: 'There was a punt to and from the island,' Garech would recall. 'Anthony and I found the punt very agreeable so we went backwards and forwards until the punters threw us off.'

RIGHT: One of the finest uilleann pipers of his generation Séamus Ennis (1919-1982) was also a notable collector of folklore and traditional music. After working in a number of professions he finally devoted himself full-time to music from the late 1950s onwards, playing on a set of early 19th-century pipes bought by his father. In the drawing room at Luggala is a bronze cast of his hands made by Edward Delaney.

9-13 September 1990
Bards aplenty, of
Northern origin,
gathered here for
a few days discussion
seeking to find
words to heal the nation
(though some had reservations)
Mahon, Longley, Deane
minds fertile & keen,
and Francis of the Stuart clan,
an ancient thoughtful man:
– where was the singer Van? –
melodism as the stags bellowing,
our solitary yelling.
John Montague

15 September 1990.
Today I came back, after
25 years. Twenty five
years of madness
And I remember Tara
feeling me to the little
temple by the lake
and showing me the
baby's grave – And to
day I came back and
saw his grave – And
I know he was happy
that Marlon and
me were here and
remembered the years
of madness that we
did not love to live.
Anita Pallenberg

Mid summer night
We lit a fire by the
Loch's edge against the
brief darkness of the
night and planted
a tree to take the place
of Merlin's tree, fallen and
dead. The chosen
place proved hard
digging. A huge rock
embraced by sinuous
roots had to be dug out
with much sweat and
sorrow. At midnight I
intoned Merlin's charm of
making and it was done
John Boorman.

Today I planted
a wych-elm
(weeping) by
~~the~~ house. it was
very cold. I talked
to Poorna about
change & love &
illness. it got
dark. I went home
Marianne Faithfull
x.

October 11th 1993
To.day I came to
Luggala with Diane.
My portrait of Garech
finished at last will
hang at the R.H.A.
next sunday. I am
a happy fellow.
Anthony Palliser

May 6 97
During the days
I stayed we
cried and broke
down (Literally as
we ran out of
Petrol) but
most importantly
we found the
final resting
place for
Caroline: she would approve!
Love Ivana xx

ABOVE AND OPPOSITE: As well as the capacious visitors' book, Luggala also has a much smaller, leather-bound book bearing the initials GB. Inside this, friends are sometimes invited to write their thoughts after spending time in the house or planting a tree in the grounds. Among those who have done so are two of Garech's oldest friends, poet John Montague, who has been coming to stay at Luggala since the 1950s, and director John Boorman, who bought a house not far away more than forty years ago. Anita Pallenberg and Marianne Faithfull both originally came to stay at Luggala through their friendships with Garech's brother, Tara. Artist Anthony Palliser first met Garech at a wedding in Paris and would later act as best man when Garech married the Maharajkumari Harshad Purna Devi in India in 1981. Writer Ivana Lowell is a daughter of Garech's cousin Caroline Blackwood who died in 1996 and whose ashes she intends one day to scatter at Luggala. In June 1993 John Hurt wrote of planting 'the demented "Tortuosa" beech on a glorious day surrounded by friends...'

That encounter occurred too late for Palliser to have captured the visit of Robert Graves to Luggala in May 1975. Then almost eighty, Graves gave a reading in Dublin, and recorded some of his work with Claddagh. On his return to Majorca, where he then lived, he wrote to Garech, 'You gave us an extraordinary holiday – we will never forget a square yard of your domain. Nor the herds of deer, nor the fish jumping from the lake, nor the shining mica on the sand...The long splendid table where we dined and the proud position you gave me at your side which implied my gift of the first helping of food – this sentence I'm afraid lacks a main verb but it was all unforgettable.' Among those who met Graves at Luggala were poet and future Nobel Laureate Seamus Heaney and his wife Marie. She had long cherished the idea of having a volume in which living poets would inscribe their own work. Just such a book was started for her by Graves on that day in Luggala.

Three years earlier, in August 1972, the Heaneys and their children had moved from Belfast to the gate lodge of Glanmore Castle, County Wicklow. They already knew Garech from his visits to Northern Ireland with John Montague, 'a boy with the long hair, the Aran sweater and the crios,' Heaney remembers. 'He used to be about the Bohemian public houses – not that we were averse to following him inside.' While not regular callers to Luggala, the Heaneys found themselves there on various significant occasions, such as the party for Robert Graves in May 1975. 'It was a beautiful day,' says Marie Heaney. 'We were outside and there was a whole lamb roasting on a spit. I remember all the little lambs cavorting around their brother, a very Greek event.'

Another visitor to Luggala they recall was Mick Jagger and his then-wife Bianca. This happened soon after the Heaneys had moved to Glanmore. 'We'd no shower or anything in the house at that time and I remember feeling very grubby compared to them. She was extraordinarily beautiful,

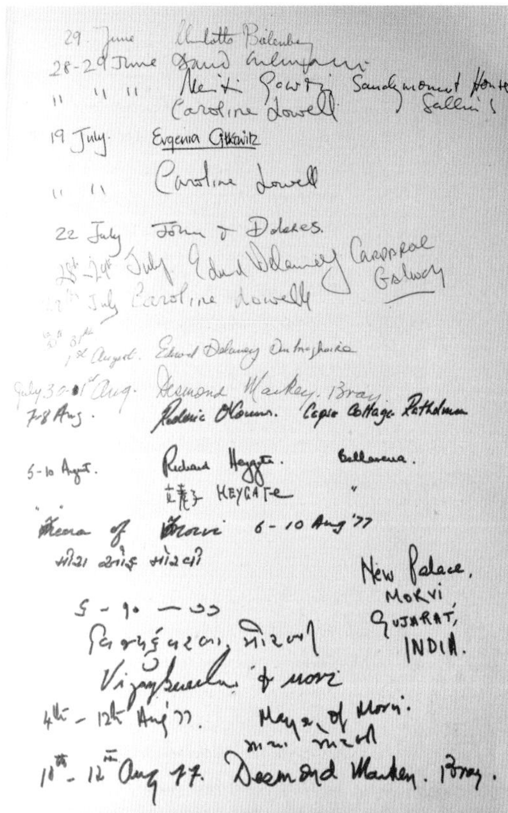

29 June

19 July. Eugenia Citkowitz

" " Caroline Lowell

22 July John & Dolores.

1st August. Edward Delaney

5-10 Aug. Richard Heygate. Belleoreia.

New Palace, Morvi Gujarat, India.

11th – 12th Aug 77. Desmond MacKay. Bray.

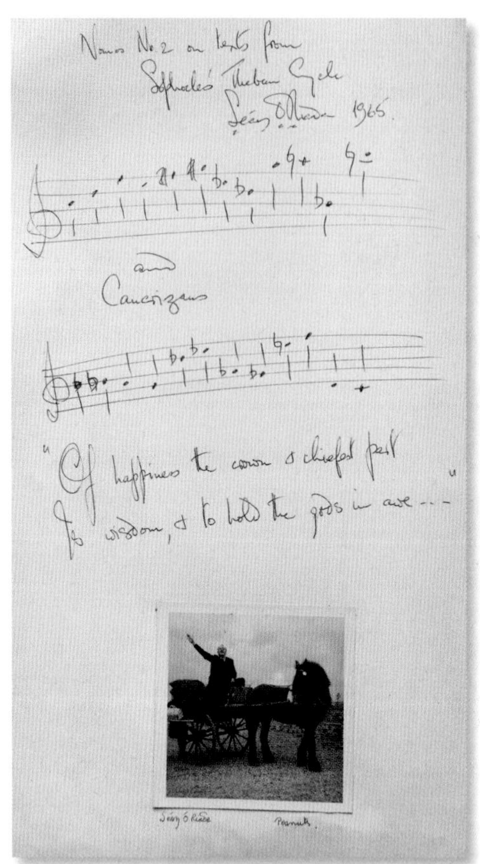

Nous No. 2 on texts from Sophocles' Theban Cycle Seán Ó Riada 1965.

and Canzoni

"Of happiness the crown & chiefest part Is wisdom, & to hold the gods in awe . . ."

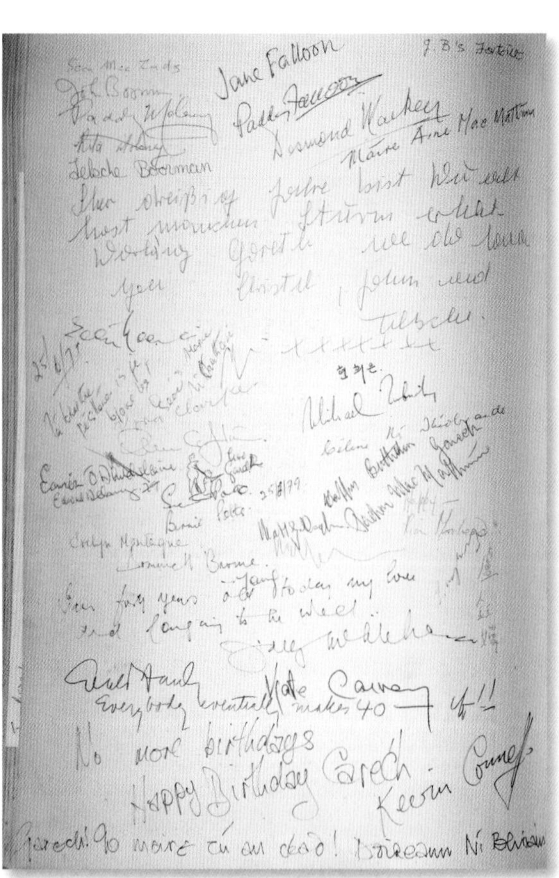

J. B.'s portrait

Jane Falloon

Desmond MacKay

Everybody eventually makes 40

No more birthdays

Happy Birthday Garech

Kevin Conolly

Garech! go maire tú an céad!

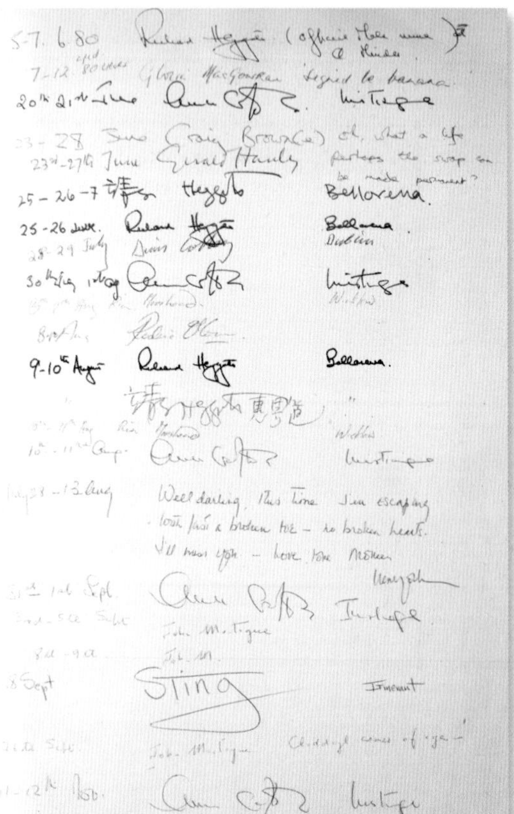

5-7. 6 80

Well darling, this time I'm escaping with just a broken toe – no broken heart.

Sting

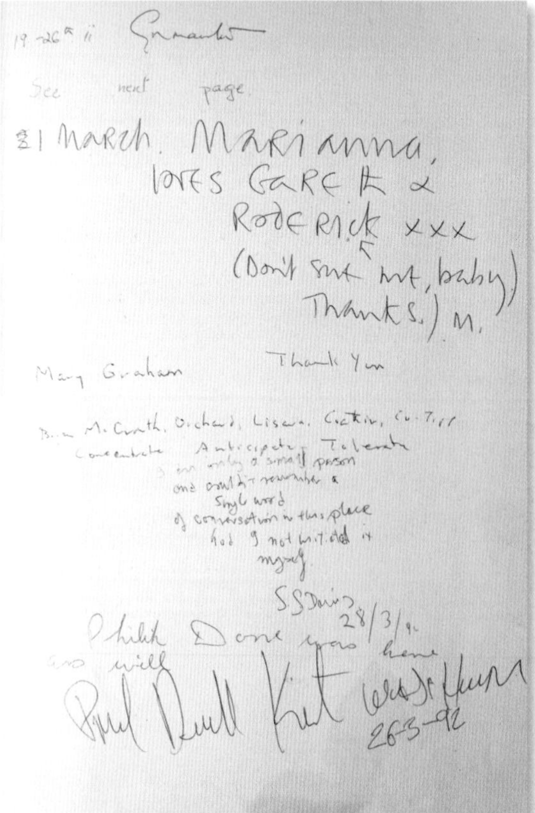

See next page

21 March. Marianna, loves Garech & Roderick xxx (Don't sue me, baby) Thanks.) M.

Mary Graham Thank you

I'm only a small person and couldn't remember a single word of conversation in this place had I not written it myself

S S Davis 28/3/92

Philip Donne was here

26-3-92

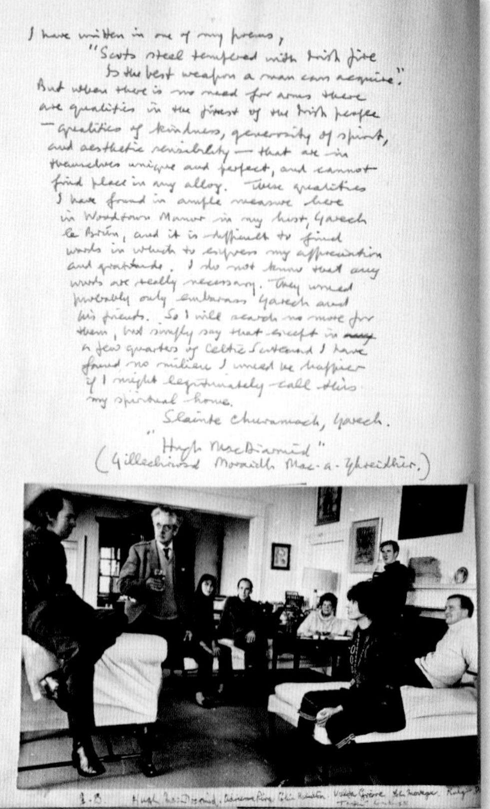

I have written in one of my poems,

"Scots steel tempered with Irish fire
Is the best weapon a man can acquire".

But when there is no need for arms there are qualities in the finest of the Irish people – qualities of kindness, generosity of spirit, and aesthetic sensibility – that are in themselves unique and perfect, and cannot find place in any alloy. These qualities I have found in ample measure here in Woodtown Manor in my host, Garech de Brún, and it is difficult to find words in which to express my appreciation and gratitude. I do not know that any words are really necessary. They would probably only embarrass Garech and his friends. So I will search no more for them, but simply say that except in ~~many~~ a few quarters of Celtic Scotland I have found no milieu I would be happier if I might legitimately call this my spiritual home.

Slainte chuvamach, Garech.

"Hugh MacDiarmid"
(Gillechriosd Moraidh Mac-a-Ghreidhir.)

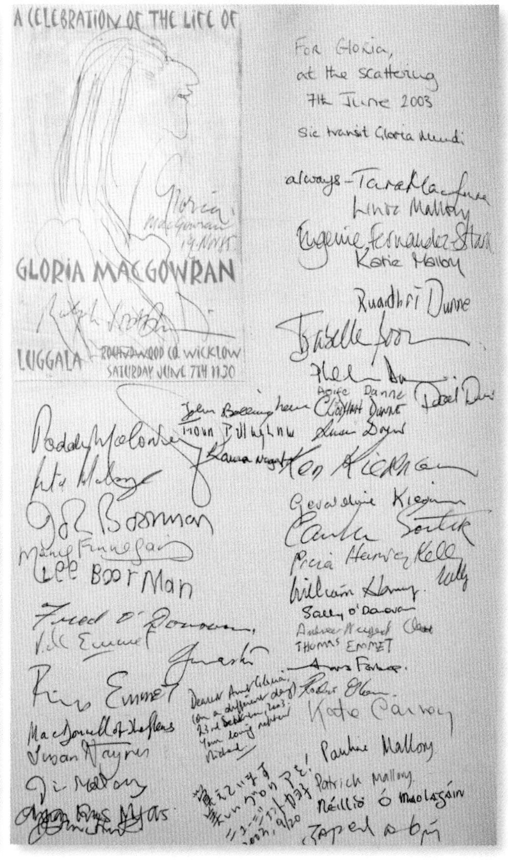

OPPOSITE AND LEFT:
Garech's visitors' book is a record of Irish cultural history over the past half-century, featuring an extraordinary cross-section of writers, musicians, actors, singers, composers and even a few colourful charlatans. For all of them, Luggala and its present owner have exerted an irresistible allure, as well as a source of support and inspiration. During the time of both Oonagh and Garech, Luggala has proven to be a crucible of creativity. Here are just a few of the people who have passed through the house in recent decades and have left a record of their stay, not least one of Garech's cousins, writer Caroline Blackwood who through three successive marriages was a regular guest at Luggala. Then there was Irish composer Seán Ó Riada, who made his last recording in the house, and another composer Frederick May who found the happiness and succour at Luggala he rarely knew elsewhere. The house has been the location for many celebrations, those to mark Garech's birthdays or the loss of friends such as actor Jack MacGowran's wife Gloria. Its fame overseas means an opportunity to visit Luggala has been eagerly sought by many people passing through Ireland such as Sting, who signed himself simply 'Itinerant'.

ABOVE: Director John Boorman moved to Ireland in 1970, buying a house in Wicklow not far from Luggala. In 1991 he made a 20-minute film for the BBC called *I Dreamt I Woke Up* in which John Hurt says of Garech, 'He is the custodian of this valley of Luggala. He nurtures it as he nurtures Irish music and poetry.' Here Boorman and Hurt are seen swimming in Lough Tay with another of Garech's oldest friends, the poet John Montague.

wearing a white tux suit with nothing beneath.' Garech was not at Luggala at the time, but Paddy Moloney, who had telephoned the Heaneys and asked them over, was then staying in a cottage on the estate. 'Mick and Bianca came to visit me for tea and scones with little Jade aged nine months,' he says. 'My mother, who was eighty, was there at the time and after they left she said to me, 'Who was that weirdo?'

Richard Ryan remembers meeting the Jaggers at Luggala. In the early 1970s he often stayed in the house by himself, rising early to pass the day deer stalking. One night when already in bed he heard a commotion as other people arrived at the house but, having turned the front door key to allow entry, went to sleep. The following day, passing through one of the bedrooms on his way downstairs, he saw two figures asleep. It was only that night, on returning to the house with his gun, covered in blood and carrying the liver of a deer he had shot, he discovered the Jaggers in the entrance hall looking understandably startled at his appearance. 'That's really the point about Luggala,' he says. 'The ebb and flow is so unpredictable. But there was a combustible certainty about every occasion.'

Among the most fascinating entries in Luggala's visitors' book are those provided by poets. Seamus Heaney has left several examples of his work, as have Derek Mahon, Michael Longley, Thomas Kinsella, Richard Ryan, Seamus Deane, and, of course, John Montague. In a piece entitled *Luggala* and written to mark Garech's 50th birthday in June 1989, the second stanza opens with a succinct description of the place: 'The road leading from the white wedding cake of the hunting lodge is lined with late blooming daffodils. As you leave, it fades back into its mountain setting, a folly nestling under boulder-strewn granite cliffs, with a stream rushing down by its side.' Few places can have drawn so many poets as Luggala, and few men been friends with so many poets as the house's present owner. Garech, observed Anthony Palliser in 2007, 'is very much the pivot, the great introducer with everything Irish.' And for Palliser and many others, Luggala has been the place where an introduction to all things Irish has taken place. It serves to mark a beginning, but also an end, since Garech has never allowed the death of an old friend to pass unacknowledged. Novelist and travel writer Gerald Hanley, who had lived in East Africa, India and Pakistan before coming to Ireland and settling in County Wicklow,

1st Oct - 4th Oct.
Back to the splendours of Luggala and its surroundings – wonderful. So long ago – so good to be back. Sonja.
2nd-4th X There are so many pieces to the jigsaw puzzle!
Thank you
11-10-93 Claude
SUPRÊME COURT Bruxelles
13/10/93 Le lieu est à l'image de son Maître d'une beauté surprenante et d'une magie sans pareil
Anthony Palliser
Ambre Thiaw
3-4th NOV Sarah Owens XX Beautiful Autumn –

RIGHT AND ABOVE: Although based in Paris, painter Anthony Palliser has been a regular visitor to Luggala for 30 years. 'It is probably the most beautiful place I know,' he says. 'It truly is enhanced reality. There's something about the perspectives from the house to the lake and the mountains beyond, something I never tire of.' Here Palliser is seen rowing with Garech across the lake in 1991 and outside the house in 2011. Inside the house's visitors' book he has also left his own impression of Luggala.

— The Beds of Grainne & Diarmuid —

How many secret nooks in copse or glen
We sained for ever with our pure embraces,
No man shall know; though indeed master-poets
Reckon one such for every eve of the year,
To sain their calendar —

Robert Graves

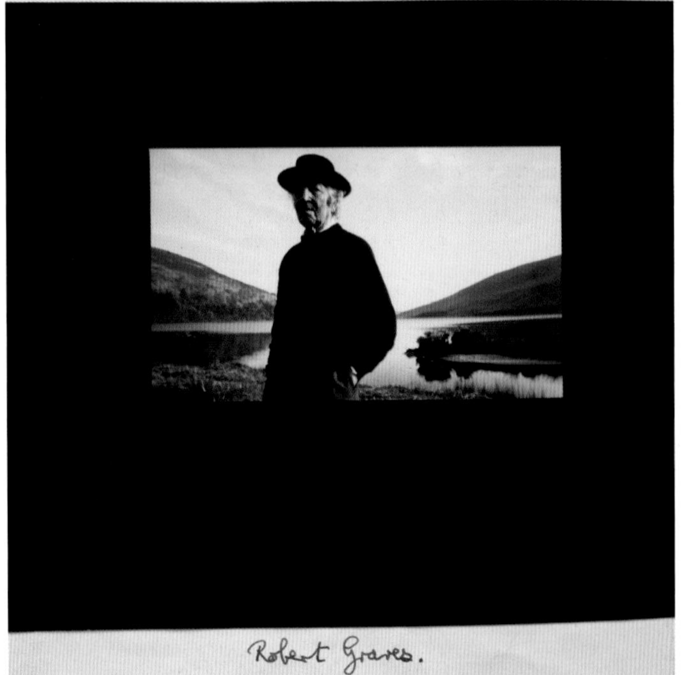

died in September 1992 at the age of 76. 'When I was a child,' remembers Hanley's daughter Maya, 'my father would quite often disappear, sometimes for days at a time, and the place he'd go was Luggala.' She and her siblings never went there, it was their father's retreat and a portrait of him, painted by Anthony Palliser, still hangs in one of the house's bedrooms. Following Gerald Hanley's funeral, Garech invited everyone back to Luggala to celebrate the deceased by writing their names, their thoughts and messages in the visitors' book. 'After that,' says Maya, 'we all had lunch together in The Roundwood Inn, with Ronan Browne playing the uilleann pipes for us and lots of laughter, tears and reminiscing. We didn't know we were supposed to be at John Boorman's house that afternoon too and ended up arriving very late.'

The variable timekeeping displayed on the day of Gerald Hanley's funeral is one of the features of life at Luggala. While much of place's character has remained unchanged since responsibility passed from Oonagh to her son, the latter has a more fluid approach to time. Friends soon discover his relaxed attitude towards punctuality. Pierre Joannon recalls an evening he and his wife Annick were invited to dinner at Woodtown and, as bidden, turned up at 8pm. The door was opened by an unshaven, poorly-dressed man, leading the Joannons to question whether they had come on the right occasion. Reassured the invitation was for that night, they were brought into the drawing room and then left, eventually finding themselves offering drinks to other guests as these arrived. 'Around 9.30,' says Joannon, 'we saw the guy who'd opened the door, now shaved and dressed like a butler. "Oh," he said, "Mr Browne never appears before 10 for dinner at 8".'

LEFT: In May 1975 writer Robert Graves came to stay at Luggala and also gave a reading of his work in Dublin. After returning to his home in Majorca, he wrote to Garech, 'You gave us an extraordinary holiday – we will never forget a square yard of your domain. Nor the herds of deer, nor the fish jumping from the lake, nor the shining mica on the sand...The long splendid table where we dined and the proud position you gave me at your side which implied my gift of the first helping of food...'

OPPOSITE: Mick Jagger photographed in the drawing room at Luggala by Michael Cooper in 1966 when he came to stay for Tara Browne's 21st birthday. Jagger came back several times later, not least in August 1972 when he was accompanied by then-wife Bianca and the couple's baby daughter, Jade. Paddy Moloney, then staying with his family in a cottage on the estate, invited the Jaggers over for tea. He remembers, 'My mother, who was eighty, was there at the time and after they left she said to me, 'Who was that weirdo?'

Exile's Return

We came off the Ozarks at night,
Dreaming the motels we stayed in,
Skirted the snow and parked
On the edge of the Grand Canyon.

Now it is the tinder of border towns,
Greened ruins, locked headlands,
Cow-quilted fields and scattered squalls
Scouting for winter. Honey thins

Out of the blood. At four o'clock
The rivers are dark. Yet, desert-bright,
Sensation is not removed here
From what it loves. The last oasis

Before civilisation, condensed
Out of ocean, malingering far
West of Eden, its truest colour
Nettle-green. Here the heart begins.

Seamus Deane
Sept, 90.

The Last Mummer

Carries a stone in his pocket,
An ash plant under his arm.

Moves out of the fog
On the lawn, pads up the terrace.

The luminous screen in the corner
Has them charmed in a ring

So he stands a long time behind them.
St. George, Beelzebub and Jack Straw

Can't be conjured from mist.
He catches the stick in his fist

And, shrouded, starts beating
The bars of the gate.

His boots crack the road. The stone
Clatters down off the slates.

For Garech, who allows the mummers to possess the floor

Seamus Heaney
6th July 1970.

ABOVE AND OPPOSITE: A remarkable number of Ireland's finest poets – John Montague, Seamus Deane, Seamus Heaney – have written examples of their work in the Luggala visitors' book. From 1972 Heaney was living with his wife Marie and their children in County Wicklow, not far from Luggala. They already knew Garech – ''He used to be about the Bohemian public houses,' Heaney recalls, 'not that we were averse to following him inside' – and so were invited over the house. Like everyone else, they were seduced by the special character of the place. 'I think it's a sense of crossing the border once you enter that glen,' says Heaney. 'The minute you start going down, you do cross a line into a slight otherwhere. And when the house appears, there's a sense of destination; it's a beautiful aspect.'

In August 1981 the *Irish Times'* Kevin Myers wrote of a lunch given by Garech to mark the 85th birthday of Liam O'Flaherty at which the host managed to be absent for almost the entire occasion. 'Oh, Garech has no sense of time, none at all.' one of the guests informed Myers. Garech finally arrived just as the meal came to a close.

'There's an anarchic quality to events at Luggala,' says John Boorman. 'And the late meal is very much part of it. Garech is always late: on one occasion in order to get him to come to me in time for dinner I told him it was a late lunch.' Richard Ryan agrees that once Garech took over responsibility for Luggala, 'Things became a little more dishevelled probably...Things didn't always happen on time.' Pierre and Annick Joannon tell of another occasion when, travelling in Ireland with friends, they happened to meet Garech in the Roundwood Inn and were encouraged to call to Luggala later that day. Duly arriving, the group knocked repeatedly on the front door but got no response. Spotting an open window, they pushed this up and all clambered into the drawing room where 'we made ourselves at ease and got drinks.' After about 45 minutes, the Joannons thought they should look for their putative host, and found him upstairs asleep in bed with his wife: 'We went back downstairs, wrote a note and then left by the window.'

Asked by an *Irish Times* journalist in October 1979 whether he ever intended to marry, Garech responded, 'Who would want to have anything to do with me?' Fourteen months later his question was answered as he finally became a husband at the age of 41. Since the 1950s there had been a succession of girlfriends, among the earliest a maid at Luggala called Margaret McCabe. When Garech wanted to bring her to a fashion show presented by Dublin couturier Sybil Connolly in February 1958, he asked John Montague's wife Madeleine to attend the event as well in order to act as a decoy for the press. She agreed to do so and was duly photographed with Garech, an article appearing in the following morning's *Daily Express* with the headline 'Garech Browne and his Girlfriend Show up with the Fashions.' As a result of this error, the Montagues were able to sue the newspaper for libel and, as John Montague wrote in his 2001 memoir *Company*, 'On the principle of *noblesse oblige*, I thought that some of the resulting spoils should go into the company [Claddagh Records], and so we got started.'

Other girlfriends followed, among the most notable being Jamaican actress and dress designer Tessa Welborn, today best remembered for creating the bikini worn by Ursula Andress in the 1962 James Bond film *Dr No*. She later went on to own a private drinking club in London's Shepherd Market frequented by Garech and friends like John Hurt and Nicholas Gormanston. Then there was Welsh-born Janet Elizabeth Aiyar, commonly known as Tiger. In 1961 she had married as his third wife Denis Wellesley, Earl Cowley. However the couple were divorced shortly before his death in 1968. For several years Tiger Cowley and Garech enjoyed a lively relationship, much of which seemed to be played out in newspaper headlines, and while marriage seemed imminent on a number of occasions, it never happened; in 1976 Tiger Cowley married Pierson Dixon (after five years this also ended in divorce).

In November 1977 *Harper's & Queen* described Garech as 'Ireland's most eligible bachelor.' Four years later, in December 1981 he married Princess Harshad Purna Devi of Morvi, known as Purna, in a ceremony in Mumbai that lasted several days. Purna is the youngest daughter of the Maharaja of Morvi, a former princely state on the Kathiawar peninsula in Gujarat. From the late 17th century until Indian independence in 1947 it had been ruled by the Jadeja clan of Rajputs. Their enlightened policy of modernisation ensured the state's prosperity from the late 19th century onwards. Purna's grandfather, Maharaja Shri Sir Lakhdhiraji Waghji Lakhdhirji, is especially remembered for his endeavours to improve Morvi. In 1948 he abdicated in favour of her father, Mahendrasinhji, who had already been responsible for commissioning the construction of an immense Art Deco palace in Morvi, on which work began in 1931. Designed by the Indian architect Ram Singh and inspired by Le Corbusier and Mallet-Stevens, the two-storey granite building has six drawing rooms, six dining rooms, and fourteen bedrooms. A number of the interiors contain murals by the Polish artist Julius Stefan Norblin whose work can also be seen in other former princely residences in India, albeit with women's breasts covered due to their owners' primness. The palace with its Norblin interiors remains in Morvi. Purna's now-deceased brother Mayurdhwaj succeeded their father in 1957 and at the age of five was the last Maharaja to be crowned in India; in 1971 the country's government amended the Indian Constitution to remove his position as a ruler and his right to receive privy-purse payments.

Marriage meant that Garech spent more time in India. Always an inveterate traveller, he was frequently away from Luggala in the late 1970s and 1980s. But this did not mean he neglected the place or failed to keep an eye on any potential threat to its special character. From the time of the La Touches, one of the features setting Luggala apart has been its remoteness, allowing for an element of surprise whenever the area is discovered by visitors. This seclusion applies not just to the estate but to the entire region in which it is located. Here, unlike much of the rest of Ireland, the landscape's appearance and personality has remained almost unaltered since the 18th century. Yet the very traits making Luggala so distinctive came under threat in 1989. The Office of Public Works, a state body, announced its intention to build a visitor centre in the immediate vicinity, one of three such new public amenities planned for Ireland thanks to an EU-funded tourism 'operational programme.' All three projects would inspire violent and widespread antipathy.

In the case of the Luggala centre, the entrance was to be located directly opposite the present estate gates. Garech was far from being the only party publicly opposed to the scheme, with resistance to the OPW's plans coming from a wide range of individuals and organisations, not just in the immediate area but throughout Ireland. The essence of the argument against the proposed centre was that it would attract large quantities of traffic onto what has always been a minor road. This would have to be widened to accommodate the greater number of cars and buses, which would in turn draw still more visitors to the district, thereby destroying forever precisely the environment that the centre was intended to celebrate and support. Instead, the project's opponents argued, the new facility should be located in an existing population centre, the nearest and most obvious being the village of Roundwood just a few miles away.

The battle against the Luggala visitor centre went on for more than five years, with the OPW – which stood to draw 75 per cent of funding for the project from the EU – determined to go ahead despite consistent hostility to its proposals. In 1991 an environmental impact study commissioned by the state organisation took the chosen location as given and did not consider alternatives. Although the local authority's own senior planner advised against the scheme, warning it would create traffic hazards and be 'seriously injurious' to the area, contractors were brought onto the site the following year and started work on the centre's concrete structure. Marianne Faithfull remembers going with Garech and his mother to see Chekhov's *The Cherry Orchard* at the Gate Theatre in Dublin. 'It was the time when everyone thought things didn't look good and the centre looked like it was going to happen. At the end of the play, with the sound of the axes chopping down the trees, I looked at Garech and Oonagh and said, 'We're living in the Cherry Orchard"!'

In 1993, however, Ireland's High and Supreme Courts successively ruled thatr the OPW had no power to build visitor centres, thereby making the development at Luggala

illegal. In 1994 the organisation lodged a planning application to go ahead with the centre and duly received permission from Wicklow County Council. The scheme's opponents then appealed to the state planning authority, An Bord Pleanala, the ultimate arbiter in such matters. It held oral hearings into the case in November 1994 and issued judgement in February 1995: sanction was refused for a visitor centre on which £1.6 million had already been spent. Over two years later the OPW finally promised to initiate work to restore the site to its condition before clearance had taken place for the controversial centre.

In retrospect, the plan to erect such a building in the intended location looks grotesquely ill-conceived, not least because of the irrevocable damage it would have wrought to the landscape. But for much of the period in which the centre was under consideration, there seemed to be every possibility

ABOVE: Irish painter Edward McGuire (1932-1986) was the finest portraitist of his generation and responsible for painting likenesses of many notable figures at the time. Now hanging in the dining room at Luggala, this large picture of Garech dates from 1968, and presents the sitter in traditional Irish dress and surrounded by many of the instruments, like harp and uilleann pipes that could be heard on the LPs issued by his company Claddagh Records. McGuire also painted Garech's girlfriend of the time, Welsh-born Janet Elizabeth Aiyar, commonly known as Tiger. In 1961 she had married Lord Cowley as his third wife, but the couple were divorced shortly before his death in 1968. Her grandfather Seshandri Iyer had been Dewan of Mysore and her uncle brought the first hydro-electric scheme to India.

Edward Delaney
Anne Sullivan. Carraroe Co. Galway.
Emer Delaney (25 Feb. 1991)
Rónán

20 Wed. and 21 Thurs. Feb. 1991.
The night that decided Djouce Mountain
will not have an Interpritive Centre
to educate the Dubliners about the
Wicklow Mountains.
Maria Simonds-Gooding Dún-Chaoin

Ger Mac Donald

G. Mac Donald
24–28 Feb Anne Sullivan. CARRAROE. C. GALWAY
24–28 Feb Emer Delaney & CARRAROE 24–28 Feb 1991
Rohan Co. Galway
Sarah Sheart LARAGH
Peter Farrell Roundwood
4/3/91 Thanks for the warm bed and cottage pie, and all went well at the meeting against the interpretative centre we hope!

ABOVE: In 1989 the unique character of Luggala and its surrounding countryside came under threat from plans by a state body, the Office of Public Works, to build a visitor centre in the immediate vicinity. Garech was heavily involved in the battle against this intrusive project, a fight that often looked as though it would be lost but continued until the proposed centre was decisively rejected by the official planning authority in 1995, thereby preserving Luggala for future generations. Here in the visitors' book, artist Maria Simonds-Gooding records a moment in the middle of the struggle.

the scheme's advocates would win the day. It was only thanks to the determination of adversaries like Garech that this was not the outcome. 'There is no question that without Garech's dogged determination the centre's development would have gone ahead,' says Sarah Owens, 'and that would have been a total travesty. The country on many levels owes him much more than people may realise.'

Garech's involvement against the visitor centre did not damage his relations with the Irish state. In March 2006, he sold over 1,600 acres of the Luggala estate to the government, so allowing two previously separated blocks of Wicklow Mountains National Park to be joined and giving a continuous area of national parkland along the spine of the Wicklow Mountains from the Dublin border to just short of Lugnaquilla mountain. 'It's only a little bit of a land,' Garech told a reporter from the *Irish Times*, 'but it's of some strategic importance. It's something I've wanted to do from the very beginning.'

Even without a visitor centre, Luggala continues to be a magnet for all sorts of people who find their way there. Among the most extraordinary was singer Michael Jackson, who rented the house during 2006. Here he remained for eight weeks with his three children, Prince, Paris and Blanket, and his manager Grace Rwaramba. For much of the period, while rumours circulated about Jackson's rental of the estate, few beyond its boundaries actually saw him. One of those who did so was Luggala's Project Manager, Tony Boylan, who remembers that while almost nobody visited the place, there were regular telephone calls from Bill and Hilary Clinton, the Williams sisters and Oprah Winfrey. No photography was permitted and one day, when someone arrived to deliver heating oil, Jackson lay on the drawing-room floor, convinced the paparazzi had tracked him down. Irish puppeteer Conor Lambert was hired to give a performance for the singer and his children in the house, but only discovered who had asked for him when handed a confidentiality agreement to sign once inside the entrance hall. On the other hand, a group of musicians also invited to play at Luggala got as far as the entrance gates before being told their services were no longer required.

'He absolutely loved the house,' says Boylan, 'and at one stage he said he'd like to make an offer for it.' Although this did not happen, the following year Irish music magazine *Hot Press* announced that Jackson had bought Luggala for €20

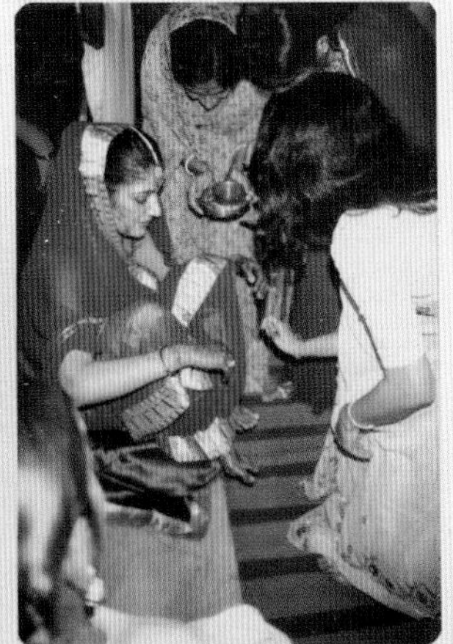

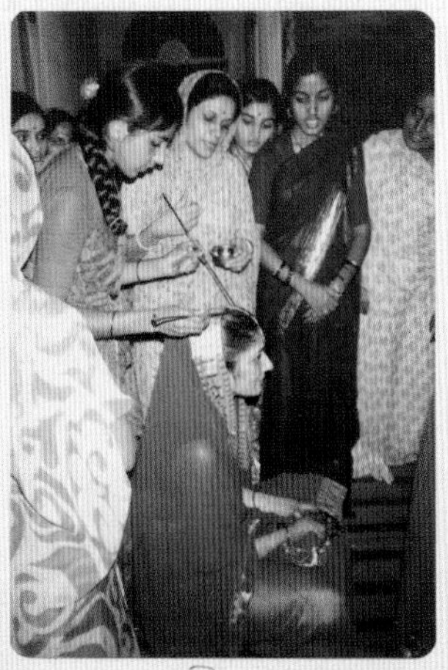

LEFT AND BELOW:
Asked by an *Irish Times* journalist in October 1979 whether he ever intended to marry, Garech replied, 'Who would want to have anything to do with me?' Fourteen months later his question was answered when he wed Princess Harshad Purna Devi of Morvi, known as Purna, youngest daughter of the Maharaja of Morvi, a former princely city-state on the Kathiawar peninsula in Gujarat. The marriage took place over several days in Mumbai.

Luggala Resurgens

'On one visit to Luggala,' remembers Bono, 'I tried to straighten a Francis Bacon hanging in the salon only to discover it was covering a hole in the wall that literally let the light in. When asked, Garech replied "great art has to be seen from all sides".'

In 1996, a year after his mother's death and four decades after it had last been restored, Garech decided to undertake a complete refurbishment of Luggala. As indicated by Bono's anecdote, the house was beginning to show signs of wear, scarcely surprising when its history of intensive use is considered. A feature on the house published by Ireland's *Image* magazine in the mid-1980s noted that 'Garech's hospitality at Luggala is warm, never ending and very hard on the carpets.' The time had come for the place to be revamped and redecorated. 'Well you see,' explains Garech, 'I was sort of in charge of Mr Hope in 1956 after it got burnt down. And then [Irish documentary film maker] George Morrison gave me a set of photographs of the house in the 19th century and I was distressed it didn't look like it should have.' Here Garech refers to a photograph taken by the Hon. Lewis Wingfield in the 1860s which shows Luggala with windows rising to the top of each Gothic arch and not with the tops squared off, as happened at some date in the second half of the 19th century. Garech now decided the time had come to reinstate the original style of fenestration.

In June 1996 Marion Cashman of Dublin architects Sheehan & Barry received a full brief for the job at Luggala. As well as the windows, this involved a number of practical issues such as the

OPPOSITE AND ABOVE: Luggala has always been a welcoming house, frequently overflowing with visitors, many of whom come for a drink and stay for several days. This takes an inevitable toll on the building and as a result in 1996, 40 years after its last refurbishment, Garech decided to embark on a comprehensive overhaul of the entire structure. One of the most substantial alterations was the recreation of the original arched windows which had been squared off at some date in the late 19th century, as well as the reinstatement of chimneys and battlements to their correct height and scale, and the recreation of a long-lost wing on the north side of the courtyard. Then there was all the necessary but largely invisible work, such as installation of new electrics and plumbing. It was a slow process and took more than four years, but the outcome is that Luggala now looks as well as it did when first occupied by Peter and Elizabeth La Touche.

entire property being rewired and the installation of a new water treatment system. On 5th June 1997 the ashes of Garech's mother were scattered at Luggala and afterwards the house was closed for restoration. Like Oonagh before him, for the project's duration Garech moved into the Cowshed behind the main house.

As is often the case with enterprises of this kind, much of the work undertaken over the next few years was necessary but invisible. Among the more noticeable structural alterations, however, was the restoration of chimneys and battlements to their original height and scale since parts of both had been altered, perhaps around the same time as were the windows. Suggested by David Mlinaric, the return of the latter to their earlier form is the most immediately dramatic modification of the building and the one that demanded the greatest assault on the structure, since sections of the external walls had to be removed. Once that work was completed, the coved ceilings of rooms affected were re-done. The result was even more radical than had been anticipated: the south-facing rooms are now inundated with light as the spectacular landscape beyond almost seems to enter the house.

In addition to the reinstatement of arched windows, a new staircase – in fact one salvaged from an 18th-century house in Dublin – was installed to replace the rather mundane stairs created by Alan Hope. Similarly his uninspired drawing room and dining room chimneypieces were replaced with specially commissioned examples from Dick Reid of York, who had worked on the restoration of Spencer House in London. The substitutes were copied from those lost in the 1956 fire. Although not visible from the front of the house, another significant change was that made to the immediate north where a long wing, evident from old Ordnance Survey maps but not easily visible, was now reinstated, thereby largely enclosing the courtyard as must once have been the case.

Internally the house was thoroughly redecorated, albeit in a style that recalled its previous incarnation. For this assignment, Garech called on the services of two people who knew Luggala well and were sympathetic to its distinctive character: David Mlinaric and Amanda Douglas. Their brief was to make the house look much as it had before, 'the same, only different.' 'It was clear that Garech wanted it to feel like the old Luggala,' comments David Mlinaric. 'But also Woodtown as well, he did that all by himself.' Garech was by no means a passive client. 'I was taught to use my eyes by Lucian Freud,' he has commented. 'Lucian took me round the Louvre when I was about fourteen. He didn't tell me how to use my eyes, but allowed me to use them – and then told me I was right!' The house's restoration was very much a collaborative process. 'What Garech has,' says John Boorman, 'is exquisite taste in almost everything.' It is a verdict with which David Mlinaric would concur. Of Luggala's redecoration he says, 'Garech really led it because he's very certain about what he wants and likes. His taste is pretty similar to mine.'

Mlinaric and Douglas looked to source identical successors for much of what had been in the house, such as the Pugin-designed drawing room paper. This was hand printed by London firm Cole & Son using the original blocks made in the 19th century by J. C. Crace & Son. Other papers for the house were printed by Irish specialist David Skinner.

'The Library curtain fabric was made by Atkinsons in Northern Ireland,' explains Amanda Douglas. 'They had not made this beautiful watered poplin for years but agreed to do it for Garech and to match the colour of his grandfather's robes as a Knight of St. Patrick. I found the Gothic braid in an archive at Clermont, and had it made up in off-white/cream for the dining room curtains, which had never been done before. The red silk velvet for the drawing room curtains came from France, and the silk for the inner curtains was made in England by Humphries Weavers... Every single item in the house was a "special" in some way – nothing "off the peg". Even the carpets were specially dyed.' As an instance of the trouble taken over the furnishings, the drawing room settee, originally made for Russborough, is now covered in luscious burgundy-coloured velvet. This fabric was gauffraged, or stamped, by a firm in Lyons using surviving 18th-century wooden cylinders, which broke during the process, meaning this technique can never be repeated.

An entry in the Luggala visitors' book notes that in August 2000 a 'christening of the chamber' took place in the presence of Garech and several old friends like Paddy Moloney and John Hurt. The process of moving back into the house began the following month, but refurbishment work went on for some time longer. Indeed parts of the building, such as the double-height library created in the west range, still await further attention. As recently as September 2011, when David Mlinaric and his wife Martha came to stay for a few days, pictures and furniture were moved around the house to produce more satisfying results. 'Somebody said to me that Luggala could be beautiful also if done very simply,' remarks Mlinaric. 'The answer to which is yes, but not for Garech.' It is justifiable to describe Luggala as a work in progress, one that may never be definitive. But after its most recent restoration, the fabric of the building is now fit to survive another two centuries of occupation.

ABOVE: Post-restoration, Luggala resumed its old character as a place where friends gathered and music was performed. In October 2000 a party took place to mark the visit of Garech's mother-in-law the Maharani Vijaykuverba and two of her daughters, Uma and Purna, the latter being Garech's wife. Among the musicians playing on that occasion were uilleann piper Ronan Browne and Éamon de Buitléar, a founder member of Ceoltóirí Chualann, the folk-orchestra created by the composer Seán Ó Riada.

million. Despite being erroneous and quickly denied, the news item spread around the world, and still turns up on the internet. It is easy to see why such a story would attract widespread interest – and seem to have credibility – not least because of Luggala's fame, national and international, as a place of wonderment. This perception of the estate has only increased in recent decades, perhaps in part thanks to its use as a film location. 'I can understand why people who shoot films are so fascinated by the place,' says Pierre Joannon, who saw Luggala in the cinema before he ever went there. 'It has a cinematic strangeness unlike anythere else.'

Luggala's landscape is not static, but continually evolving, thanks to Garech's policy of planting trees which, while rare and exotic, nevertheless look at home in their new environment. In 2004 Patrick Bowe described some of this work: 'A group of majestic old lime trees is the setting for a new collection of exotic young limes...Browne has chosen a grove of native Scots pine as the setting for a planting of conifers including the outstanding Japanese Umbrella Pine...Among a group of mature native oaks, he has planted a small collection of other members of the oak family including a Korean form of the Japanese Daimyo oak.'

Luggala's grounds were first extensively used in 1967 for the filming of *Sinful Davey* by John Huston, an old friend of Oonagh Oranmore. Six years later John Boorman, by then living nearby, used it for the filming of *Zardoz* with Sean Connery and Charlotte Rampling, and again in 1981 for *Excalibur*, the cast of which included Helen Mirren, Liam Neeson, Gabriel Byrne and Patrick Stewart. Another film on the same theme, Touchstone Picture's *King Arthur* with Kiera Knightley and Clive Owen was filmed at Luggala, as was the 2010 television series *Camelot*. Other films that have been filmed, in whole or in part, at Luggala include *Braveheart* (1995), *Animal Farm* (1998), *Becoming Jane* (2006)and *P.S. I Love You* (2007). Then there are long-running television series like *The Tudors*, which continued for four years from 2007 and regularly featured Luggala.

Manus Hingerty has worked as a film locations manager in Ireland for 20 years. Luggala, he says, 'is a bit like Lugga-world: it has its own micro-climate and atmosphere, and because it's set in a valley, you pretty much own the world around you. Outside the gates there's nothing but rolling bog land and suddenly you're in this lush green environment. Because Luggala is awkward to get to, that makes it very private. You don't have to worry about people taking photographs or snooping because there's only one way in or out.' Above all, Hingerty explains, it is the atmosphere of Luggala which makes the estate so attractive to film directors. He cites the instance of Laurent Tirard, director of *Asterix and Obelix* who came to Ireland to investigate possible locations for the fourth in the film series, shot in 2011. 'There was nothing in the script story-boarded for Luggala,' says Hingerty, 'but when he got there, he decided he had to use it.'

In 1991 John Boorman made a 20-minute film for the BBC called *I Dreamt I Woke Up*, much of it shot at Luggala. At one point John Hurt, speaking Boorman's script, says of Garech, 'He is the custodian of this valley of Luggala. He nurtures it as he nurtures Irish music and poetry...Here he collects poets

ABOVE: While filming in Ireland in November 1996, actor Pierce Brosnan came to visit Garech Browne at Luggala, writing in the visitors' book 'Bloody Marys and...more.'

and pipers, Druids, drunks, landed and stranded gentry. He likes to have his friends about him; when they die he keeps their death mask close at hand. And indeed their hands. His own likeness by Lucian Freud is a death mask of his youth...'

Since assuming responsibility for Luggala, Garech has loved and cared for the estate and nothing within its boundaries escapes his attention. Anthony Palliser remembers one day when he and Garech were going up the drive in the latter's car, 'and there was a wild turkey sitting in the middle of the road. Garech got out, looked at it and said, "Now, what should we do?" I always think that's the epitome of his attitude to wildlife at Luggala.'

Like his mother before him, Garech has made the house a veritable crucible of creativity, an inspirational meeting place for composers, painters and writers, musicians and actors, singers and dancers, performers and perhaps a few poseurs along the way. Just as it did during the time of Oonagh Oranmore, Luggala often serves as a private theatre: guests staying in the house feel free to act in a way they might not outside its walls. Libation brings liberation and the chance to escape, if only temporarily, from obligations and responsibilities. The attraction of surrendering to the enchanted moment – of being 'Luggala'ed' – remains as potent as ever. Luggala leaves an indelible impact on everyone.

For this the house's owner can claim some responsibility. Ever since he was a young man, Garech has made an impression not least thanks to his physical appearance. *Forbes* correspondent Oliver Bath provided the following description of Garech in October 2005: 'Luggala's master is diminutive but dominates a room by stepping into it. I couldn't decide – man, leprechaun, hobbit...wizard? He carried a walking stick and had a bald pate, long gray wispy beard and hair tied in an unkempt ponytail, and he was impeccably dressed in a baby-blue tweed three-piece suit. I wouldn't have been surprised if

he'd reached into his pocket and produced either a flintlock pistol or a mandrake root. His eyes gleamed with intelligence and hospitality, but a trace of sadness...Garech looks at you with a sly half-smile, as though daring you to blurt out whatever fugitive thought you're withholding.'

These are the observations of somebody who was only given a glimpse of Garech but they chime with the sentiments of long-standing friends and admirers. Garech, says Bono, 'is different, a true bohemian, he dresses like a remnant of a more romantic time in our country, woven in cheviot by some god of tweed who was perhaps distracted in the process by the mischief in the eyes of his subject. His mischief and the grand madness of the Claddagh project made much sense of us, of Ireland, and we owe him a debt of gratitude for the high times and dizzy ceilis he fastidiously recorded. "The beerage" his family have been hailed and heckled, but though his aura is perfumed with the kind of noble rot reserved for the best

OPPOSITE AND ABOVE: Garech is an indefatigable collector, be it of books, of music, of people and even of buttons. Here he can be seen going through the last of these, sitting on the floor of Luggala's drawing room. The two chairs to his right are part of a set which have always been in the house and are believed to date back to the time of the La Touches. Garech is also a discerning collector of clothing and footwear. Lined below the dressing room sofa are some of his boots, made for him by John Lobb of London not just from leather but also the skins of sika deer and ostrich, and even from elephant ears.

claret and the best vintage, he is strangely not out of touch with earthier concerns. He is much more savvy and punk rock than his Bilbo Baggins silver whiskers suggest. Intellectual curiosity is at the centre of who he is and I'm sure has cost him some holes in his pockets...'

'What I find fascinating about Garech,' says John Hurt, 'is that he was never concerned what anybody in the world thought about him, or what mood he was in. There could be really important people there and he doesn't give a damn. Somehow he is the definition of a character.' Marianne Faithfull says of him, 'I don't think I've ever known anyone quite so distinct. It comes out in every way: in his homes, his friends, his love of musicians – that's the way we connected. I always sing to Garech if he wants, I'm part of his caravanserai... I know I'm very privileged with him. I'm allowed to take liberties with Garech and so is he with me. I know we're not family, but there are times when we feel connected.'

'Garech is unique,' confirms Anjelica Huston. 'First of all, there's his incredible sensibility and depth, he feels very, very deeply. His passions are very ardent as is his nationalism. I adore him and think he's a really fine person, he belongs to the best of this and of the former centuries.'

He also belongs to Luggala and its surroundings, a point made by Sarah Owens. 'What I most admire and love about him,' she says, 'is that for all the extraordinary people he has encountered in his very privileged life, he places no importance on the standing of one person over the next. Yes, like many he responds well to the company of those who have either national or international prominence in their cultural or public fields, but the conversation, knowledge and friendship of his local community is as paramount in importance.'

For people who have come to know them over the past four decades, Luggala and Garech Browne are synonymous. 'I realise that Luggala in the absence of Garech is a fine place but missing its soul,' says musician Ronan Browne, 'yet when Garech is away from Luggala all that magic is still there with him – in Dublin, London or any of his haunts, being with Garech is the very same as being with him in Luggala... Of course this is only to be expected – a place takes on the persona of its inhabitant but in the case of Garech Browne and Luggala that reality is amplified.' It has become impossible to conceive of one without the other. As Garech told Mirabel Cecil in 2008, 'Luggala made me and I, in part, made Luggala.'

OPPOSITE LEFT AND RIGHT: Since birth Garech has been ceaselessly photographed, despite a certain reticence which is evident in many of these pictures. As he says, 'I'm a shy man who likes attention,' and he has received this all his life, not least thanks to his inherent elegance whether wearing traditional Irish clothing or, as here, formal dress. The picture on the left shows him wearing mourning clothes in June 2003 at a gathering to celebrate the life of Gloria MacGowran, widow of actor Jack MacGowran. Joining Garech at the temple is the outstanding uilleann piper Liam O'Flynn.

ABOVE: For his long-standing friends, it has become inconceivable to imagine Luggala and Garech Browne apart: the bond between place and person appears indissoluble. Each has enhanced the other, each helped to define the other's character.

Postscript

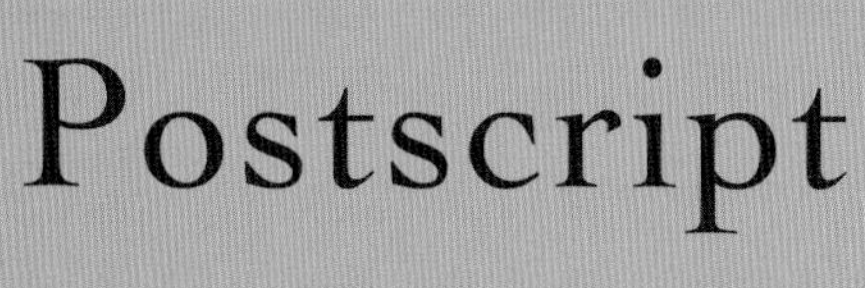

In his 1934 book *Things to Live For: Notes for an Autobiography* Francis Stuart wrote, 'On a wild part of the mountains several miles from here there is a certain big boulder. From it one can see down into the valley of Luggelaw and a corner of Lough Dan. At moments of especial happiness I go there. The first time I came on it was by chance and it seemed such a wild secret spot that I thought: "Whenever things are going really well I will go there; I will keep it as a place only to be happy."' More than seventy years later in September 2007 *New York Times* journalist Lynn Hirschberg, then writing a profile of Daniel Day-Lewis, visited County Wicklow where he owns a house. The actor invited her for a drive 'through the narrow country roads in the gorgeous, undeveloped tree-covered mountains south of Dublin. We took a crossroad called Sally Gap, heading up a steep climb toward a spot called Luggala, where the view, Day-Lewis hinted, would, in some fundamental way, explain all that he loved about this country.'

For those privileged to know it, Luggala is truly Francis Stuart's place of especial happiness. And, like Daniel Day-Lewis, it represents all that is most engaging about Ireland. 'I think of people that I love who have never seen Luggala,' says Anthony Palliser, 'and I want to show it to them... there's something about the perspectives from the house to the lake and mountains beyond, something I never tire of.' Like many others, Palliser uses the word enchantment when speaking of Luggala. So too does Anjelica Huston. 'For me,' she comments, 'Luggala is a sort of dream of peace, it's an enchanted place. Because of the way the house looks it has its place in the illustrations of Arthur Rackham but there's also an almost zen feeling, like a configuration of all the forces that come together right. The way the lake is embraced on the left by woods and on the right by rocks, the way the house sits in the cleft...Luggala is unique. It's like a unicorn.'

For more than two centuries Luggala has served as stimulus and muse, and continues to do so. 'This valley of Luggala,' wrote John Boorman in *I Dreamt I Woke Up*, 'is an enchanted place, a chalice cupped by mountains. I felt sure it was here, the heart of her mystery that the Lady of the Lake might offer up the sword of power, Excalibur.' In March 2005 *Vogue* contributing editor Robert Sullivan reported Bono telling Garech, 'Look, we just wanted you to know that your place has turned out to be our inspiration.'

Luggala is also somewhere capable of inspiring near-fanatical devotion. No wonder the term magical is so often used in descriptions: Luggala casts a spell over visitors almost as soon as they pass through the first entrance gate. 'I think it's a sense of crossing the border once you enter that glen,' says Seamus Heaney. 'The minute you start going down, you do cross a line into a slight otherwhere. And when the house appears, there's a sense of destination; it's a beautiful aspect.' 'It has a beautiful magic,' agrees Paddy Moloney, 'an enchanted feeling, you're in another world. You can almost hear the trees playing music and whistling tunes.'

House and setting each enhance the other. Luggala's beauty constantly surprises the habitué even as it stirs unexpected emotions in the jaded voyager. Patrick Bowe has written that Luggala remains etched on the memory: 'It is a landscape of many moods, changing with the light and the seasons. From certain viewpoints, it is expansive and sublime, from others intimate and touched by melancholy.' Luggala, says Pierre Joannon, 'is a dreamland: the setting at the end of this valley with the mountains and the lake, the rocks and the trees. The natural beauty of the setting is out of this world.' For Nicholas

OVERLEAF: Luggala seen looking north across Lough Tay, the near barren lower slopes of Fancy Mountain to the west contrasting with the dense woodland on the eastern approach to the valley.

RIGHT: In 1965 the Knight of Glin called Luggala an example of 'that special brand of eighteenth-century gothick that rejoices in little battlements, crochets, trefoil and quatrefoil windows and ogee mantelpieces,' a description that still holds good almost half a century later.

Gormanston Luggala possesses 'the mystique of the hidden away.' It is, says Marianne Faithfull, 'the most beautiful place in the world. It has everything you need but without any external stimulant.'

In June 2011 the Marquis of Huntly, husband of Garech's niece Catheryn Kindersley, wrote following a visit to Luggala, 'I have been lucky enough to visit houses in wild and wonderful places before but none can compare. It felt to me as if a higher hand had gently placed the fragile little building in the heart of this most sensational of vistas – as if they had just stooped to place it there in the hollow of the park as an artist might reach across a canvas to deliver his brushstroke of genius. Your commitment and love for the place echoes between those hills for all to see and hear and I know, because I have been told, that your active and scholarly contribution to the arts has been a constant in the social pulse of the house for many years. The inspiration and guidance you have shown must be all the greater for the theatre in which you perform.'

RIGHT: A place that is impossible to forget. As the Rev. Michael O'Ferrall wrote in 1873:

'Lake and lawn, and circling highland,
Wooded slope, and heath-clad hill,
Fairest spot of this fair island,
Luggelaw! I love thee still.'

Index

Italic page numbers refer to picture captions

Picture credits

The publishers would like to thank the following for permission to reproduce these illustrations and photographs:

Page 3: painting by Francis Hastings, 16th Earl of Huntingdon, in 1947–48
Page 7: Joe St Leger © The Irish Times
Page 9: Peter Knaup
Page 11: Marion Cashman
Page 32: © National Gallery of Ireland
Page 40: Courtesy of The National Library
Page 41: M Davies
Page 45: © The British Library Board (Maps K.Top.55.45.c)
Page 63: de Laszlo Trust/ © Christopher Wood Ltd
Page 95: Cosmo Brockway
Page 183: Michael Cooper
Page 193: Head of A Boy © The Lucien Freud Archive
Page 197, 198, 199: Joe St Leger © The Irish Times
Page 203: Jeffrey Craig, © Ceirnini Cladaig/Claddagh Records Ltd
Page 208, top: Doug McKenzie
Pages 208, bottom, and 209: Perry Ogden
Page 215, right: Colm Henry
Page 218, top right and bottom right: Sarah Owens
Page 220, right: Anthony Palliser
Page 224, top and bottom: Sarah Owens
Page 226, top: Doug McKenzie
Page 227 Michael Cooper
Pages 234 and 235, right: Marion Cashman
Page 238: Sarah Owens
Page 240: Sarah Owens
Page 243, right: Joe St Leger © The Irish Times
Oonagh's photograph albums photographed by Gavin Kingcombe, by kind permission of Dorian Browne.
Architectural plans on endpapers courtesy of Marion Cashman.

Acknowledgments

Above all, to the Hon. Garech Browne for his kindness, tolerance and hospitality during the research and writing of this book. Also to Frances Gillespie, Kristina Jambrovich and John Welsby for their equal goodness and patience during my many visits and telephone calls to Luggala.

And to the following: John Boorman; Tony Boylan; Ciara Brennan; Lady Brinckman; Cosmo Brockway; Dorian and Alison Browne; Koo and Freddie Browne; Ronan Browne; Sean Byrne; Godfrey Carey; Marion Cashman; Michael and Louisa de las Casas; Lady Cochrane; Andrew Cockburn; Adam Cooper; Chris Corlett; Anna Cotter; Mary Davies; Amanda Douglas; Marianne Faithfull; Lord Gormanston; Lord Gowrie; Maya Hanley; Susan Haynes; Seamus and Marie Heaney; Bono and Ali Hewson; Manus Hingerty; Paul Howard; John Hurt; Anjelica Huston; Pierre and Annick Joannon; Robin Kindersley and Jane Clarke; Tania Kindersley; Peter Knaup; Conor Lambert; Lady Lucinda Lambton; the Hon. Lady Langrishe; Jeremy Lewis; Ivana Lowell; Anne Madden; David Mlinaric; John Montague; Paddy Moloney; Madeleine Mottuel; Perry Ogden; Sarah Owens; Anthony Palliser; David Ryan; Richard Ryan; Michael Seery; Francis Wyndham. Also, sincerest thanks to anyone who may have been inadvertently omitted.

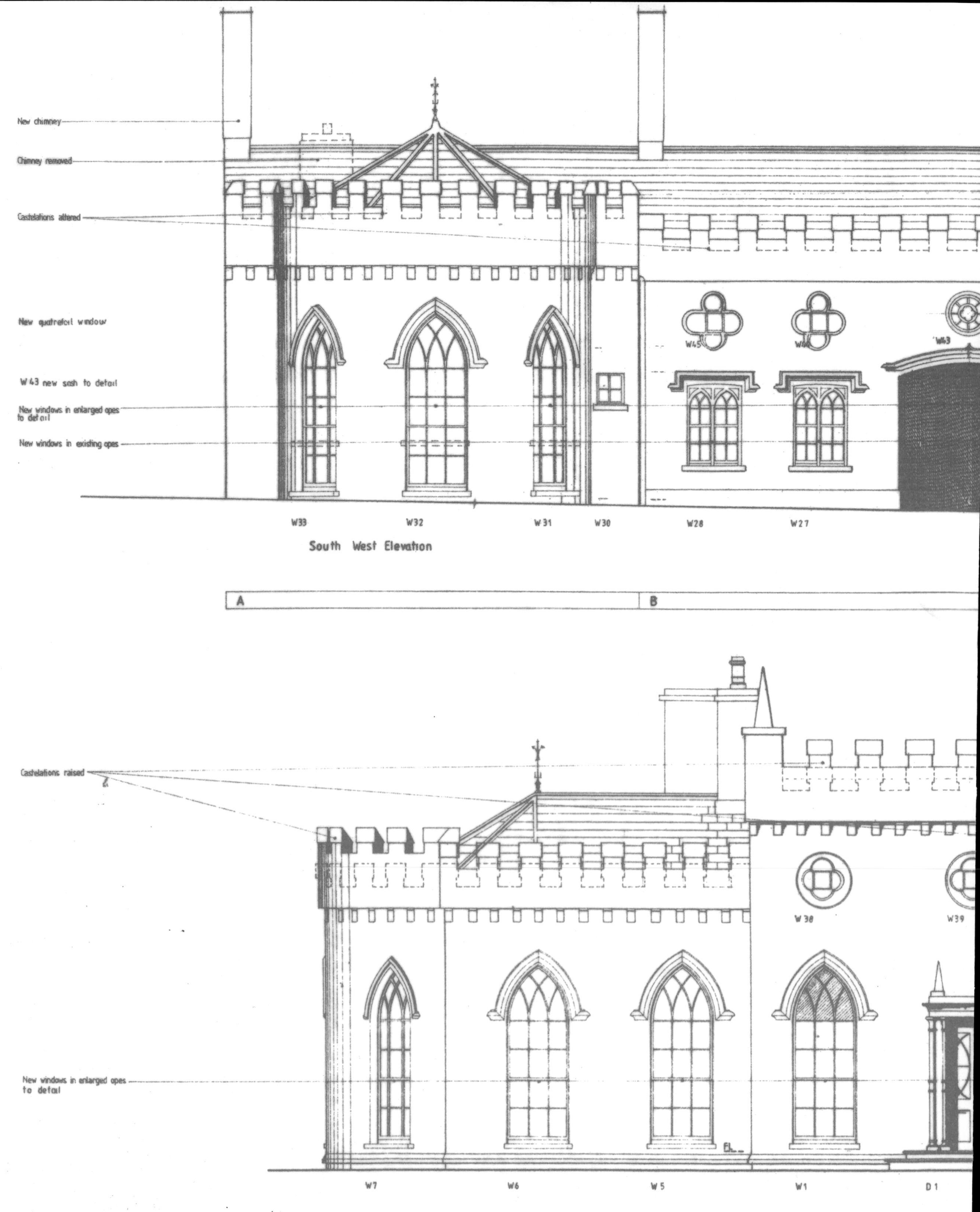

New chimney
Chimney removed
Castelations altered
New quatrefoil window
W43 new sash to detail
New windows in enlarged opes to detail
New windows in existing opes
W45
W43
W33
W32
W31
W30
W28
W27
South West Elevation
A
B
Castelations raised
W 38
W39
New windows in enlarged opes to detail
FL
W7
W6
W5
W1
D1
South East Elevation